SILENCE

Lectures

and

writings

by

JOHN

CAGE

SILENCE

THE M.I.T. PRESS
Massachusetts Institute of Technology
Cambridge, Massachusetts, and London, England

Many of these lectures and articles have been delivered or published elsewhere in the past two decades. The headnote preceding each one makes grateful acknowledgment of its precise source.

First edition published by The Wesleyan University Press, 1961

First M.I.T. Press paperback edition, August, 1966

Fourth Paperback Printing, April 1970

ISBN 0 262 53003 1

Library of Congress Catalog Card Number: 61-14238
Manufactured in the United States of America

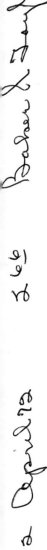

To Whom It May Concern

CONTENTS

FOREWORD

For over twenty years I have been writing articles and giving lectures. Many of them have been unusual in form—this is especially true of the lectures—because I have employed in them means of composing analogous to my composing means in the field of music. My intention has been, often, to say what I had to say in a way that would exemplify it; that would, conceivably, permit the listener to experience what I had to say rather than just hear about it. This means that, being as I am engaged in a variety of activities, I attempt to introduce into each one of them aspects conventionally limited to one or more of the others.

So it was that I gave about 1949 my *Lecture on Nothing* at the Artists' Club on Eighth Street in New York City (the artists' club started by Robert Motherwell, which predated the popular one associated with Philip Pavia, Bill de Kooning, et al.). This *Lecture on Nothing* was written in the same rhythmic structure I employed at the time in my musical compositions (*Sonatas and Interludes, Three Dances,* etc.). One of the structural divisions was the repetition, some fourteen times, of a single page in which occurred the refrain, "If anyone is sleepy let him go to sleep." Jeanne Reynal, I remember, stood up part way through, screamed, and then said, while I continued speaking, "John, I dearly love you, but I can't bear another minute." She then walked out. Later, during the question period, I gave one of six previously prepared answers regardless of the question asked. This was a reflection of my engagement in Zen.

At Black Mountain College in 1952, I organized an event that involved the paintings of Bob Rauschenberg, the dancing of Merce Cunningham, films, slides, phonograph records, radios, the poetries of Charles Olson and M. C. Richards recited from the tops of ladders, and the pianism of David Tudor, together with my *Juilliard* lecture, which ends: "A piece of string, a sunset, each acts." The audience was seated in the center of all this activity. Later that summer, vacationing in New England, I visited America's first synagogue, to discover that the congregation was there seated precisely the way I had arranged the audience at Black Mountain.

As I look back, I realize that a concern with poetry was early with me. At Pomona College, in response to questions about the Lake poets, I wrote in the manner of Gertrude Stein, irrelevantly and repetitiously. I got an A. The second time I did it I was failed. Since the *Lecture on Nothing* there have been more than a dozen pieces that were unconventionally written, including some that were done by means of chance operations and one that was largely a series of questions left unanswered. When M. C. Richards asked me why I didn't one day give a conventional informative lecture, adding that that would be the most shocking thing I could do, I said, "I don't give these lectures to surprise people, but out of a need for poetry."

As I see it, poetry is not prose simply because poetry is in one way or another formalized. It is not poetry by reason of its content or ambiguity but by reason of its allowing musical elements (time, sound) to be introduced into the world of words. Thus, traditionally, information no matter how stuffy (e. g., the sutras and shastras of India) was transmitted in poetry. It was easier to grasp that way. Karl Shapiro may have been thinking along these lines when he wrote his *Essay on Rime* in poetry.

Committing these formalized lectures to print has presented certain problems, and some of the solutions reached are compromises between what would have been desirable and what was practicable. The lecture *Where Are We Going? and What Are We Doing?* is an example. In this and other cases, a headnote explains the means to be used in the event of oral delivery.

Not all these pieces, of course, are unusual in form. Several were written to be printed—that is, to be seen rather than to be heard. Several others were composed and delivered as conventional informative lectures (without shocking their audiences for that reason, so far as I could determine).

This collection does not include all that I have written; it does reflect what have been, and continue to be, my major concerns.

Critics frequently cry "Dada" after attending one of my concerts or hearing one of my lectures. Others bemoan my interest in Zen. One of the liveliest lectures I ever heard was given by Nancy Wilson Ross at the Cornish School in Seattle. It was called *Zen Buddhism and Dada*. It is possible to make a connection between the two, but neither Dada nor Zen is a fixed tangible. They change; and in quite different ways in different places and times, they invigorate action. What was Dada in the 1920's is now, with the exception of the work of Marcel Duchamp, just art. What I do, I do not wish blamed on Zen, though without my engagement with Zen (attendance at lectures by Alan Watts and D. T. Suzuki, reading of the literature) I doubt whether I would have done what I have done. I am told that Alan Watts has questioned the relation between my work and Zen. I mention this in order to free Zen of any responsibility for my actions. I shall continue making them, however. I often point out that Dada nowadays has in it a space, an emptiness, that it formerly lacked. What nowadays, America mid-twentieth century, is Zen?

I am grateful to Richard K. Winslow, composer, whose musical ways are different from mine, who seven years ago, as Professor of Music at Wesleyan University, engaged David Tudor and me for a concert and who, at the time as we were walking along, introduced me without warning to his habit of suddenly quietly singing. Since then, he has twice invited us back to Wesleyan, even though our programs were consistently percussive, noisy, and silent, and the views which I expressed were consistently antischolastic and anarchic. He helped obtain for me the Fellowship at the Wesleyan Center for Advanced Studies which, in spite of the air-conditioning, I have enjoyed during the last academic year. And he inspired the University Press to publish this book. The reader may argue the propriety of this support, but he must admire, as I do, Winslow's courage and unselfishness.

—J. C.

June 1961

The text below was written for Julian Beck and Judith Malina, directors of the Living Theatre, for use in their program booklet when they were performing at the Cherry Lane Theatre, Greenwich Village, New York.

written in response
to a request for   } instantaneous   and unpredictable
a manifesto on
music, 1952

nothing is accomplished by writing a piece of music }   our ears are
     "   "   "   " hearing "   "   "   "   now
     "   "   "   " playing "   "   "   "   in excellent condition

—JOHN CAGE

SILENCE

The following text was delivered as a talk at a meeting of a Seattle arts society organized by Bonnie Bird in 1937. It was printed in the brochure accompanying George Avakian's recording of my twenty-five-year retrospective concert at Town Hall, New York, in 1958.

THE FUTURE OF MUSIC: CREDO

I BELIEVE THAT THE USE OF NOISE

Wherever we are, what we hear is mostly noise. When we ignore it, it disturbs us. When we listen to it, we find it fascinating. The sound of a truck at fifty miles per hour. Static between the stations. Rain. We want to capture and control these sounds, to use them not as sound effects but as musical instruments. Every film studio has a library of "sound effects" recorded on film. With a film phonograph it is now possible to control the amplitude and frequency of any one of these sounds and to give to it rhythms within or beyond the reach of the imagination. Given four film phonographs, we can compose and perform a quartet for explosive motor, wind, heartbeat, and landslide.

TO MAKE MUSIC

If this word "music" is sacred and reserved for eighteenth- and nineteenth-century instruments, we can substitute a more meaningful term: organization of sound.

WILL CONTINUE AND IN-
CREASE UNTIL WE REACH A MUSIC PRODUCED THROUGH THE AID OF ELECTRICAL INSTRUMENTS

Most inventors of electrical musical instruments have attempted to imitate eighteenth- and nineteenth-century instruments, just as early automobile designers copied the carriage. The Novachord and the

Solovox are examples of this desire to imitate the past rather than construct the future. When Theremin provided an instrument with genuinely new possibilities, Thereministes did their utmost to make the instrument sound like some old instrument, giving it a sickeningly sweet vibrato, and performing upon it, with difficulty, masterpieces from the past. Although the instrument is capable of a wide variety of sound qualities, obtained by the turning of a dial, Thereministes act as censors, giving the public those sounds they think the public will like. We are shielded from new sound experiences.

The special function of electrical instruments will be to provide complete control of the overtone structure of tones (as opposed to noises) and to make these tones available in any frequency, amplitude, and duration.

WHICH WILL MAKE AVAILABLE FOR MUSICAL PURPOSES ANY AND ALL SOUNDS THAT CAN BE HEARD. PHOTOELECTRIC, FILM, AND MECHANICAL MEDIUMS FOR THE SYNTHETIC PRODUCTION OF MUSIC

It is now possible for composers to make music directly, without the assistance of intermediary performers. Any design repeated often enough on a sound track is audible. Two hundred and eighty circles per second on a sound track will produce one sound, whereas a portrait of Beethoven repeated fifty times per second on a sound track will have not only a different pitch but a different sound quality.

WILL BE EXPLORED. WHEREAS, IN THE PAST, THE POINT OF DISAGREEMENT HAS BEEN BETWEEN DIS- SONANCE AND CONSONANCE, IT WILL BE, IN THE IMMEDIATE FUTURE, BETWEEN NOISE AND SO-CALLED MUSICAL SOUNDS.

THE PRESENT METHODS OF WRITING MUSIC, PRINCIPALLY THOSE WHICH EMPLOY HARMONY AND ITS REFERENCE TO PARTICULAR STEPS IN THE FIELD OF SOUND, WILL BE INADEQUATE FOR THE COMPOSER, WHO WILL BE FACED WITH THE ENTIRE FIELD OF SOUND.

The composer (organizer of sound) will be faced not only with the entire field of sound but also with the entire field of time. The "frame" or fraction of a second, following established film technique, will probably be the basic unit in the measurement of time. No rhythm will be beyond the composer's reach.

NEW METHODS WILL BE DISCOVERED, BEARING A DEFINITE RELATION TO SCHOEN-
BERG'S TWELVE-TONE SYSTEM

Schoenberg's method assigns to each material, in a group of equal materials, its function with respect to the group. (Harmony assigned to each material, in a group of unequal materials, its function with respect to the fundamental or most important material in the group.) Schoenberg's method is analogous to a society in which the emphasis is on the group and the integration of the individual in the group.

AND PRESENT METHODS OF WRITING PERCUSSION
MUSIC

Percussion music is a contemporary transition from keyboard-influenced music to the all-sound music of the future. Any sound is acceptable to the composer of percussion music; he explores the academically forbidden "non-musical" field of sound insofar as is manually possible.

Methods of writing percussion music have as their goal the rhythmic structure of a composition. As soon as these methods are crystallized into one or several widely accepted methods, the means will exist for group improvisations of unwritten but culturally important music. This has already taken place in Oriental cultures and in hot jazz.

AND ANY OTHER METHODS WHICH ARE FREE FROM THE CONCEPT OF A
FUNDAMENTAL TONE.

THE PRINCIPLE OF
FORM WILL BE OUR ONLY CONSTANT CONNECTION WITH THE PAST. ALTHOUGH
THE GREAT FORM OF THE FUTURE WILL NOT BE AS IT WAS IN THE PAST, AT

Before this happens, centers of experi-
mental music must be established. In these centers, the new materials,
oscillators, turntables, generators, means for amplifying small sounds, film
phonographs, etc., available for use. Composers at work using twentieth-
century means for making music. Performances of results. Organization
of sound for extra-musical purposes (theatre, dance, radio, film).

THROUGH
THE PRINCIPLE OF ORGANIZATION OR MAN'S COMMON ABILITY TO THINK.

· ·

It was a Wednesday. I was in the sixth grade. I overheard Dad saying to Mother, "Get ready: we're
going to New Zealand Saturday." I got ready. I read everything I could find in the school library about
New Zealand. Saturday came. Nothing happened. The project was not even mentioned, that day or any
succeeding day.

M. C. Richards went to see the Bolshoi Ballet. She was delighted with the dancing. She said, "It's not
what they do; it's the ardor with which they do it." I said, "Yes: composition, performance, and audition or
observation are really different things. They have next to nothing to do with one another." Once, I told her,
I was at a house on Riverside Drive where people were invited to be present at a Zen service conducted by
a Japanese Roshi. He did the ritual, rose petals and all. Afterwards tea was served with rice cookies. And
then the hostess and her husband, employing an out-of-tune piano and a cracked voice, gave a wretched
performance of an excerpt from a third-rate Italian opera. I was embarrassed and glanced towards the Roshi
to see how he was taking it. The expression on his face was absolutely beatific.

A young man in Japan arranged his circumstances so that he was able to travel to a distant island to
study Zen with a certain Master for a three-year period. At the end of the three years, feeling no sense of
accomplishment, he presented himself to the Master and announced his departure. The Master said, "You've
been here three years. Why don't you stay three months more?" The student agreed, but at the end of the
three months he still felt that he had made no advance. When he told the Master again that he was leaving,
the Master said, "Look now, you've been here three years and three months. Stay three weeks longer." The
student did, but with no success. When he told the Master that absolutely nothing had happened, the Master
said, "You've been here three years, three months, and three weeks. Stay three more days, and if, at the
end of that time, you have not attained enlightenment, commit suicide." Towards the end of the second
day, the student was enlightened.

The following statement was given as an address to the convention of the Music Teachers National Association in Chicago in the winter of 1957. It was printed in the brochure accompanying George Avakian's recording of my twenty-five-year retrospective concert at Town Hall, New York, in 1958.

EXPERIMENTAL MUSIC

Formerly, whenever anyone said the music I presented was experimental, I objected. It seemed to me that composers knew what they were doing, and that the experiments that had been made had taken place prior to the finished works, just as sketches are made before paintings and rehearsals precede performances. But, giving the matter further thought, I realized that there is ordinarily an essential difference between making a piece of music and hearing one. A composer knows his work as a woodsman knows a path he has traced and retraced, while a listener is confronted by the same work as one is in the woods by a plant he has never seen before.

Now, on the other hand, times have changed; music has changed; and I no longer object to the word "experimental." I use it in fact to describe all the music that especially interests me and to which I am devoted, whether someone else wrote it or I myself did. What has happened is that I have become a listener and the music has become something to hear. Many people, of course, have given up saying "experimental" about this new music. Instead, they either move to a halfway point and say "controversial" or depart to a greater distance and question whether this "music" is music at all.

For in this new music nothing takes place but sounds: those that are notated and those that are not. Those that are not notated appear in the written music as silences, opening the doors of the music to the sounds that happen to be in the environment. This openness exists in the fields of modern sculpture and architecture. The glass houses of Mies van der Rohe reflect their environment, presenting to the eye images of clouds, trees, or grass, according to the situation. And while looking at the constructions in wire of the sculptor Richard Lippold, it is inevitable that one will see other things, and people too, if they happen to be there at the same time, through the network of wires. There is no such thing as an empty space or an empty time. There is always something to see, something to hear. In fact, try as we may to make a silence, we cannot. For certain engineering purposes, it is desirable to have as silent a situation as possible. Such a room is called an anechoic chamber, its six walls made of special material, a room without echoes. I entered one at Harvard University several years ago and heard two sounds, one high and one low. When I described them to the engineer in charge, he informed me that the high one was my nervous system in operation, the low one my blood in circulation. Until I die there will be sounds. And they will continue following my death. One need not fear about the future of music.

But this fearlessness only follows if, at the parting of the ways, where it is realized that sounds occur whether intended or not, one turns in the direction of those he does not intend. This turning is psychological and seems at first to be a giving up of everything that belongs to humanity—for a musician, the giving up of music. This psychological turning leads to the world of nature, where, gradually or suddenly, one sees that humanity and nature, not separate, are in this world together; that nothing was lost when everything was given away. In fact, everything is gained. In musical terms, any sounds may occur in any combination and in any continuity.

And it is a striking coincidence that just now the technical means to produce such a free-ranging music are available. When the Allies entered Germany towards the end of World War II, it was discovered that improvements had been made in recording sounds magnetically such that tape had become suitable for the high-fidelity recording of music. First in France with the work of Pierre Schaeffer, later here, in Germany, in Italy, in Japan, and perhaps, without my knowing it, in other places, magnetic tape was used not simply to record performances of music but to make a new music that was possible only because of it. Given a minimum of two tape recorders and a disk recorder, the following processes are possible: 1) a single recording of any sound may be made; 2) a rerecording may be made, in the course of which, by means of filters and circuits, any or all of the physical characteristics of a given recorded sound may be altered; 3) electronic mixing (combining on a third machine sounds issuing from two others) permits the presentation of any number of sounds in combination; 4) ordinary splicing permits the juxtaposition of any sounds, and when it includes unconventional cuts, it, like rerecording, brings about alterations of any or all of the original physical characteristics. The situation made available by these means is essentially a total sound-space, the limits of which are ear-determined only, the position of a particular sound in this space being the result of five determinants: frequency or pitch, amplitude or loudness, overtone structure or timbre, duration, and morphology (how the sound begins, goes on, and dies away). By the alteration of any one of these determinants, the position of the sound in sound-space changes. Any sound at any point in this total sound-space can move to become a sound at any other point. But advantage can be taken of these possibilities only if one is willing to change one's musical habits radically. That is, one may take advantage of the appearance of images without visible transition in distant places, which is a way of saying "television," if one is willing to stay at home instead of going to a theatre. Or one may fly if one is willing to give up walking.

Musical habits include scales, modes, theories of counterpoint and harmony, and the study of the timbres, singly and in combination of a limited number of sound-producing mechanisms. In mathematical terms these all concern discrete steps. They resemble walking—in the case of pitches, on steppingstones twelve in number. This cautious stepping is not characteristic of the possibilities of magnetic tape, which is revealing to us that musical action or existence can occur at any point or along any line or curve or what have you in total sound-space; that we are, in fact, technically equipped to transform our contemporary awareness of nature's manner of operation into art.

Again there is a parting of the ways. One has a choice. If he does not wish to give up his attempts to control sound, he may complicate his musical technique towards an approximation of the new possibilities and awareness. (I use the word "approximation" because a measuring mind can never finally measure nature.) Or, as before, one may give up the desire to control sound, clear his mind of music, and set about discovering means to let sounds be themselves rather than vehicles for man-made theories or expressions of human sentiments.

This project will seem fearsome to many, but on examination it gives no cause for alarm. Hearing sounds which are just sounds immediately sets the theorizing mind to theorizing, and the emotions of human beings are continually aroused by encounters with nature. Does not a mountain unintentionally evoke in us a sense of wonder? otters along a stream a sense of mirth? night in the woods a sense of fear? Do not rain falling and mists rising up suggest the love binding heaven and earth? Is not decaying flesh loathsome? Does not the death of someone we love bring sorrow? And is there a greater hero than the least plant that grows? What is more angry than the flash of lightning and the sound of thunder? These responses to nature are mine and will not necessarily correspond with another's. Emotion takes place in the person who has it. And sounds, when allowed to be themselves, do not require that those who hear them do so unfeelingly. The opposite is what is meant by response ability.

New music: new listening. Not an attempt to understand something that is being said, for, if something were being said, the sounds would be given the shapes of words. Just an attention to the activity of sounds.

Those involved with the composition of experimental music find ways and means to remove themselves from the activities of the sounds they make. Some employ chance operations, derived from sources as ancient as the Chinese *Book of Changes,* or as modern as the tables of random numbers used also by physicists in research. Or, analogous to the Rorschach tests of psychology, the interpretation of imperfections in the paper upon which one is writing may provide a music free from one's memory and imagination. Geometrical means employing spatial superimpositions at variance with the ultimate performance in time may be used. The total field of possibilities may be roughly divided and the actual sounds within these divisions may be indicated as to number but left to the performer or to the splicer to choose. In this latter case, the composer resembles the maker of a camera who allows someone else to take the picture.

Whether one uses tape or writes for conventional instruments, the present musical situation has changed from what it was before tape came into being. This also need not arouse alarm, for the coming into being of something new does not by that fact deprive what was of its proper place. Each thing has its own place, never takes the place of something else; and the more things there are, as is said, the merrier.

But several effects of tape on experimental music may be mentioned. Since so many inches of tape equal so many seconds of time, it has become more and more usual that notation is in space rather than in symbols of quarter, half, and sixteenth notes and so on. Thus where on a page a note appears will correspond to when in a time it is to occur. A stop watch is used to facilitate a performance; and a rhythm results which is a far cry from horse's hoofs and other regular beats.

Also it has been impossible with the playing of several separate tapes at once to achieve perfect synchronization. This fact has led some towards the manufacture of multiple-tracked tapes and machines with a corresponding number of heads; while others—those who have accepted the sounds they do not intend—now realize that the score, the requiring that many parts be played in a particular togetherness, is not an accurate representation of how things are. These now compose parts but not scores, and the parts may be combined in any unthought ways. This means that each performance of such a piece of music is unique, as interesting to its composer as to others listening. It is easy to see again the parallel with nature, for even with leaves of the same tree, no two are exactly alike. The parallel in art is the sculpture with moving parts, the mobile.

It goes without saying that dissonances and noises are welcome in this new music. But so is the dominant seventh chord if it happens to put in an appearance.

Rehearsals have shown that this new music, whether for tape or for instruments, is more clearly heard when the several loud-speakers or performers are separated in space rather than grouped closely together. For this music is not concerned with harmoniousness as generally understood, where the quality of harmony results from a blending of several elements. Here we are concerned with the coexistence of dissimilars, and the central points where fusion occurs are many: the ears of the listeners wherever they are. This disharmony, to paraphrase Bergson's statement about disorder, is simply a harmony to which many are unaccustomed.

Where do we go from here? Towards theatre. That art more than music resembles nature. We have eyes as well as ears, and it is our business while we are alive to use them.

And what is the purpose of writing music? One is, of course, not dealing with purposes but dealing with sounds. Or the answer must take the form of paradox: a purposeful purposelessness or a purposeless play. This play, however, is an affirmation of life—not an attempt to bring order out of chaos nor to suggest improvements in creation, but simply a way of waking up to the very life we're living, which is so excellent once one gets one's mind and one's desires out of its way and lets it act of its own accord.

. . . .

When Xenia and I came to New York from Chicago, we arrived in the bus station with about twenty-five cents. We were expecting to stay for a while with Peggy Guggenheim and Max Ernst. Max Ernst had met us in Chicago and had said, "Whenever you come to New York, come and stay with us. We have a big house on the East River." I went to the phone booth in the bus station, put in a nickel, and dialed. Max Ernst answered. He didn't recognize my voice. Finally he said, "Are you thirsty?" I said, "Yes." He said, "Well, come over tomorrow for cocktails." I went back to Xenia and told her what had happened. She said, "Call him back. We have everything to gain and nothing to lose." I did. He said, "Oh! It's you. We've been waiting for you for weeks. Your room's ready. Come right over."

Dad is an inventor. In 1912 his submarine had the world's record for staying under water. Running as it did by means of a gasoline engine, it left bubbles on the surface, so it was not employed during World War I. Dad says he does his best work when he is sound asleep. I was explaining at the New School that the way to get ideas is to do something boring. For instance, composing in such a way that the process of composing is boring induces ideas. They fly into one's head like birds. Is that what Dad meant?

This article, there titled Experimental Music, *first appeared in* The Score and I. M. A. Magazine, *London, issue of June 1955. The inclusion of a dialogue between an uncompromising teacher and an unenlightened student, and the addition of the word "doctrine" to the original title, are references to the* Huang-Po Doctrine of Universal Mind.

EXPERIMENTAL MUSIC: DOCTRINE

Objections are sometimes made by composers to the use of the term *experimental* as descriptive of their works, for it is claimed that any experiments that are made precede the steps that are finally taken with determination, and that this determination is knowing, having, in fact, a particular, if unconventional, ordering of the elements used in view. These objections are clearly justifiable, but only where, as among contemporary evidences in serial music, it remains a question of making a thing upon the boundaries, structure, and expression of which attention is focused. Where, on the other hand, attention moves towards the observation and audition of many things at once, including those that are environmental—becomes, that is, inclusive rather than exclusive—no question of making, in the sense of forming understandable structures, can arise (one is tourist), and here the word "experimental" is apt, providing it is understood not as descriptive of an act to be later judged in terms of success and failure, but simply as of an act the outcome of which is unknown. What has been determined?

For, when, after convincing oneself ignorantly that sound has, as its clearly defined opposite, silence, that since duration is the only characteristic of sound that is measurable in terms of silence, therefore any valid structure involving sounds and silences should be based, not as occidentally traditional, on frequency, but rightly on duration, one enters an anechoic chamber, as silent as technologically possible in 1951, to discover that one hears two sounds of one's own unintentional making (nerve's systematic operation, blood's circulation), the situation one is clearly in is not objective (sound-silence), but rather subjective (sounds only), those intended and those others (so-called silence) not intended. If, at this point, one says, "Yes! I do not discriminate between intention and non-intention," the splits, subject-object, art-life, etc., disappear, an identification has been made with the material, and actions are then those relevant to its nature, i.e.:

A sound does not view itself as thought, as ought, as needing another sound for its elucidation, as etc.; it has no time for any consideration—it is occupied with the performance of its characteristics: before it has died away it must have made perfectly exact its frequency, its loudness, its length, its overtone structure, the precise morphology of these and of itself.

Urgent, unique, uninformed about history and theory, beyond the imagination, central to a sphere without surface, its becoming is unimpeded, energetically broadcast. There is no escape from its action. It does not exist as one of a series of discrete steps, but as transmission in all directions from the field's center. It is inextricably synchronous with all other, sounds, non-sounds, which latter, received by other sets than the ear, operate in the same manner.

A sound accomplishes nothing; without it life would not last out the instant.

Relevant action is theatrical (music [imaginary separation of hearing from the other senses] does not exist), inclusive and intentionally purposeless. Theatre is continually becoming that it is becoming; each human being is at the best point for reception. Relevant response (getting up in the morning and discovering oneself musician) (action, art) can be made with any number (including none [none and number, like silence and music, are unreal]) of sounds. The automatic minimum (see above) is two.

Are you deaf (by nature, choice, desire) or can you hear (externals, tympani, labyrinths in whack)?

Beyond them (ears) is the power of discrimination which, among other confused actions, weakly pulls apart (abstraction), ineffectually establishes as not to suffer alteration (the "work"), and unskillfully protects from interruption (museum, concert hall) what springs, elastic, spontaneous, back together again with a beyond that power which is fluent (it moves in or out), pregnant (it can appear when- where- as what-ever [rose, nail, constellation, 485.73482 cycles per second, piece of string]), related (it is you yourself in the form you have that instant taken), obscure (you will never be able to give a satisfactory report even to yourself of just what happened).

In view, then, of a totality of possibilities, no knowing action is commensurate, since the character of the knowledge acted upon prohibits all but some eventualities. From a realist position, such action, though cautious, hopeful, and generally entered into, is unsuitable. An *experimental* action, generated by a mind as empty as it was before it became one, thus in accord with the possibility of no matter what, is, on the other hand, practical. It does not move in terms of approximations and errors, as "informed" action by its nàture must, for no mental images of what would happen were set up beforehand; it sees things directly as they are: impermanently involved in an infinite play of interpenetrations. Experimental music—

QUESTION: —in the U.S.A., if you please. Be more specific. What do you have to say about rhythm? Let us agree it is no longer a question of pattern, repetition, and variation.

ANSWER: There is no need for such agreement. Patterns, repetitions, and variations will arise and disappear. However, rhythm is durations of any length coexisting in any states of succession and synchronicity. The latter is liveliest, most unpredictably changing, when the parts are not fixed by a score but left independent of one another, no two performances yielding the same resultant durations. The former, succession, liveliest when (as in Morton Feldman's *Intersections*) it is not fixed but presented in situation-form, entrances being at any point within a given period of time.——Notation of durations is in space, read as corresponding to time, needing no reading in the case of magnetic tape.

QUESTION: What about several players at once, an orchestra?

ANSWER: You insist upon their being together? Then use, as Earle Brown suggests, a moving picture of the score, visible to all, a static vertical line as coordinator, past which the notations move. If you have no particular togetherness in mind, there are chronometers. Use them.

QUESTION: I have noticed that you write durations that are beyond the possibility of performance.

ANSWER: Composing's one thing, performing's another, listening's a third. What can they have to do with one another?

*   *   *

QUESTION: And about pitches?

ANSWER: It is true. Music is continually going up and down, but no longer only on those stepping stones, five, seven, twelve in number, or the quarter tones. Pitches are not a matter of likes and dislikes (I have told you about the diagram Schillinger had stretched across his wall near the ceiling: all the scales, Oriental and Occidental, that had been in general use, each in its own color plotted against, no one of them identical with, a black one, the latter the scale as it would have been had it been physically based on the overtone series) except for musicians in ruts; in the face of habits, what to do? Magnetic tape opens the door providing one doesn't immediately shut it by inventing a *phonogène,* or otherwise use it to recall or extend known musical possibilities. It introduces the unknown with such sharp clarity that anyone has the opportunity of having his habits blown away like dust.——For this purpose the prepared piano is also useful, especially in its recent forms where, by alterations during a performance, an otherwise static gamut situation becomes changing. Stringed instruments (not string-players) are very instructive, voices too; and sitting still anywhere (the stereophonic, multiple-loud-speaker manner of operation in the everyday production of sounds and noises) listening...

QUESTION: I understand Feldman divides all pitches into high, middle, and low, and simply indicates how many in a given range are to be played, leaving the choice up to the performer.

ANSWER: Correct. That is to say, he used sometimes to do so; I haven't seen him lately. It is also essential to remember his notation of super- and subsonic vibrations (*Marginal Intersection No. 1*).

QUESTION: That is, there are neither divisions of the "canvas" nor "frame" to be observed?

ANSWER: On the contrary, you must give the closest attention to everything.
*   *   *

QUESTION: And timbre?

ANSWER: No wondering what's next. Going lively on "through many a perilous situation." Did you ever listen to a symphony orchestra?
*   *   *

QUESTION: Dynamics?

ANSWER: These result from what actively happens (physically, mechanically, electronically) in producing a sound. You won't find it in the books. Notate that. As far as too loud goes: "follow the general outlines of the Christian life."

QUESTION: I have asked you about the various characteristics of a sound; how, now, can you make a continuity, as I take it your intention is, without intention? Do not memory, psychology——

ANSWER: "——never again."

QUESTION: How?

ANSWER: Christian Wolff introduced space actions in his compositional process at variance with the subsequently performed time actions. Earle Brown devised a composing procedure in which events, following tables of random numbers, are written out of sequence, possibly anywhere in a total time now and possibly anywhere else in the same total time next. I myself use chance operations, some derived from the *I-Ching*, others from the observation of imperfections in the paper upon which I happen to be writing. Your answer: by not giving it a thought.

QUESTION: Is this athematic?

ANSWER: Who said anything about themes? It is not a question of having something to say.

QUESTION: Then what is the purpose of this "experimental" music?

ANSWER: No purposes. Sounds.

QUESTION: Why bother, since, as you have pointed out, sounds are continually happening whether you produce them or not?

ANSWER: What did you say? I'm still——

QUESTION: I mean—— But is this *music*?

ANSWER: Ah! you like sounds after all when they are made up of vowels and consonants. You are slow-witted, for you have never brought your mind to the location of urgency. Do you need me or someone else to hold you up? Why don't you realize as I do that nothing is accomplished by writing, playing, or listening to music? Otherwise, deaf as a doornail, you will never be able to hear anything, even what's well within earshot.

QUESTION: But, seriously, if this is what music is, I could write it as well as you.

ANSWER: Have I said anything that would lead you to think I thought you were stupid?

The following three lectures were given at Darmstadt (Germany) in September 1958. The third one, with certain revisions, is a lecture given earlier that year at Rutgers University in New Jersey, an excerpt from which was published in the Village Voice, New York City, *in April 1958.*

COMPOSITION AS PROCESS
I. Changes

Having been asked by Dr. Wolfgang Steinecke, Director of the Internationale Ferienkurse für Neue Musik at Darmstadt, to discuss in particular my Music of Changes, *I decided to make a lecture within the time length of the* Music of Changes *(each line of the text whether speech or silence requiring one second for its performance), so that whenever I would stop speaking, the corresponding part of the* Music of Changes *itself would be played. The music is not superimposed on the speech but is heard only in the interruptions of the speech—which, like the lengths of the paragraphs themselves, were the result of chance operations.*

This is a lecture on changes that have taken place in my composition means, with particular reference to what, a decade ago, I termed "structure" and "method." By "structure" was meant the division of a whole into parts; by "method," the note-to-note procedure. Both structure and method (and also

"material"— the sounds and silences of a composition)

were, it seemed to me then, the proper concern of the mind (as opposed to the heart) (one's ideas of order as opposed to one's spontaneous actions); whereas the two last

of these, namely method and material, together with form (the morphology of a continuity) were equally the proper concern of the heart. Composition, then, I viewed, ten years ago, as an activity integrating the opposites, the rational and the irrational, bringing about, i-

deally, a freely moving continuity within a strict division of parts, the sounds, their combination and succession being either logically related or arbitrarily chosen. ¶The strict division of parts, the structure, was a function of the duration aspect of sound, since, of all the aspects of sound including frequency, amplitude, and timbre, duration, alone, was also a characteristic of silence. The structure, then, was a division of actual time by conventional metrical means, meter taken as simply the measurement of quantity. ¶In the case of the *Sonatas and Interludes* (which I finished in nineteen forty-eight), only structure was organized, quite roughly for the work as a whole, exactly, however, within each single piece. The method was that of considered improvisation (mainly at the piano, though ideas came to me at some moments away from the instrument.

The materials, the piano preparations, were chosen as one chooses shells while walking along a beach. The form was as natural as my taste permitted: so that where, as in all of the *Sonatas* and two of the *Interludes,* parts were to be repeated, the formal concern was to make the progress from the end of a section to its beginning seem inevitable. ¶The structure of one of the *Sonatas,* the fourth, was one hundred measures of two-two time, divided into ten units of ten measures each. These units were combined in the proportion three, three, two, two, to give the piece large parts, and they were subdivided in the same proportion to give small parts to each unit. In contrast to a structure based on the frequency aspect of sound, tonality, that is, this rhythmic structure was as hospitable to non-musical sounds, noises, as it was to those of the conventional scales and instruments. For nothing about the structure was determined by the materials which were to occur in it; it was conceived, in fact, so that it could be as well expressed by the absence of these materials as by their presence. ¶In terms of the opposition of freedom and law, a piece written ten years before the *Sonatas and Interludes, Construction in Metal*, presents the same relationship, but reversed: structure, method, and materials were all of them subjected to organization. The morphology of the continuity, form, alone was free. Drawing a straight line between this situation and that presented by the later work, the deduction might be made that there is a tendency in my composition means away from ideas of order towards no ideas of order. And though when examined the history would probably not read as a straight line, recent works, beginning with the *Music of Changes*, support the accuracy of this deduction. ¶For, in the *Music of Changes*, the note-to-note procedure, the method, is the function of chance operations. And the structure, though planned precisely as those of the *Sonatas and Interludes*, and more thoroughly since it encompassed the whole span of the composition, was only a series of numbers, three, five, six and three quarters, six and three quarters, five, three and one eighth, which became, on the one hand, the number of units within each section, and, on the other, number of measures of four-four within each unit. At each small structural division in the *Music of Changes*, at the beginning, for example, and again at the fourth and ninth measures and so on, chance operations determined stability or change of tempo. Thus, by introducing the action of method into the body of the structure, and these two opposed in terms of order and freedom, that structure became indeterminate: it was not possible to know the total time-length of the piece until the final chance operation, the last toss of coins affecting the rate of tempo, had been made. Being indeterminate, though still present, it became apparent that structure was not necessary, even though it had certain uses. ¶One of these uses was the determination of density, the determination, that is, of how many of the potentially present eight lines, each composed of sounds and silences, were actually to be present within a given small structural part. ¶Another use of the structure affected the charts of sounds and silences, amplitudes, durations, potentially active in the continuity. These twenty-four charts, eight for sounds and silences, eight for amplitudes, eight for durations, were, throughout the course of a single structural unit, half of them mobile and half of them immobile. Mobile meant that once any of the elements in a chart was used it disappeared to be replaced by a new one. Immobile meant that though an element in a chart had been used, it remained to be used again. At each unit structural point, a chance operation determined which of the charts, numbers one, three, five, and seven or numbers two, four, six, and eight, were mobile and which of the charts were immobile—not changing. ¶The structure, therefore, was in these respects useful. Furthermore, it determined the beginning and ending of the composition-al process. But this process, had it in the end brought about a division of parts the time-lengths of which were pro-portional to the origi-nal series of numbers, would have been extraordi-nary. And the presence of the mind as a rul-ing factor, e-ven by such an extraordina-ry eventu-ality, would not have been es-tablished. For what happened came a-bout only through the tossing of coins. ¶It be-came clear, therefore, I repeat, that structure was not necessary. And, in *Music for Piano,* and subsequent pieces, indeed, structure is no longer a part of the compo-sition means. The view taken is not of an ac-tivity the purpose of which is to inte-grate the oppo-sites, but rather of an activ-ity charac-terized by process and es-sentially purposeless. The mind, though stripped of its right to control, is still present. What does it do, having nothing to do? And what happens to a piece of music when it is purposeless-ly made? ¶What hap-pens, for instance, to silence? That is, how does the mind's perception of it change? For-merly, silence was the time lapse between sounds, use-ful towards a va-riety of ends, among them that of tasteful arrangement, where by separat-ing two sounds or two groups of sounds their differen-ces or rela-tionships might re-ceive emphasis; or that of ex-pressivity, where silences in a musi-cal discourse might provide pause or punctuation; or again, that of architec-ture, where the in-troduction or interruption of silence might give defini-tion either to a predeter-mined structure or to an organi-ically de-veloping one. Where none of these or other goals is present, si-lence becomes some-thing else—not si-lence at all, but sounds, the ambi-ent sounds. The na-ture of these is unpredicta-ble and changing. These sounds (which are

called silence on-
ly because they
do not form part
of a musi-
cal intention)
may be depen-
ded upon to
exist. The world
teems with them, and
is, in fact, at
no point free of
them. He who has
entered an an-
echoic cham-
ber, a room made
as silent as
technologi-
cally possible,
has heard there two
sounds, one high, one
low—the high the
listener's ner-
vous system in
operation,
the low his blood
in circula-
tion. There are, dem-
onstrably, sounds
to be heard and
forever, giv-
en ears to hear.
Where these ears are
in connection

with a mind that
has nothing to
do, that mind is
free to enter
into the act
of listening,
hearing each sound
just as it is,
not as a phe-
nomenon more
or less approx-
imating a
preconception.

¶What's the histo-
ry of the chan-
ges in my com-
position means
with particu-
lar reference
to sounds? I had
in mind when I
chose the sounds for
*Construction in
Metal* that they
should be sixteen
for each player.
The number six-
teen was also
that of the num-
ber of measures

of four-four in
each unit of
the rhythmic struc-
ture. In the case
of the structure
this number was
divided four,
three, two, three, four;
in the case of
the materi-
als the gamuts
of sixteen sounds
were divided
into four groups
of four. The plan,
as preconceived,
was to use four
of the sounds in
the first sixteen
measures, intro-
ducing in each
succeeding struc-
tural unit
four more until
the exposi-
tion involving
all sixteen and
lasting through the
first four units
was completed.
The subsequent
parts, three, two, three,
four, were composed

as develop-
ment of this in-
itial situ-
ation. In ac-
tuality,
this simple plan
was not real-
ized, although it
was only re-
cently that I
became fully
aware that it
was not. I had
known all along
that one of the
players used three
Japanese tem-
ple gongs rather
than four, but the
fact that only
three of these rel-
atively rare
instruments were
then availa-
ble to me, to-
gether with the
attachment I
felt towards their sound,
had convinced me
of the rightness
of this change in
number. More se-
rious, however,
it seems to
me now, was the
effect of beat-
ers: playing cow-
bells first with rub-
ber and then with
metal multi-
plied by two the
number of sounds
actually
used. Sirenlike
piano trills
which sound as one
were counted as
two. Various
other devi-
ations from the
original
plan could be dis-
covered on an-
alysis: for
instance, the ad-
dition of met-
al thundersheets
for background noise
bringing the num-
ber sixteen, for
those players who
enjoyed it

to seventeen. One might conclude that in composing *Construction in Metal* the organization of sounds was imperfectly realized. Or he might conclude that the composer had not actually listened to the sounds he used. ¶I have already compared the selection of the sounds for the *Sonatas and Interludes* to a selection of shells while walking along a beach. They are therefore a collection exhibiting taste. Their number was increased by use of the *una corda*, this pedal bringing about alterations of timbre and frequency for many of the prepared keys. In terms of pitch, however, there is no change from the sounds of the *Construction*. In both cases a static gamut of sounds is presented, no two octaves repeating relations. However, one could hear interesting differences between certain of these sounds. On depressing a key, sometimes a single frequency was heard. In other cases depressing a key produced an interval; in still others an aggregate of pitches and timbres. Noticing the nature of this gamut led to selecting a comparable one for the *String Quartet:* the inclusion there of rigidly scored conventional harmonies is a matter of taste, from which a conscious control was absent. Before writing the *Music of Changes,* two pieces were written which also used gamuts of sounds: single sounds, double sounds and others more numerous, some to be played simultaneously, others successively in time. These pieces were *Sixteen Dances* and *Concerto for Prepared Piano and Chamber Orchestra.* The elements of the gamuts were arranged unsystematically in charts and the method of composition involved moves on these charts analagous to those used in constructing a magic square. Charts were also used for the *Music of Changes,* but in contrast to the method which involved chance opera-

tions, these charts were
subjected to
a rational
control: of the
sixty-four el-
ements in a
square chart eight times
eight (made in this
way in order
to interpret
as sounds the co-
in oracle
of the Chinese
Book of Changes)
thirty-two were
sounds, thirty-two
silences. The
thirty-two sounds
were arranged in
two squares one a-
bove the other,
each four by four.
Whether the charts
were mobile or
immobile, all
twelve tones were pres-
ent in any
four elements
of a given
chart, whether a
line of the chart
was read hori-
zontally or
vertically.
Once this dodec-
aphonic re-

quirement was sat-
isfied, noises
and repeti-
tions of tones were
used with freedom.

One may conclude
from this that in
the *Music of
Changes* the ef-
fect of the
chance operations
on the structure

(making very
apparent its
anachronis-
tic character)

was balanced by
a control of
the materials.
Charts remain in
the *Imagi-
nary Landscape
Number IV*, and
in the *Williams*

Mix, but, due to
the radios
of the first piece
and the librar-
y of record-
ed sounds of the
second, and for
no other rea-
son, no twelve-tone
control was used.
The question "How
do we need to
cautiously pro-
ceed in dual-
istic terms?" was
not consciously
answered until
the *Music for
Piano.* In
that piece notes were
determined by
imperfections
in the paper
upon which the
music was writ-
ten. The number
of imperfec-
tions was deter-
mined by chance.

The origi-
nal notation
is in ink, and
the actual
steps that were tak-
en in compo-
sition have been
described in an
article in
Die Reihe. ¶Though
in the *Music*
for Piano
I have affirmed
the absence of
the mind as a
ruling agent
from the structure
and method of the
composing
means, its presence
with regard to
material
is made clear on
examining
the sounds themselves:
they are only
single tones of
the convention-
al grand pia-
no, played at the
keyboard, plucked or
muted on the
strings, together
with noises in-
side or outside
the piano
construction. The
limited na-
ture of this u-
niverse of pos-
sibilities
makes the events
themselves compa-
rable to the
first attempts at
speech of a child
or the fumblings
about of a
blind man. The mind
reappears as
the agent which
established the
boundaries with-
in which this small
play took place. Some-
thing more far-reach-
ing is neces-
sary: a com-
posing of sounds
within a u-
niverse predi-
cated upon the
sounds themselves

rather than up-
on the mind which
can envisage
their coming in-
to being. ¶Sounds,
as we know, have
frequency, am-
plitude, dura-
tion, timbre, and in
a composi-
tion, an order
of succession.
Five lines repre-
senting these five
characteris-
tics may be drawn

in India ink
upon trans-
parent plastic
squares. Upon an-
other such square
a point may be
inscribed. Placing
the square with the
lines over the
square with the point,
a determi-
nation may be
made as to the
physical na-
ture of a sound

and its place with-
in a deter-
mined program sim-
ply by dropping
a perpendi-
cular from the
point to the line
and measuring
according to
any method
of measurement.
Larger points will
have the meaning
of intervals
and largest points
that of aggre-
gates. In order
to make the sev-
eral measure-
ments necessar-
y for inter-
vals and aggre-
gates, further squares
having five lines
are made and the
meaning of an-
y of the lines
is left unde-
termined, so that
a given one
refers to an-
y of the five
characteris-
tics. These squares are
square so that they
may be used in

any posi-
tion with respect
to one anoth-
er. This describes
the situa-
tion obtaining

in a recent
composition,
Variations,
the composing
means itself one
of the eighty-
four occurring
in the part for
piano of
Concert for Pi-

*ano and Or-
chestra.* In this
situation,
the universe
within which the
action is to
take place is not
preconceived. Fur-
thermore, as we
know, sounds are e-
vents in a field
of possibil-
ities, not on-
ly at the dis-
crete points conven-
tions have favored.
The notation
of *Varia-
tions* departs from
music and im-
itates the phys-
ical real-
ity. ¶It is
now my inten-
tion to relate
the history
of the changes
with regard to
duration of
sounds in my com-
posing means. Be-
yond the fact that
in the *Construc-
tion in Metal*
there was a con-
trol of dura-

tion patterns parallel to that
of the number
of sounds chosen,
nothing unconventional took
place. Quantities
related through
multiplication by two or
addition of
one-half together with grupettos of three, five,
seven, and nine
were present. The
same holds for the
*Sonatas and
Interludes,* though
no rhythmic patterns were rationally controlled.
In the *String Quartet* the rhythmic
interest drops,
movements being
nearly characterized by the
predominance
of a single
quantity. Not
until the *Music of Changes*
do the quantities
and their notation change. They

are there measured
in space, a quarter note equalling two and onehalf centimeters. This made possible the notation of a
fraction, for example one-third
of an eighth, without the necessity of notating the remainder of the
fraction, the remaining two-thirds,
following the
same example.
This possibility is directly analogous to the
practice of cutting magnetic
tape. In the duration charts of
the *Music of
Changes* there were
sixty-four elements, all of
them durations
since they were both

applicable

to sound and silence (each of which
had thirty-two
elements). These
were segmented
(for example
one-half plus onethird of an eighth
plus six-sevenths
of a quarter)
and were expressible wholly
or in part. This
segmentation
was a practical measure taken to avoid
the writing of
an impossible situation which might arise during a
high density
structural area due to
the chance oper-

ations. ¶The same
segmentation
of durations
took place in the
Williams Mix, since
a maximum
of eight machines
and loudspeakers
had been pre-established. When the
density rose
from one to sixteen, it was often necessary to express
durations by
their smallest parts,
there being no
room left on the
tape for the larger segments. ¶Exact measurement
and notation

of durations
is in reality mental:

imaginary exactitude. In the case
of tape, many

circumstances enter which ever so slightly, but nonetheless profoundly, alter the intention (even though it was only the carrying out of an action indicated by chance operations). Some of these circumstances are the effects of weather upon the material; others follow from human frailty— the inability to read a ruler and make a cut at a given point— still others are due to mechanical causes, eight machines not running at precisely the same speed. ¶Given these circumstances, one might be inspired towards greater heights of dura-

tion control or he might renounce the need to control durations at all. In *Music for Piano* I took the latter course. Structure no longer being present, that piece took place in any length of time whatsoever, according to the exigencies of an occasion. The duration of single sounds was therefore also left indeterminate. The notation took the form of whole notes in space, the space suggesting but not measuring time. Noises were crotchets without stems. ¶When a

performance of *Music for Piano* involves more than one pianist, as it may from two to twenty, the succession of sounds becomes completely indeterminate. Though each page is read from left to right conventionally, the combination is unpredictable in terms of succession. ¶The history of changes with reference to timbre is short. In the *Construction in Metal* four sounds had a single timbre; while the prepared piano of the *Sonatas and Interludes* provided by its nature a *klangfarbenmelodie*. This interest in changing timbres is evi-

dent in the *String Quartet*. But this matter of timbre, which is largely a question of taste, was first radically changed for me in the *Imaginary Landscape Number IV*. I had, I confess, never enjoyed the sound of radios. This piece opened my ears

to them, and was essentially a giving up of personal taste about timbre. I now frequently compose with the radio turned on, and my friends are no longer embarrassed when visiting them I interrupt their receptions. Several other kinds of sound have been distasteful to me: the works of Beethoven, Italian *bel canto*, jazz, and the vibraphone. I used Beethoven in the *Williams Mix*, jazz in the *Imaginary Landscape Number V*, *bel canto* in the recent part for voice in the *Concert for Piano and Orchestra*. It remains for me to come to terms with the vibraphone. In other words, I find my taste for timbre

lacking in necessity, and I discover that in the proportion I give it up, I find I hear more and more accurate-

ly. Beethoven now is a surprise, as acceptable to the ear as a cowbell. What are the orchestral timbres of the *Concert for Piano and Orchestra*? It is impossible to predict, but this may be said: they invite the timbres of jazz, which more than serious music has explored the possibilities of instruments. ¶With tape and music-synthesizers, action with the overtone structure of sounds can be less a matter of taste and more thoroughly an action in a field of possibilities. The notation I have described for *Variations* deals with it as such.

¶The early works have beginnings, middles, and endings. The later ones do not. They begin anywhere, last any length of time, and involve more or fewer instruments and players. They are therefore not preconceived objects, and to approach them as objects is to utterly miss

the point. They are

occasions for experience, and this experience is not only received by the ears but by the eyes too. An ear alone is not a being. I have noticed listening to a record

that my attention moves to a moving object or a play of light, and at a rehearsal of the *Williams Mix* last May when all eight machines were in operation the attention of those present was engaged by a sixty-year-old piano tuner who was busy tuning the instrument for the evening's concert. It becomes evident that music itself is an ideal situation, not a real one. The mind may be used either to ignore ambient sounds, pitches other than the eighty-eight, durations which are not counted, timbres which are unmusical or distasteful, and in general to control and understand an available experience. Or the mind may give up its desire to improve on creation and function as a faithful receiver of experience. ¶I have not yet told any stories and yet when I give a talk I generally do. The subject certainly suggests my telling something

irrelevant

but my inclination is to tell something apt. That reminds me: Several years ago I was present at a lecture given by Dr. Daisetz Teitaro Suzuki. He spoke quietly when he spoke. Sometimes, as I was telling a friend yesterday evening, an airplane

would pass overhead. The lecture was at Columbia University and the campus is directly in line with the departure from La Guardia of planes bound for the west. When the weather was good, the windows were open: a plane passing above drowned out Dr. Daisetz Teitaro Suzuki. Nevertheless, he never raised his voice, never paused, and never informed his listeners of what they missed of the lecture, and no one ever asked him what he had said while the airplanes passed above. Any-

way, he was explaining one day the meaning of a Chinese character—Yu, I believe it was—spending the whole time explaining it and yet its meaning as close as he could get to it in English was "unexplainable." Finally he laughed and then said, "Isn't it strange that having come all the way from Japan I spend my time explaining to you that which is not to be explained?" ¶That was not the story I was going to tell when I first thought I would tell one, but it reminds me of another.

Years ago when I was studying with Arnold Schoenberg someone asked him to explain his technique of twelve-tone composition. His reply was immediate: "That is none of your business." ¶Now I remember the story I was going to tell when I first got the idea to tell one. I hope I can tell it well. Several men, three as a matter of fact, were out walking one day, and as they were walking along and talking one of them noticed another man standing on a hill ahead of them. He turned to his friends and said, "Why do you think that man is standing up there on that hill?" One said, "He must be up there because it's cooler there and he's enjoying the breeze." He turned to another and repeated his question, "Why do you think that man's standing up there on that hill?" The second said, "Since the hill is elevated above the rest of the land, he must be up there in order to see something in the distance." And the third said, "He must have lost his friend and that is why he is standing there alone on that hill." After some time walking along, the men came up the hill and the one who had been standing there was still there: standing there. They asked him to say which one was right concerning his reason for standing where he was standing. ¶"What reasons do you have for my standing here?" he asked. "We have three," they answered. "First, you are standing up here because it's cooler here and you are enjoying the breeze. Second, since the hill is elevated above the rest of the land, you are up here in order to

see something in the distance. Third, you have lost your friend and that is why you are standing here alone on this hill. We have walked this way; we never meant to climb this hill; now we want an

answer: Which one
of us is right?"
¶The man answered,
"I just stand." ¶When
I was studying
with Schoenberg
one day as he was
writing some
counterpoint to
show the way to
do it, he used
an eraser.
And then while he
was doing this

he said, "This end
of the pencil
is just as im-
portant as the
other end." I
have several
times in the course
of this lecture
mentioned ink. Com-
posing, if it
is writing notes,
is then actu-

ally writing,
and the less one
thinks it's thinking
the more it be-
comes what it is:
writing. Could mu-
sic be composed
(I do not mean
improvised) not
writing it in
pencil or ink?

The answer is
no doubt Yes and
the changes in
writing are pro-
phetic. The *So-
natas and In-
terludes* were com-
posed by playing
the piano,
listening to
differences,
making a choice,
roughly writing
it in pencil;
later this sketch

was copied, but
again in pen-
cil. Finally
an ink manuscript
was made care-
fully. The *Mu-
sic of Changes*
was composed in
almost the same
way. With one change:
the origi-
nal pencil sketch
was made exact-
ly, an era-
ser used whenev-
er necessar-
y, elimin-
ating the need
for a neat pen-
cil copy. In
the case of the
*Imaginar-
y Landscape Num-
ber IV*, the first
step of playing
the instrument
was elimin-
ated. The oth-
ers kept. *Music
for Piano*
was written di-
rectly in ink.

The excessively small type in the following pages is an attempt to emphasize the intentionally pontifical character of this lecture.

II. Indeterminacy

This is a lecture on composition which is indeterminate with respect to its performance. The *Klavierstück XI* by Karlheinz Stockhausen is an example. *The Art of the Fugue* by Johann Sebastian Bach is an example. In *The Art of the Fugue*, structure, which is the division of the whole into parts; method, which is the note-to-note procedure; and form, which is the expressive content, the morphology of the continuity, are all determined. Frequency and duration characteristics of the material are also determined. Timbre and amplitude characteristics of the material, by not being given, are indeterminate. This indeterminacy brings about the possibility of a unique overtone structure and decibel range for each performance of *The Art of the Fugue*. In the case of the *Klavierstück XI*, all the characteristics of the material are determined, and so too is the note-to-note procedure, the method. The division of the whole into parts, the structure, is determinate. The sequence of these parts, however, is indeterminate, bringing about the possibility of a unique form, which is to say a unique morphology of the continuity, a unique expressive content, for each performance.

The function of the performer, in the case of *The Art of the Fugue,* is comparable to that of someone filling in color where outlines are given. He may do this in an organized way which may be subjected successfully to analysis. (Transcriptions by Arnold Schoenberg and Anton Webern give examples pertinent to this century.) Or he may perform his function of colorist in a way which is not consciously organized (and therefore not subject to analysis)—either arbitrarily, feeling his way, following the dictates of his ego; or more or less unknowingly, by going inwards with reference to the structure of his mind to a point in dreams, following, as in automatic writing, the dictates of his subconscious mind; or to a point in the collective unconscious of Jungian psychoanalysis, following the inclinations of the species and doing something of more or less universal interest to human beings; or to the "deep sleep" of Indian mental practice—the Ground of Meister Eckhart—identifying there with no matter what eventuality. Or he may perform his function of colorist arbitrarily, by going outwards with reference to the structure of his mind to the point of sense perception, following his taste; or more or less unknowingly by employing some operation exterior to his mind: tables of random numbers, following the scientific interest in probability; or chance operations, identifying there with no matter what eventuality

The function of the performer in the case of the *Klavierstück XI* is not that of a colorist but that of giving form, providing, that is to say, the morphology of the continuity, the expressive content. This may not be done in an organized way: for form unvitalized by spontaneity brings about the death of all the other elements of the work. Examples are provided by academic studies which copy models with respect to all their compositional elements: structure, method, material, and form. On the other hand, no matter how rigorously controlled or conventional the structure, method, and materials of a composition are, that composition will come to life if the form is not controlled but free and original. One may cite as examples the sonnets of Shakespeare and the *haikus* of Basho. How then in the case of the *Klavierstück XI* may the performer fulfill his function of giving form to the music? He must perform his function of giving form to the music in a way which is not consciously organized (and therefore not subject to analysis), either arbitrarily, feeling his way, following the dictates of his ego, or more or less unknowingly, by going inwards with reference to the structure of his mind to a point in dreams, following, as in automatic writing, the dictates of his subconscious mind; or to a point in the collective unconscious of Jungian psychoanalysis, following the inclinations of the species and doing something of more or less universal interest to human beings; or to the "deep sleep" of Indian mental practice—the Ground of Meister Eckhart—identifying there with no matter what eventuality. Or he may perform his function of giving form to the music arbitrarily, by going outwards with reference to the structure of his mind to the point of sense perception, following his taste; or more or less unknowingly by employing some operation exterior to his mind: tables of random numbers, following the scientific interest in probability; or chance operations, identifying there with no matter what eventuality.

However, due to the presence in the *Klavierstück XI* of the two most essentially conventional aspects of European music—that is to say, the twelve tones of the octave (the frequency characteristic of the material) and regularity of beat (affecting the element of method in the composing means), the performer—in those instances where his procedure follows any dictates at all (his feelings, his automatism, his sense of universality, his taste)—will be led to give the form aspects essentially conventional to European music. These instances will predominate over those which are unknowing where the performer wishes to act in a way consistent with the composition as written. The form aspects essentially conventional to European music are, for instance, the presentation of a whole as an object in time having a beginning, a middle, and an ending, progressive rather than static in character, which is to say possessed of a climax or climaxes and in contrast a point or points of rest.

The indeterminate aspects of the composition of the *Klavierstück XI* do not remove the work in its performance from the body of European musical conventions. And yet the purpose of indeterminacy would seem to be to bring about an unforseen situation. In the case of *Klavierstück XI*, the use of indeterminacy is in this sense unnecessary since it is ineffective. The work might as well have been written in all of its aspects determinately. It would lose, in this case, its single unconventional aspect: that of being printed on an unusually large sheet of paper which, together with an attachment that may be snapped on at several points enabling one to stretch it out flat and place it on the music rack of a piano, is put in a cardboard tube suitable for safekeeping or distribution through the mails.

This is a lecture on composition which is indeterminate with respect to its performance. The *Intersection 3* by Morton Feldman is an example. The *Music of Changes* is not an example. In the *Music of Changes*, structure, which is the division of the whole into parts; method, which is the note-to-note procedure; form, which is the expressive content, the morphology of the continuity; and materials, the sounds and silences of the composition, are all determined. Though no two performances of the *Music of Changes* will be identical (each act is virgin, even the repeated one, to refer to René Char's thought), two performances will resemble one another closely. Though chance operations brought about the determinations of the composition, these operations are not available in its performance. The function of the performer in the case of the *Music of Changes* is that of a contractor who, following an architect's blueprint, constructs a building. That the *Music of Changes* was composed by means of chance operations identifies the composer with no matter what eventuality. But that its notation is in all respects determinate does not permit the performer any such identification: his work is specifically laid out before him. He is therefore not able to perform from his own center but must identify himself insofar as possible with the center of the work as written. The *Music of Changes* is an object more inhuman than human, since chance operations brought it into being. The fact that these things that constitute it, though only sounds, have come together to control a human being, the performer, gives the work the alarming aspect of a Frankenstein monster. This situation is of course characteristic of Western music, the masterpieces of which are its most frightening examples, which when concerned with humane communication only move over from Frankenstein monster to Dictator.

In the case of the *Intersection 3* by Morton Feldman, structure may be viewed as determinate or as indeterminate; method is definitely indeterminate. Frequency and duration characteristics of the material are determinate only within broad limits (they are with respect to narrow limits indeterminate); the timbre characteristic of the material, being given by the instrument designated, the piano, is determinate; the amplitude characteristic of the material is indeterminate. Form conceived in terms of a continuity of various weights—that is, a continuity of numbers of sounds, the sounds themselves particularized only with respect to broad range limits (high, middle, and low)—is determinate, particularly so due to the composer's having specified boxes as time units. Though one might equally describe it as indeterminate for other reasons. The term "boxes" arises from the composer's use of graph paper for the notation of his composition. The function of the box is comparable to that of a green light in metropolitan thoroughfare control. The performer is free to play the given number of sounds in the range indicated at any time during the duration of the box, just as when driving an automobile one may cross an intersection at any time during the green light. With the exception of method, which is wholly indeterminate, the compositional means are characterized by being in certain respects determinate, in others indeterminate, and an interpenetration of these opposites obtains which is more characteristic than either. The situation is therefore essentially non-dualistic; a multiplicity of centers in a state of non-obstruction and interpenetration.

The function of the performer in the case of the *Intersection 3* is that of a photographer who on obtaining a camera uses it to take a picture. The composition permits an infinite number of these, and, not being mechanically constructed, it will not wear out. It can only suffer disuse or loss. How is the performer to perform the *Intersection 3*? He may do this in an organized way which may be subjected successfully to analysis. Or he may perform his function of photographer in a way which is not consciously organized (and therefore not subject to analysis)—either arbitrarily, feeling his way, following the dictates of his ego; or more or less unknowingly, by going inwards with reference to the structure of his mind to a point in dreams, following, as in automatic writing, the dictates of his subconscious mind; or to a point in the collective unconsciousness of Jungian pyschoanalysis, following the inclinations of the species and doing something of more or less universal interest to human beings; or to the "deep sleep" of Indian mental practice—the Ground of Meister Eckhart—identifying there with no matter what eventuality. Or he may perform his function of photographer arbitrarily, by going outwards with reference to the structure of his mind to the point of sense perception, following his taste; or more or less unknowingly by employing some operation exterior to his mind: tables of random numbers, following the scientific interest in probability; or chance operations, identifying there with no matter what eventuality.

One evening Morton Feldman said that when he composed he was dead; this recalls to me the statement of my father, an inventor, who says he does his best work when he is sound asleep. The two suggest the "deep sleep" of Indian mental practice. The ego no longer blocks action. A fluency obtains which is characteristic of nature. The seasons make the round of spring, summer, fall, and winter, interpreted in Indian thought as creation, preservation, destruction, and quiescence. Deep sleep is comparable to quiescence. Each spring brings no matter what eventuality. The performer then will act in any way. Whether he does so in an organized way or in any one of the not consciously organized ways cannot be answered until his action is a reality. The nature of the composition and the knowledge of the composer's own view of his action suggest, indeed, that the performer act sometimes consciously, sometimes not consciously and from the Ground of Meister Eckhart, identifying there with no matter what eventuality.

This is a lecture on composition which is indeterminate with respect to its performance. *Indices* by Earle Brown is not an example. Where the performance involves a number of players, as it does in the case of *Indices*, the introduction of a score—that is, a fixed relation of the parts—removes the quality of indeterminacy from the performance. Though tables of random numbers (used in a way which introduces bias) brought about the determinations of the composition (structure, method, materials, and form are in the case of *Indices* all thus determined), those tables are not available in its performance. The function of the conductor is that of a contractor, who, following an architect's blueprint, constructs a building. The function of the instrumentalists is that of workmen who simply do as they are bid. That the *Indices* by Earle Brown was composed by means of tables of random numbers (used in a way which introduces bias) identifies the composer with no matter what eventuality, since by the introduction of bias he has removed himself from an association with the scientific interest in probability. But that the notation of the parts is in all respects determinate, and that, moreover, a score provides a fixed relation of these parts, does not permit the conductor or the players any such identification. Their work is laid out before them. The conductor is not able to conduct from his own center but must identify himself insofar as possible with the center of the work as written. The instrumentalists are not able to perform from their several centers but are employed to identify themselves insofar as possible with the directives given by the conductor. They identify with the work itself, if at all, by one remove. From that point of view from which each thing and each being is seen as moving out from its own center, this situation of the subservience of several to the directives of one who is himself controlled, not by another but by the work of another, is intolerable.

(In this connection it may be remarked that certain Indian traditional practices prohibit ensemble, limiting performance to the solo circumstance. This solo, in traditional Indian practice, is not a performance of something written by another but an improvisation by the performer himself within certain limitations of structure, method, and material. Though he himself by the morphology of the continuity brings the form into being, the expressive content does not reside in this compositional element alone, but by the conventions of Indian tradition resides also in all the other compositional elements.)

The intolerable situation described is, of course, not a peculiarity of *Indices*, but a characteristic of Western music, the masterpieces of which are its most imposing examples, which, when they are concerned not with tables of random numbers (used in a way which introduces bias) but rather with ideas of order, personal feelings, and the integration of these, simply suggest the presence of a man rather than the presence of sounds. The sounds of *Indices* are just sounds. Had bias not been introduced in the use of the tables of random numbers, the sounds would have been not just sounds but elements acting according to scientific theories of probability, elements acting in relationship due to the equal distribution of each one of those present—elements, that is to say, under the control of man.

This is a lecture on composition which is indeterminate with respect to its performance. The *4 Systems* by Earle Brown is an example. This piece may be performed by one or several players. There is no score, either for the solo circumstance or for that of ensemble. The quality of indeterminacy is for this reason not removed from the performance even where a number of players are involved, since no fixed relation of the parts exists. The original notation is a drawing of rectangles of various lengths and widths in ink on a single cardboard having four equal divisions (which are the systems). The vertical position of the rectangles refers to relative time. The width of the rectangles may be interpreted either as an interval where the drawing is read as two-dimensional, or as amplitude where the drawing is read as giving the illusion of a third dimension. Any of the interpretations of this material may be superimposed in any number and order and, with the addition or not of silences between them, may be used to produce a continuity of any time-length. In order to multiply the possible interpretations the composer gives a further permission—to read the cardboard in any of four positions: right side up, upside down, sideways, up and down.

This further permission alters the situation radically. Without it, the composition was highly indeterminate of its performance. The drawing was not consciously organized. Drawn unknowingly, from the Ground of Meister Eckhart, it identified the composer with no matter what eventuality. But with the further permission—that of reading the cardboard right side up, upside down, sideways, up and down—the drawing became that of two different situations or groups of situations and their inversions. Inversions are a hallmark of the conscious mind. The composer's identification (though not consciously so according to him) is therefore no longer with no matter what eventuality but rather with those events that are related by inversion. What might have been non-dualistic becomes dualistic. From a non-dualistic point of view, each thing and each being is seen at the center, and these centers are in a state of interpenetration and non-obstruction. From a dualistic point of view, on the other hand, each thing and each being is not seen: relationships are seen and interferences are seen. To avoid undesired interferences and to make one's intentions clear, a dualistic point of view requires a careful integration of the opposites.

If this careful integration is lacking in the composition, and in the case of *4 Systems* it is (due to the high degree of indeterminacy), it must be supplied in the performance. The function of the performer or of each performer in the case of *4 Systems* is that of making something out of a store of raw materials. Structure, the division of the whole into parts, is indeterminate. Form, the morphology of the continuity, is also indeterminate. In given interpretations of the original drawing (such as those made by David Tudor sufficient in number to provide a performance by four pianists lasting four minutes) method is determinate and so too are the amplitude, timbre, and frequency characteristics of the material. The duration characteristic of the material is both determinate and indeterminate, since lines extending from note-heads indicate exact length of time, but the total length of time of a system is indeterminate. The performer's function, in the case of *4 Systems*, is dual: to give both structure and form; to provide, that is, the division of the whole into parts and the morphology of the continuity.

Conscious only of his having made a composition indeterminate of its performance, the composer does not himself acknowledge the necessity of this dual function of the performer which I am describing. He does not agree with the view here expressed that the permission given to interpret the drawing right side up, upside down, and sideways, up and down obliges the integration of the opposites: conscious organization and its absence. The structural responsibility must be fulfilled in an organized way, such as might be subjected successfully to analysis. (The performers in each performance have, as a matter of record, given to each system lengths of time which are related as modules are in architecture: fifteen seconds and multiples thereof by two or four.) The formal responsibility must be fulfilled in one or several of the many ways which are not consciously organized. However, due to the identification with the conscious mind indicated in *4 Systems* by the presence of inversions, though not acknowledged by the composer, those ways which are not consciously organized that are adjacent to the ego are apt to be used, particularly where the performer wishes to act in a way consistent with the composition as here viewed. He will in these cases perform arbitrarily, feeling his way, following the dictates of his ego; or he will perform arbitrarily, following his taste, in terms of sense perception.

What might have given rise, by reason of the high degree of indeterminacy, to no matter what eventuality (to a process essentially purposeless) becomes productive of a time-object. This object, exceedingly complex due to the absence of a score, a fixed relation of the parts, is analogous to a futurist or cubist painting, perhaps, or to a moving picture where flicker makes seeing the object difficult.

From the account which appears to be a history of a shift from non-dualism to dualism (not by intention, since the composer does not attach to the inversions the importance here given them, but as a by-product of the action taken to multiply possibilities) the following deduction may be made: To ensure indeterminacy with respect to its performance, a composition must be determinate of itself. If this indeterminacy is to have a non-dualistic nature, each element of the notation must have a single interpretation rather than a plurality of interpretations which, coming from a single source, fall into relation. Likewise—though this is not relevant to *4 Systems*—one may deduce that a single operation within the act of composition itself must not give rise to more than a single notation. Where a single operation is applied to more than one notation, for example to those of both frequency and amplitude characteristics, the frequency and amplitude characteristics are by that operation common to both brought into relationship. These relationships make an object; and this object, in contrast to a process which is purposeless, must be viewed dualistically. Indeterminacy when present in the making of an object, and when therefore viewed dualistically, is a sign not of identification with no matter what eventuality but simply of carelessness with regard to the outcome.

This is a lecture on composition which is indeterminate with respect to its performance. *Duo II for Pianists* by Christian Wolff is an example. In the case of *Duo II for Pianists*, structure, the division of the whole into parts, is indeterminate. (No provision is given by the composer for ending the performance.) Method, the note-to-note procedure, is also indeterminate. All the characteristics of the materials (frequency, amplitude, timbre, duration) are indeterminate within gamut limitations provided by the composer. The form, the morphology of the continuity, is unpredictable. One of the pianists begins the performance: the other, noticing a particular sound or silence which is one of a gamut of cues, responds with an action of his own determination from among given possibilities within a given time bracket. Following this beginning, each panist responds to cues provided by the other, letting no silence fall between responses, though these responses themselves include silences. Certain time brackets are in zero time. There is no score, no fixed relation of the parts. *Duo II for Pianists* is evidently not a time-object, but rather a process the beginning and ending of which are irrelevant to its nature. The ending, and the beginning, will be determined in performance, not by exigencies interior to the action but by circumstances of the concert occasion. If the other pieces on the program take forty-five minutes of time and fifteen minutes more are required to bring the program to a proper length, *Duo II for Pianists* may be fifteen minutes long. Where only five minutes are available, it will be five minutes long.

The function of each performer in the case of *Duo II for Pianists* is comparable to that of a traveler who must constantly be catching trains the departures of which have not been announced but which are in the process of being announced. He must be continually ready to go, alert to the situation, and responsible. If he notices no cue, that fact itself is a cue calling for responses indeterminate within gamut limitations and time brackets. Thus he notices (or notices that he does not notice) a cue, adds time bracket to time bracket, determines his response to come (meanwhile also giving a response), and, as the second hand of a chronometer approaches the end of one bracket and the beginning of the next, he prepares himself for the action to come (meanwhile still making an action), and, precisely as the second hand of a chronometer begins the next time bracket, he makes the suitable action (meanwhile noticing or noticing that he does not notice the next cue), and so on. How is each performer to fulfill this function of being alert in an indeterminate situation? Does he need to proceed cautiously in dualistic terms? On the contrary, he needs his mind in one piece. His mind is too busy to spend time splitting itself into conscious and not-conscious parts. These parts, however, are still present. What has happened is simply a complete change of direction. Rather than making the not-conscious parts face the conscious part of the mind, the conscious part, by reason of the urgency and indeterminacy of the situation, turns towards the not-conscious parts. He is therefore able, as before, to add two to two to get four, or to act in organized ways which on being subjected to analysis successfully are found to be more complex. But rather than concentrating his attention here, in the realm of relationships, variations, approximations, repetitions, logarithms, his attention is given inwardly and outwardly with reference to the structure of his mind to no matter what eventuality. Turning away from himself and his ego-sense of separation from other beings and things, he faces the Ground of Meister Eckhart, from which all impermanencies flow and to which they return. "Thoughts arise not to be collected and cherished but to be dropped as though they were void. Thoughts arise not to be collected and cherished but to be dropped as though they were rotten wood. Thoughts arise not to be collected and cherished but to be dropped as though they were pieces of stone. Thoughts arise not to be collected and cherished but to be dropped as though they were the cold ashes of a fire long dead." Similarly, in the performance of *Duo II for Pianists*, each performer, when he performs in a way consistent with the composition as written, will let go of his feelings, his taste, his automatism, his sense of the universal, not attaching himself to this or to that, leaving his performance no traces, providing by his actions no interruption to the fluency of nature. The performer therefore simply does what is to be done, not splitting his mind in two, not separating it from his body, which is kept ready for direct and instantaneous contact with his instrument.

This is a lecture on composition which is indeterminate with respect to its performance. That composition is necessarily experimental. An experimental action is one the outcome of which is not forseen. Being unforseen, this action is not concerned with its excuse. Like the land, like the air, it needs none. A performance of a composition which is indeterminate of its performance is necessarily unique. It cannot be repeated. When performed for a second time, the outcome is other than it was. Nothing therefore is accomplished by such a performance, since that performance cannot be grasped as an object in time. A recording of such a work has no more value than a postcard; it provides a knowledge of something that happened, whereas the action was a non-knowledge of something that had not yet happened.

There are certain practical matters to discuss that concern the performance of music the composition of which is indeterminate with respect to its performance. These matters concern the physical space of the performance. These matters also concern the physical time of the performance. In connection with the physical space of the performance, where that performance involves several players (two or more), it is advisable for several reasons to separate the performers one from the other, as much as is convenient and in accord with the action and the architectural situation. This separation allows the sounds to issue from their own centers and to interpenetrate in a way which is not obstructed by the conventions of European harmony and theory about relationships and interferences of sounds. In the case of the harmonious ensembles of European musical history, a fusion of sound was of the essence, and therefore players in an ensemble were brought as close together as possible, so that their actions, productive of an object in time, might be effective. In the case, however, of the performance of music the composition of which is indeterminate of its performance so that the action of the players is productive of a process, no harmonious fusion of sound is essential. A non-obstruction of sounds is of the essence. The separation of players in space when there is an ensemble is useful towards bringing about this non-obstruction and interpenetration, which are of the essence. Furthermore, this separation in space will facilitate the independent action of each performer, who, not constrained by the performance of a part which has been extracted from a score, has turned his mind in the direction of no matter what eventuality. There is the possibility when people are crowded together that they will act like sheep rather than nobly. That is why separation in space is spoken of as facilitating independent action on the part of each performer. Sounds will then arise from actions, which will then arise from their own centers rather than as motor or psychological effects of other actions and sounds in the environment. The musical recognition of the necessity of space is tardy with respect to the recognition of space on the part of the other arts, not to mention scientific awareness. It is indeed astonishing that music as an art has kept performing musicians so consistently huddled together in a group. It is high time to separate the players one from another, in order to show a musical recognition of the necessity of space, which has already been recognized on the part of the other arts, not to mention scientific awareness. What is indicated, too, is a disposition of the performers, in the case of an ensemble in space, other than the conventional one of a huddled group at one end of a recital or symphonic hall. Certainly the performers in the case of an ensemble in space will be disposed about the room. The conventional architecture is often not suitable. What is required perhaps is an architecture like that of Mies van der Rohe's School of Architecture at the Illinois Institute of Technology. Some such architecture will be useful for the performance of composition which is indeterminate of its performance. Nor will the performers be huddled together in a group in the center of the audience. They must at least be disposed separately around the audience, if not, by approaching their disposition in the most radically realistic sense, actually disposed within the audience itself. In this latter case, the further separation of performer and audience will facilitate the independent action of each person, which will include mobility on the part of all.

There are certain practical matters to discuss that concern the performance of music the composition of which is indeterminate with respect to its performance. These matters concern the physical space of the performance. These matters also concern the physical time of the performance. In connection with the physical time of the performance, where that performance involves several players (two or more), it is advisable for several reasons to give the conductor another function than that of beating time. The situation of sounds arising from actions which arise from their own centers will not be produced when a conductor beats time in order to unify the performance. Nor will the situation of sounds arising from actions which arise from their own centers be produced when several conductors beat different times in order to bring about a complex unity to the performance. Beating time is not necessary. All that is necessary is a slight suggestion of time, obtained either from glancing at a watch or at a conductor who, by his actions, represents a watch. Where an actual watch is used, it becomes possible to foresee the time, by reason of the steady progress from second to second of the second hand. Where, however, a conductor is present, who by his actions represents a watch which moves not mechanically but variably, it is not possible to foresee the time, by reason of the changing progress from second to second of the conductor's indications. Where this conductor, who by his actions represents a watch, does so in relation to a part rather than a score—to, in fact, his own part, not that of another—his actions will interpenetrate with those of the players of the ensemble in a way which will not obstruct their actions. The musical recognition of the necessity of time is tardy with respect to the recognition of time on the part of broadcast communications, radio, television, not to mention magnetic tape, not to mention travel by air, departures and arrivals from no matter what point at no matter what time, to no matter what point at no matter what time, not to mention telephony. It is indeed astonishing that music as an art has kept performing musicians so consistently beating time together like so many horseback riders huddled together on one horse. It is high time to let sounds issue in time independent of a beat in order to show a musical recognition of the necessity of time which has already been recognized on the part of broadcast communications, radio, television, not to mention magnetic tape, not to mention travel by air, departures and arrivals from no matter what point at no matter what time, to no matter what point at no matter what time, not to mention telephony.

. . . .

An Indian lady invited me to dinner and said Dr. Suzuki would be there. He was. Before dinner I mentioned Gertrude Stein. Suzuki had never heard of her. I described aspects of her work, which he said sounded very interesting. Stimulated, I mentioned James Joyce, whose name was also new to him. At dinner he was unable to eat the curries that were offered, so a few uncooked vegetables and fruits were brought, which he enjoyed. After dinner the talk turned to metaphysical problems, and there were many questions, for the hostess was a follower of a certain Indian yogi and her guests were more or less equally divided between allegiance to Indian thought and to Japanese thought. About eleven o'clock we were out on the street walking along, and an American lady said, "How is it, Dr. Suzuki? We spend the evening asking you questions and nothing is decided." Dr. Suzuki smiled and said, "That's why I love philosophy: no one wins."

The following text is made up of questions and quotations. The quotations are some from the writings of others and some from my own writings. (That from Christian Wolff is from his article "New and Electronic Music," copyright 1958 by the Audience Press, and reprinted by permission from Audience, *Volume V, Number 3, Summer 1958.) The order and quantity of the quotations were given by chance operations. No performance timing was composed. Nevertheless, I always prescribe one before delivering this lecture, sometimes adding by chance operations indications of when, in the course of the performance, I am obliged to light a cigarette.*

III. Communication

Nichi nichi kore ko nichi: Every day is a beautiful day
What if I ask thirty-two questions?
What if I stop asking now and then?
Will that make things clear?
Is communication something made clear?
What is communication?
Music, what does it communicate?
Is what's clear to me clear to you?
Is music just sounds?
Then what does it communicate?
Is a truck passing by music?
If I can see it, do I have to hear it too?
If I don't hear it, does it still communicate?
If while I see it I can't hear it, but hear something else, say an egg-beater, because I'm
    inside looking out, does the truck communicate or the egg-beater, which communicates?
Which is more musical, a truck passing by a factory or a truck
    passing by a music school?
Are the people inside the school musical and the ones outside unmusical?
What if the ones inside can't hear very well, would that change my question?
Do you know what I mean when I say inside the school?
Are sounds just sounds or are they Beethoven?
People aren't sounds, are they?

Is there such a thing as silence?

Even if I get away from people, do I still have to listen to something?

Say I'm off in the woods, do I have to listen to a stream babbling?

Is there always something to hear, never any peace and quiet?

If my head is full of harmony, melody, and rhythm, what happens to
      me when the telephone rings, to my piece and quiet, I mean?

And if it was European harmony, melody, and rhythm in my head, what has happened
      to the history of, say, Javanese music, with respect, that is to say, to my head?

Are we getting anywhere asking questions?

Where are we going?

Is this the twenty-eighth question?

Are there any important questions?

"How do you need to cautiously proceed in dualistic terms?"

Do I have two more questions?

And, now, do I have none?

Now that I've asked thirty-two questions, can I ask forty-four more?

I can, but may I?

Why must I go on asking questions?

Is there any reason in asking why?

Would I ask why if questions were not words but were sounds?

If words are sounds, are they musical or are they just noises?

If sounds are noises but not words, are they meaningful?

Are they musical?

Say there are two sounds and two people and one of each is beautiful,
      is there between all four any communication?

And if there are rules, who made them, I ask you?

Does it begin somewhere, I mean, and if so, where does it stop?

What will happen to me or to you if we have to be somewhere where beauty isn't?

I ask you, sometime, too, sounds happening in time, what will happen to our experience
      of hearing, yours, mine, our ears, hearing, what will happen if sounds being
      beautiful stop sometime and the only sounds to hear are not beautiful to hear
      but are ugly, what will happen to us?

Would we ever be able to get so that we thought the ugly sounds were beautiful?

If we drop beauty, what have we got?

Have we got truth?

Have we got religion?

Do we have a mythology?

Would we know what to do with one if we had one?

Have we got a way to make money?

And if money is made, will it be spent on music?

If Russia spends sixty million for the Brussels Fair, lots of it for music and dance, and
    America spends one-tenth of that, six million about, does that mean that one out of
    ten Americans is as musical and kinesthetic as all the Russians put together?

If we drop money, what have we got?

Since we haven't yet dropped truth, where shall we go looking for it?

Didn't we say we weren't going, or did we just ask where we were going?

If we didn't say we weren't going, why didn't we?

If we had any sense in our heads, wouldn't we know the truth instead
    of going around looking for it?

How otherwise would we, as they say, be able to drink a glass of water?

We know, don't we, everybody else's religion, mythology, and philosophy
    and metaphysics backwards and forwards, so what need would we have
    for one of our own if we had one, but we don't, do we?

But music, do we have any music?

Wouldn't it be better to just drop music too?

Then what would we have?

Jazz?

What's left?

Do you mean to say it's a purposeless play?

Is that what it is when you get up and hear the first sound of each day?

Is it possible that I could go on monotonously asking questions forever?

Would I have to know how many questions I was going to ask?

Would I have to know how to count in order to ask questions?

Do I have to know when to stop?

Is this the one chance we have to be alive and ask a question?

How long will we be able to be alive?

CONTEMPORARY MUSIC   IS NOT THE MUSIC OF THE FUTURE
                    NOR THE MUSIC OF THE PAST   BUT SIMPLY
MUSIC PRESENT WITH US: THIS MOMENT,   NOW,
              THIS NOW MOMENT.

Something remarkable has happened: I was asking questions; now I'm quoting from a lecture I gave years ago. Of course I will ask some more questions later on, but not now: I have quoting to do.

THAT MOMENT IS ALWAYS CHANGING.   (I WAS SILENT: NOW I AM
SPEAKING.)   HOW CAN WE POSSIBLY TELL WHAT CONTEMPORARY
MUSIC IS, SINCE NOW WE'RE NOT LISTENING TO IT, WE'RE LISTENING
TO A LECTURE ABOUT IT. AND THAT ISN'T IT.
THIS IS "TONGUE-WAGGING." REMOVED AS WE ARE THIS MOMENT FROM
CONTEMPORARY MUSIC (WE ARE ONLY THINKING ABOUT IT) EACH ONE OF US
IS THINKING HIS OWN THOUGHTS, HIS OWN EXPERIENCE, AND EACH
EXPERIENCE IS DIFFERENT AND EACH EXPERIENCE IS CHANGING AND WHILE
WE ARE THINKING I AM TALKING AND CONTEMPORARY MUSIC IS CHANGING.
       LIKE LIFE IT CHANGES.   IF IT WERE NOT CHANGING
IT WOULD BE DEAD, AND, OF COURSE, FOR SOME OF US,   SOMETIMES
IT IS DEAD, BUT AT ANY MOMENT IT CHANGES AND IS LIVING AGAIN.
       TALKING FOR A MOMENT ABOUT CONTEMPORARY MILK:
       AT ROOM TEMPERATURE IT IS CHANGING, GOES SOUR ETC., AND
THEN A NEW BOTTLE ETC., UNLESS BY SEPARATING IT FROM ITS CHANGING
BY POWDERING IT OR REFRIGERATION   (WHICH IS A WAY OF SLOWING
DOWN ITS LIVELINESS)   (THAT IS TO SAY MUSEUMS AND ACADEMIES ARE
WAYS OF PRESERVING)   WE TEMPORARILY SEPARATE THINGS FROM LIFE
(FROM CHANGING) BUT AT ANY MOMENT DESTRUCTION MAY COME SUDDENLY
AND THEN WHAT HAPPENS IS FRESHER

WHEN WE SEPARATE MUSIC FROM LIFE WHAT WE GET IS ART (A COMPENDIUM
OF MASTERPIECES). WITH CONTEMPORARY MUSIC, WHEN IT IS ACTUALLY
CONTEMPORARY, WE HAVE NO TIME TO MAKE THAT SEPARATION (WHICH
PROTECTS US FROM LIVING), AND SO   CONTEMPORARY MUSIC IS
NOT SO MUCH ART AS IT IS LIFE AND ANY ONE MAKING IT NO SOONER
FINISHES ONE OF IT THAN HE BEGINS MAKING ANOTHER JUST AS PEOPLE
KEEP ON WASHING DISHES, BRUSHING THEIR TEETH, GETTING SLEEPY,
AND SO ON.   VERY FREQUENTLY NO ONE KNOWS THAT
CONTEMPORARY MUSIC IS OR COULD BE ART.   HE SIMPLY THINKS IT IS
IRRITATING.   IRRITATING ONE WAY OR ANOTHER,
THAT IS TO SAY KEEPING US FROM OSSIFYING.

FOR ANY ONE OF US CONTEMPORARY MUSIC
IS OR COULD BE A WAY OF LIVING.

SEVERAL STORIES OCCUR TO ME THAT I SHOULD LIKE TO INTERPOLATE
(IN THE SAME WAY, BY THE WAY, THAT WHILE I AM WRITING THIS THAT
I AM NOW TALKING, THE TELEPHONE KEEPS RINGING AND THEN CONTEMPORARY
CONVERSATION TAKES PLACE INSTEAD OF THIS PARTICULAR WAY OF
PREPARING A LECTURE). THE FIRST STORY
IS FROM THE *Gospel of Sri Ramakrishna.* HIS LIVING AND TALKING
HAD IMPRESSED A MUSICIAN WHO BEGAN TO THINK THAT HE SHOULD GIVE
UP MUSIC AND BECOME A DISCIPLE OF RAMAKRISHNA. BUT WHEN HE PROPOSED
THIS, RAMAKRISHNA SAID, BY NO MEANS. REMAIN
A MUSICIAN: MUSIC IS A MEANS OF RAPID TRANSPORTATION.
RAPID TRANSPORTATION, THAT IS, TO LIFE "EVERLASTING,"
THAT IS TO SAY, LIFE, PERIOD. ANOTHER STORY IS THAT
WHEN I WAS FIRST AWARE THAT I WAS TO GIVE THIS TALK I CONSULTED
THE *Book of Changes* AND OBTAINED BY TOSSING COINS THE HEXAGRAM
TO INFLUENCE, TO STIMULATE. SIX AT THE TOP MEANS THE
INFLUENCE SHOWS ITSELF IN THE JAWS, CHEEKS, AND TONGUE AND THE
COMMENTARY SAYS: THE MOST SUPERFICIAL WAY OF TRYING TO INFLUENCE
OTHERS IS THROUGH TALK THAT HAS NOTHING REAL BEHIND IT. THE
INFLUENCE PRODUCED BY SUCH MERE TONGUE-WAGGING MUST NECESSARILY
REMAIN INSIGNIFICANT. HOWEVER, I FIND MYSELF IN
DISAGREEMENT WITH THE COMMENTARY. I SEE NO NECESSITY TO PUT
SOMETHING "REAL" BEHIND TONGUE-WAGGING. I DO NOT SEE THAT
TONGUE-WAGGING IS ANY MORE SIGNIFICANT OR INSIGNIFICANT THAN ANY
THING ELSE. IT SEEMS TO ME THAT IT IS SIMPLY A MATTER OF
GOING ON TALKING, WHICH IS NEITHER SIGNIFICANT NOR INSIGNIFICANT,
NOR GOOD NOR BAD, BUT SIMPLY HAPPENING TO BE THE WAY I AM RIGHT
NOW LIVING WHICH IS GIVING A LECTURE IN ILLINOIS WHICH BRINGS US
BACK TO CONTEMPORARY MUSIC. BUT TAKING OFF
AGAIN AND RETURNING TO THE *Book of Changes:* THE HEXAGRAM ON GRACE
(WHICH IS THE HEXAGRAM ON ART) DISCUSSES THE EFFECT OF A WORK
OF ART AS THOUGH IT WERE A LIGHT SHINING ON TOP OF A
MOUNTAIN PENETRATING TO A CERTAIN EXTENT THE SURROUNDING DARKNESS.
THAT IS TO SAY, ART IS DESCRIBED AS BEING ILLUMINATING,
AND THE REST OF LIFE AS BEING DARK. NATURALLY I DISAGREE.

COMPOSITION AS PROCESS / 45

IF THERE WERE A PART OF LIFE DARK ENOUGH TO KEEP OUT OF IT A LIGHT
FROM ART, I WOULD WANT TO BE IN THAT DARKNESS, FUMBLING AROUND IF
NECESSARY, BUT ALIVE   AND I RATHER THINK THAT CONTEMPORARY
MUSIC WOULD BE THERE IN THE DARK TOO, BUMPING INTO THINGS, KNOCKING
OTHERS OVER AND IN GENERAL ADDING TO THE DISORDER THAT CHARACTERIZES
LIFE (IF IT IS OPPOSED TO ART) RATHER THAN ADDING TO THE
ORDER AND STABILIZED TRUTH BEAUTY AND POWER THAT CHARACTERIZE
A MASTERPIECE (IF IT IS OPPOSED TO LIFE).   AND IS IT?   YES
IT IS.   MASTERPIECES AND GENIUSES GO TOGETHER AND WHEN BY
RUNNING FROM ONE TO THE OTHER WE MAKE LIFE SAFER THAN IT
ACTUALLY IS   WE'RE APT NEVER TO KNOW THE DANGERS OF
CONTEMPORARY MUSIC   OR   EVEN TO BE ABLE TO DRINK
A GLASS OF WATER.   TO HAVE SOMETHING BE A MASTERPIECE YOU
HAVE TO HAVE ENOUGH TIME TO CLASSIFY IT AND MAKE IT CLASSICAL.
          BUT WITH CONTEMPORARY MUSIC THERE IS NO TIME TO DO
ANYTHING LIKE CLASSIFYING.   ALL YOU CAN DO IS SUDDENLY LISTEN
          IN THE SAME WAY THAT WHEN YOU CATCH COLD ALL
YOU CAN DO IS SUDDENLY SNEEZE.   UNFORTUNATELY
EUROPEAN THINKING HAS BROUGHT IT ABOUT THAT ACTUAL THINGS THAT
HAPPEN SUCH AS SUDDENLY LISTENING OR SUDDENLY SNEEZING ARE NOT
CONSIDERED PROFOUND.   IN THE COURSE OF A
LECTURE LAST WINTER AT COLUMBIA, SUZUKI SAID THAT THERE WAS A
DIFFERENCE BETWEEN ORIENTAL THINKING AND EUROPEAN THINKING,
THAT IN EUROPEAN THINKING THINGS ARE SEEN AS CAUSING ONE
ANOTHER AND HAVING EFFECTS, WHEREAS IN ORIENTAL THINKING
          THIS SEEING OF CAUSE AND EFFECT IS NOT EMPHASIZED
BUT INSTEAD ONE MAKES AN IDENTIFICATION WITH WHAT IS HERE AND
NOW.   HE THEN SPOKE OF TWO QUALITIES: UNIMPEDEDNESS
          AND INTERPENETRATION.   NOW THIS
UNIMPEDEDNESS IS SEEING THAT IN ALL OF SPACE EACH THING AND
EACH HUMAN BEING IS AT THE CENTER AND FURTHERMORE THAT EACH
ONE BEING AT THE CENTER   IS THE MOST HONORED
ONE OF ALL.   INTERPENETRATION MEANS THAT EACH ONE OF THESE
MOST HONORED ONES OF ALL IS MOVING OUT IN ALL DIRECTIONS
PENETRATING AND BEING PENETRATED BY EVERY OTHER ONE NO MATTER
WHAT THE TIME OR WHAT THE SPACE.   SO THAT WHEN ONE SAYS

THAT THERE IS NO CAUSE AND EFFECT, WHAT IS MEANT IS THAT THERE
ARE AN INCALCULABLE INFINITY OF CAUSES AND EFFECTS, THAT IN FACT
EACH AND EVERY THING IN ALL OF TIME AND SPACE IS RELATED TO
EACH AND EVERY OTHER THING IN ALL OF TIME AND SPACE.   THIS
BEING SO THERE IS NO NEED TO CAUTIOUSLY PROCEED IN DUALISTIC
TERMS OF SUCCESS AND FAILURE OR THE BEAUTIFUL AND THE UGLY
OR GOOD AND EVIL BUT RATHER SIMPLY TO WALK ON "NOT WONDERING,"
TO QUOTE MEISTER ECKHART, "AM I RIGHT OR DOING SOMETHING WRONG."

*This is the second Tuesday in Sepember of 1958 and I still have
quite a lot to say: I'm nowhere near the end. I have four questions I must ask.*

If, as we have, we have dropped music, does that mean we have nothing to listen to?
Don't you agree with Kafka when he wrote, "Psychology—never again?"
If you had to put on ten fingers the music you would take with you
    if you were going to the North Pole, what would you put?
Is it true there are no questions that are really important?

Here's a little information you may find informative about the information theory:

FOURIER ANALYSIS ALLOWS A FUNCTION OF TIME (OR ANY OTHER INDEPENDENT VARIABLE) TO BE EX-
PRESSED IN TERMS OF PERIODIC (FREQUENCY) COMPONENTS. THE FREQUENCY COMPONENTS ARE OVER-
ALL PROPERTIES OF THE ENTIRE SIGNAL. BY MEANS OF A FOURIER ANALYSIS ONE CAN EXPRESS THE VALUE
OF A SIGNAL AT ANY POINT IN TERMS OF THE OVER-ALL FREQUENCY PROPERTIES OF THE SIGNAL; OR VICE
VERSA, ONE CAN OBTAIN THESE OVER-ALL PROPERTIES FROM THE VALUES OF THE SIGNAL AT ITS VARIOUS
POINTS.

What did I say?
Where is the "should" when they say you should have something to say?
Three. Actually when you drop something, it's still with you, wouldn't you say?
Four. Where would you drop something to get it completely away?
Five. Why do you not do as I do, letting go of each thought as though it were void?
Six. Why do you not do as I do, letting go of each thought as though it were rotten wood?
Why do you not do as I do, letting go of each thought as though it were a piece of stone?
Why do you not do as I do, letting go of each thought as though it were the cold ashes of a
    fire long dead, or else just making the slight response suitable to the occasion?

Nine. Do you really think that the discovery that a measurable entity exists, namely,
the energy which can measure mechanical, electrical, thermal, or any other kind of
physical activity, and can measure potential as well as actual activity, greatly
simplifies thinking about physical phenomena?

Do you agree with Boulez when he says what he says?

Are you getting hungry?

Twelve. Why should you (you know more or less what you're going to get)?

Will Boulez be there or did he go away when I wasn't looking?

Why do you suppose the number 12 was given up but the idea of the series wasn't?

Or was it?

And if not, why not?

In the meantime, would you like to hear the very first performance of
Christian Wolff's *For Piano with Preparations?*

What in heaven's name are they going to serve us for dinner, and what
happens afterwards?

More music?

Living or dead, that's the big question.

When you get sleepy, do you go to sleep?

Or do you lie awake?

Why do I have to go on asking questions?

Is it the same reason I have to go on writing music?

But it's clear, isn't it, I'm not writing music right now?

Why do they call me a composer, then, if all I do is ask questions?

If one of us says that all twelve tones should be in a row and another says they shouldn't,
which one of us is right?

What if a B flat, as they say, just comes to me?

How can I get it to come to me of itself, not just pop up out of my
memory, taste, and psychology?

How?

Do you know how?

And if I did or somebody else did find a way to let a sound be itself,
would everybody within earshot be able to listen to it?

Why is it so difficult for so many people to listen?

Why do they start talking when there is something to hear?

Do they have their ears not on the sides of their heads but situated inside their mouths

so that when they hear something their first impulse is to start talking?
The situation should be made more normal, don't you think?
Why don't they keep their mouths shut and their ears open?
Are they stupid?
And, if so, why don't they try to hide their stupidity?
Were bad manners acquired when knowledge of music was acquired?
Does being musical make one automatically stupid and unable to listen?
Then don't you think one should put a stop to studying music?
Where are your thinking caps?

WE'RE PASSING THROUGH TIME AND SPACE. OUR EARS ARE IN EXCELLENT CONDITION.

A SOUND IS HIGH OR LOW, SOFT OR LOUD, OF A CERTAIN TIMBRE, LASTS A CERTAIN LENGTH OF TIME, AND HAS AN ENVELOPE.

Is it high?
Is it low?
Is it in the middle?
Is it soft?
Is it loud?
Are there two?
Are there more than two?
Is it a piano?
Why isn't it?
Was it an airplane?
Is it a noise?
Is it music?
Is it softer than before?
Is it supersonic?
When will it stop?
What's coming?
Is it time?
Is it very short?
Very long?
Just medium?
If I had something to see, would it be theatre?

Is sound enough?
What more do I need?
Don't I get it whether I need it or not?
Is it a sound?
Then, again, is it music?
Is music—the word, I mean—is that a sound?
If it is, is music music?
Is the word "music" music?
Does it communicate anything?
Must it?
If it's high, does it?
If it's low, does it?
If it's in the middle, does it?
If it's soft, does it?
If it's loud, does it?
If it's an interval, does it?
What is an interval?
Is an interval a chord?
Is a chord an aggregate?
Is an aggregate a constellation?
What's a constellation?
How many sounds are there altogether?
One million?
Ten thousand?
Eighty-eight?
Do I have to ask ten more?
Do I?
Why?
Why do I?
Did I decide to ask so many?
Wasn't I taking a risk?
Was I?
Why was I?
Will it never stop?
Why won't it?

THERE IS NO SUCH THING AS SILENCE. GET THEE TO AN ANECHOIC CHAMBER AND HEAR THERE THY NERVOUS SYSTEM IN OPERATION AND HEAR THERE THY BLOOD IN CIRCULATION.

I HAVE NOTHING TO SAY AND I AM SAYING IT.

Would it be too much to ask if I asked thirty-three more?
Who's asking?
Is it I who ask?
Don't I know my own mind?
Then why do I ask if I don't know?
Then it's not too much to ask?
Right?
Then, tell me, do you prefer Bach to Beethoven?
And why?
Would you like to hear *Quantitäten* by Bo Nilsson whether it's
    performed for the first time or not?
Has any one seen Meister Eckhart lately?
Do you think serious music is serious enough?
Is a seventh chord inappropriate in modern music?
What about fifths and octaves?
What if the seventh chord was not a seventh chord?
Doesn't it seem silly to go on asking questions when there's so much
    to do that's really urgent?
But we're halfway through, aren't we?
Shall we buck up?
Are we in agreement that the field of music needs to be enlivened?
Do we disagree?
On what?
Communication?
If I have two sounds, are they related?
If someone is nearer one of them than he is to the second, is he
    more related to the first one?
What about sounds that are too far away for us to hear them?
Sounds are just vibrations, isn't that true?
Part of a vast range of vibrations including radio waves, light,
    cosmic rays, isn't that true?

Why didn't I mention that before?

Doesn't that stir the imagination?

Shall we praise God from Whom all blessings flow?

Is a sound a blessing?

I repeat, is a sound a blessing?

I repeat, would you like to hear *Quantitäten* by Bo Nilsson whether
it's performed for the first time or not?

The Belgians asked me about the avant-garde in America and this is what I told them:

IN THE UNITED STATES THERE ARE AS MANY WAYS OF WRITING MUSIC AS THERE
ARE COMPOSERS. THERE IS ALSO NO AVAILABLE INFORMATION AS TO WHAT IS
GOING ON. THERE IS NO MAGAZINE CONCERNED WITH MODERN MUSIC. PUBLISHERS
ARE NOT INQUISITIVE. THE SOCIETIES WHICH ACTIVELY EXIST (BROADCAST
MUSIC INC., AMERICAN SOCIETY OF COMPOSERS, AUTHORS AND PUBLISHERS) ARE
CONCERNED WITH ECONOMICS, CURRENTLY ENGAGED IN AN IMPORTANT LAWSUIT.
IN NEW YORK CITY, THE LEAGUE OF COMPOSERS AND THE INTERNATIONAL
SOCIETY FOR CONTEMPORARY MUSIC HAVE FUSED, THE NEW ORGANIZATION
REPRESENTING THE CURRENT INTEREST IN CONSOLIDATING THE ACQUISITIONS
OF SCHOENBERG AND STRAVINSKY. THIS CIRCLE HAS, NO DOUBT, AN AVANT-GARDE,
BUT IT IS A CAUTIOUS ONE, REFUSING RISK. ITS MOST ACCOMPLISHED
AND ADVENTUROUS REPRESENTATIVE IS PROBABLY MILTON BABBITT, WHO, IN
CERTAIN WORKS, HAS APPLIED SERIAL METHOD TO THE SEVERAL ASPECTS OF
SOUND. THE WORKS FOR MAGNETIC TAPE BY LUENING AND USSACHEVSKY, LOUIS
AND BEBE BARRON, ARE NOT PROPERLY TERMED AVANT-GARDE, SINCE THEY
MAINTAIN CONVENTIONS AND ACCEPTED VALUES. THE YOUNG STUDY WITH
NEO-CLASSICISTS, SO THAT THE SPIRIT OF THE AVANT-GARDE, INFECTING THEM,
INDUCES A CERTAIN DODECAPHONY. IN THIS SOCIAL DARKNESS, THEREFORE, THE
WORK OF EARLE BROWN, MORTON FELDMAN, AND CHRISTIAN WOLFF CONTINUES TO
PRESENT A BRILLIANT LIGHT, FOR THE REASON THAT AT THE SEVERAL POINTS
OF NOTATION, PERFORMANCE, AND AUDITION, ACTION IS PROVOCATIVE. NONE
OF THESE USES SERIAL METHOD. BROWN'S NOTATION IN SPACE EQUAL TO TIME
TENDS CURRENTLY TO FINE PRECISION OF DIRECTIVE. WOLFF'S INTRODUCTION
IN DURATIONS OF SPLIT AND PARTIAL GRUPETTOS, IN TEMPI THAT OF ZERO,
TENDS OPPOSITELY. THE GRAPHS OF FELDMAN GIVE WITHIN LIMITS EXTREME
FREEDOM OF ACTION TO THE PERFORMER.

They also—the Belgians, that is—asked me whether the American avant-garde follows the same direction as the European one and this is what I told them:

THE AMERICAN AVANT-GARDE, RECOGNIZING THE PROVOCATIVE CHARACTER OF
CERTAIN EUROPEAN WORKS, OF PIERRE BOULEZ, KARLHEINZ STOCKHAUSEN,
HENRI POUSSEUR, BO NILSSON, BENGT HAMBRAEUS, HAS IN ITS CONCERTS
PRESENTED THEM IN PERFORMANCES, NOTABLY BY DAVID TUDOR, PIANIST. THAT
THESE WORKS ARE SERIAL IN METHOD DIMINISHES SOMEWHAT THE INTEREST
THEY ENJOIN. BUT THE THOROUGHNESS OF THE METHOD'S APPLICATION BRINGING
A SITUATION REMOVED FROM CONVENTIONAL EXPECTATION FREQUENTLY
OPENS THE EAR. HOWEVER, THE EUROPEAN WORKS PRESENT A HARMONIOUSNESS,
A DRAMA, OR A POETRY WHICH, REFERRING MORE TO THEIR COMPOSERS THAN TO
THEIR HEARERS, MOVES IN DIRECTIONS NOT SHARED BY THE AMERICAN ONES.
MANY OF THE AMERICAN WORKS ENVISAGE EACH AUDITOR AS CENTRAL, SO
THAT THE PHYSICAL CIRCUMSTANCES OF A CONCERT DO NOT OPPOSE AUDIENCE
TO PERFORMERS BUT DISPOSE THE LATTER AROUND-AMONG THE FORMER, BRINGING
A UNIQUE ACOUSTICAL EXPERIENCE TO EACH PAIR OF EARS. ADMITTEDLY, A
SITUATION OF THIS COMPLEXITY IS BEYOND CONTROL, YET IT RESEMBLES
A LISTENER'S SITUATION BEFORE AND AFTER A CONCERT—DAILY EXPERIENCE,
THAT IS. IT APPEARS SUCH A CONTINUUM IS NOT PART OF THE EUROPEAN
OBJECTIVE, SINCE IT DISSOLVES THE DIFFERENCE BETWEEN "ART" AND "LIFE."
TO THE UNEXPERIENCED, THE DIFFERENCE BETWEEN THE EUROPEANS AND THE
AMERICANS LIES IN THAT THE LATTER INCLUDE MORE SILENCE IN THEIR WORKS.
IN THIS VIEW THE MUSIC OF NILSSON APPEARS AS INTERMEDIATE, THAT OF
BOULEZ AND OF THE AUTHOR AS IN OPPOSITION. THIS SUPERFICIAL DIFFERENCE
IS ALSO PROFOUND. WHEN SILENCE, GENERALLY SPEAKING, IS NOT IN
EVIDENCE, THE WILL OF THE COMPOSER IS. INHERENT SILENCE IS EQUIVALENT
TO DENIAL OF THE WILL. "TAKING A NAP, I POUND THE RICE." NEVERTHELESS,
CONSTANT ACTIVITY MAY OCCUR HAVING NO DOMINANCE OF WILL IN IT.
NEITHER AS SYNTAX NOR STRUCTURE, BUT ANALOGOUS TO THE SUM OF NATURE,
IT WILL HAVE ARISEN PURPOSELESSLY.

It's getting late, isn't it?
I still have two things to do, so what I want to know is: Would you like to hear
Quantitäten by Bo Nilsson whether it's performed for the first time or not?

I must read a little from an article by Christian Wolff. Here's what he says:

NOTABLE QUALITIES OF THIS MUSIC, WHETHER ELECTRONIC OR NOT, ARE MONOTONY
AND THE IRRITATION THAT ACCOMPANIES IT. THE MONOTONY MAY LIE IN
SIMPLICITY OR DELICACY, STRENGTH OR COMPLEXITY. COMPLEXITY TENDS TO
REACH A POINT OF NEUTRALIZATION: CONTINUOUS CHANGE RESULTS IN A CERTAIN
SAMENESS. THE MUSIC HAS A STATIC CHARACTER. IT GOES IN NO PARTICULAR
DIRECTION. THERE IS NO NECESSARY CONCERN WITH TIME AS A MEASURE OF
DISTANCE FROM A POINT IN THE PAST TO A POINT IN THE FUTURE, WITH LINEAR
CONTINUITY ALONE. IT IS NOT A QUESTION OF GETTING ANYWHERE, OF
MAKING PROGRESS, OR HAVING COME FROM ANYWHERE IN PARTICULAR, OF TRADITION
OR FUTURISM. THERE IS NEITHER NOSTALGIA NOR ANTICIPATION. OFTEN
THE STRUCTURE OF A PIECE IS CIRCULAR: THE SUCCESSION OF ITS PARTS IS
VARIABLE, AS IN POUSSEUR'S *Exercises de Piano* AND STOCKHAUSEN'S *Klavierstück XI*.
IN CAGE'S RECENT WORK THE NOTATION ITSELF CAN BE CIRCULAR,
THE SUCCESSION OF NOTES ON A STAVE NOT NECESSARILY INDICATING THEIR
SEQUENCE IN TIME, THAT IS, THE ORDER IN WHICH THEY ARE PERFORMED. ONE
MAY HAVE TO READ NOTES ON A CIRCLE, IN TWO "VOICES" GOING IN OPPOSITE
DIRECTIONS SIMULTANEOUSLY. AN ASPECT OF TIME DISSOLVES. AND THE EUROPEANS
OFTEN VIEW ORGANIZATION AS "GLOBAL," WHEREBY BEGINNINGS AND ENDS
ARE NOT POINTS ON A LINE BUT LIMITS OF A PIECE'S MATERIAL (FOR EXAMPLE,
PITCH RANGES OR POSSIBLE COMBINATIONS OF TIMBRES) WHICH MAY BE TOUCHED
AT ANY TIME DURING THE PIECE. THE BOUNDARIES OF THE PIECE ARE EXPRESSED,
NOT AT MOMENTS OF TIME WHICH MARK A SUCCESSION, BUT AS MARGINS OF A
SPATIAL PROJECTION OF THE TOTAL SOUND STRUCTURE.

AS FOR THE QUALITY OF IRRITATION, THAT IS A MORE SUBJECTIVE MATTER.
ONE MIGHT SAY THAT IT IS AT LEAST PREFERABLE TO SOOTHING, EDIFYING,
EXALTING, AND SIMILAR QUALITIES. ITS SOURCE IS, OF COURSE, PRECISELY
IN MONOTONY, NOT IN ANY FORMS OF AGGRESSION OR EMPHASIS. IT IS THE
IMMOBILITY OF MOTION. AND IT ALONE, PERHAPS, IS TRULY MOVING.

And now I have to read a story from Kwang-Tse and then I'm finished:

Yun Kiang, rambling to the East, having been borne along on a gentle breeze,
suddenly encountered Hung Mung, who was rambling about, slapping his buttocks and
hopping like a bird. Amazed at the sight, Yun Kiang stood reverentially and said to

the other, "Venerable Sir, who are you? and why are you doing this?" Hung Mung went on slapping his buttocks and hopping like a bird, but replied, "I'm enjoying myself." Yun Kiang said, "I wish to ask you a question." Hung Mung lifted up his head, looked at the stranger, and said, "Pooh!" Yun Kiang, however, continued, "The breath of heaven is out of harmony; the breath of earth is bound up; the six elemental influences do not act in concord; the four seasons do not observe their proper times. Now I wish to blend together the essential qualities of those six influences in order to nourish all living things. How shall I go about it?" Hung Mung slapped his buttocks, hopped about, and shook his head, saying, "I do not know; I do not know!"

Yun Kiang could not pursue his question; but three years afterwards, when again rambling in the East, as he was passing by the wild of Sung, he happened to meet Hung Mung. Delighted with the rencontre, he hastened to him, and said, "Have you forgotten me, O Heaven? Have you forgotten me, O Heaven?" At the same time, he bowed twice with his head to the ground, wishing to receive his instructions. Hung Mung said, "Wandering listlessly about, I know not what I seek; carried on by a wild impulse, I know not where I am going. I wander about in the strange manner which you have seen, and see that nothing proceeds without method and order—what more should I know?" Yun Kiang replied, "I also seem carried on by an aimless influence, and yet people follow me wherever I go. I cannot help their doing so. But now as they thus imitate me, I wish to hear a word from you." The other said, "What disturbs the regular method of Heaven, comes into collision with the nature of things, prevents the accomplishment of the mysterious operation of Heaven, scatters the herds of animals, makes the birds sing at night, is calamitous to vegetation, and disastrous to all insects; all this is owing, I conceive, to the error of governing men." "What then," said Yun Kiang, "shall I do?" "Ah," said the other, "you will only injure them! I will leave you in my dancing way, and return to my place." Yun Kiang rejoined, "It has been difficult to get this meeting with you, O Heaven! I should like to hear from you a word more." Hung Mung said, "Ah! your mind needs to be nourished. Do you only take the position of doing nothing, and things will of themselves become transformed. Neglect your body; cast out from you your power of hearing and sight; forget what you have in common with things; cultivate a grand similarity with the chaos of the plastic ether; unloose your mind; set your spirit free; be still as if you had no soul. Of all the multitude of things, every one returns to its root, and does not know that it is doing so. They all are as in the state of chaos, and during all their existence they do not leave it. If they knew that they were returning to their root, they would be consciously leaving it. They do not ask its name; they do not seek to spy out their nature; and thus it is that things come to life of themselves."

Yun Kiang said, "Heaven, you have conferred on me the knowledge of your operation and revealed to me the mystery of it. All my life I have been seeking for it, and now I have obtained it." He then bowed twice with his head to the ground, arose, took his leave, and walked away.

. . . .

One day when I was across the hall visiting Sonya Sekula, I noticed that she was painting left-handed. I said, "Sonya, aren't you right-handed?" She said, "Yes, but I might lose the use of my right hand, and so I'm practicing using my left." I laughed and said, "What if you lose the use of both hands?" She was busy painting and didn't bother to reply. Next day when I visited her, she was sitting on the floor, painting with difficulty, for she was holding the brush between two toes of her left foot.

Morris Graves introduced Xenia and me to a miniature island in Puget Sound at Deception Pass. To get there we traveled from Seattle about seventy-five miles north and west to Anacortes Island, then south to the Pass, where we parked. We walked along a rocky beach and then across a sandy stretch that was passable only at low tide to another island, continuing through some luxuriant woods up a hill where now and then we had views of the surrounding waters and distant islands, until finally we came to a small foot-bridge that led to our destination—an island no larger than, say, a modest home. This island was carpeted with flowers and was so situated that all of Deception Pass was visible from it, just as though we were in the best seats of an intimate theatre. While we were lying there on that bed of flowers, some other people came across the footbridge. One of them said to another, "You come all this way and then when you get here there's nothing to see."

A composer friend of mine who spent some time in a mental rehabilitation center was encouraged to do a good deal of bridge playing. After one game, his partner was criticizing his play of an ace on a trick which had already been won. My friend stood up and said, "If you think I came to the loony bin to learn to play bridge, you're crazy."

56/SILENCE

The two articles which follow are technical. Information regarding other compositional means may be found in the brochure accompanying George Avakian's recording of my twenty-five-year retrospective concert at Town Hall in 1958.

The first article was my part of Four Musicians at Work *which was published in* trans/formation, *Volume 1, Number 3 (New York City, 1952).*

COMPOSITION

To Describe the Process of Composition Used in
Music of Changes and *Imaginary Landscape No. 4*

My recent work (*Imaginary Landscape No. IV* for twelve radios and the *Music of Changes* for piano) is structurally similar to my earlier work: based on a number of measures having a square root, so that the large lengths have the same relation within the whole that the small lengths have within a unit of it. Formerly, however, these lengths were time-lengths, whereas in the recent work the lengths exist only in space, the speed of travel through this space being unpredictable.

What brings about this unpredictability is the use of the method established in the *I-Ching* (*Book of Changes*) for the obtaining of oracles, that of tossing three coins six times.

Three coins tossed once yield four lines: three heads, broken with a circle; two tails and a head, straight; two heads and a tail, broken; three tails, straight with a circle. Three coins tossed thrice yield eight trigrams (written from the base up): *chien,* three straight; *chen,* straight, broken, broken; *kan,* broken, straight, broken; *ken,* broken, broken, straight; *kun,* three broken; *sun,* broken, straight, straight; *li,* straight, broken, straight; *tui,* straight, straight, broken. Three coins tossed six times yield sixty-four hexagrams (two trigrams, the second written above the first) read in reference to a chart of the numbers 1 to 64 in a traditional arrangement having eight divisions horizontally corresponding to the eight lower trigrams and eight divisions vertically corresponding to the eight upper trigrams. A hexagram having lines with circles is read twice, first as written, then as changed. Thus, *chien-chien,* straight lines with circles, is read first as 1, then as *kun-kun,* 2; whereas *chien-chien,* straight lines without circles, is read only as 1.

Charts are made of an equal number of elements (sixty-four) which refer to Superpositions (one chart) (how many events are happening at once during a given structural space); Tempi (one chart); Durations (*n,* the number of possible superpositions, in these works, eight charts); Sounds (eight charts); Dynamics (eight charts).

Where there are eight charts, four at any instant are mobile and four immobile (mobile means an element passes into history once used, giving place to a new one; immobile means an element, though used, remains to be used again). Which charts are which is determined by the first toss at a large unit structural point, an odd number bringing about a change, an even number maintaining the previous status.

The Tempi and Superpositions charts, however, remain unchanged through the entire work.

In the charts for sounds thirty-two of the elements (the even numbers) are silences. The sounds themselves are single, aggregates (cf. the accord sometimes obtained on a prepared piano when only one key is depressed), or complex situations (constellations) in time (cf. the Chinese characters made with several strokes). Sounds of indefinite pitch (noises) are free to be used without any restriction. Those of definite pitch are taken as being twelve in number. In any chart for sounds (there being thirty-two sounds) two squares (four times four) exist, one above the other. Reading horizontally or vertically, one reads all twelve tones. In the case of the mobility of sounds (disappearance into history) four in succession also produce the twelve tones, with or without noises and repetitions. In the case of "interference" (the appearance of a sound having characteristics in common with the characteristics of the previously sounded situation) the characteristics that produce the interference are omitted from the newly appearing sound or cut short in the situation that has previously sounded. In the radio piece, numbers on a tuning dial are written instead of sounds, whatever happens being acceptable (station, static, silence).

In the charts for dynamics only sixteen numbers produce changes (one, five, nine, etc.); the others maintain the previous status. These are either dynamic levels or accents (in the piano piece); levels, diminuendi, and crescendi in the radio piece. In the piano piece, combinations of dynamic levels (e.g. fff>p) indicate accents; in the case of a sound complex in time this may become a diminuendo or (by retrograde interpretation) a crescendo, or derived complex.

In the charts for durations there are sixty-four elements (since silence also has length). Through use of fractions (e.g. ⅓; ⅓ + ⅗ + ½) measured following a standard scale (2½ cm. equals a crotchet), these durations are, for the purposes of musical composition, practically infinite in number. The note stem appears in space at a point corresponding to the appearance of the sound in time, that is if one reads at the tempo, or changing tempo indicated. Given fractions of a quarter, half, dotted half and whole note up to ⅛, simple addition of fractions is the method employed for the generating of durations. Because addition is the generating means employed, the durations may be said to be "segmented." These segments may be permuted and/or divided by two or three (simple nodes). A sound may then express the duration by beginning at any one of these several points.

A way of relating durations to sounds has been thought of in the course of this work but not in it utilized: to let four durations equal a specified length (on the chart, horizontally or vertically and in mobility four in succession)—this specified length being subject to change.

The chart for Tempi has thirty-two elements, the blanks maintaining the previous tempo.

Each one of the events one to eight is worked from the beginning to the end of the composition. For instance, the eighth one is present from beginning to end but may sound only during a structural space that has been defined by a toss (for Superpositions) of fifty-seven to sixty-four. It is then not only present but possibly audible. It becomes actually audible if a sound is tossed (rather than a silence) and if the duration tossed is of a length that does not carry the sound beyond the structural space open to it.

It is thus possible to make a musical composition the continuity of which is free of individual taste and memory (psychology) and also of the literature and "traditions" of the art. The sounds enter the time-space centered within themselves, unimpeded by service to any abstraction, their 360 degrees of circumference free for an infinite play of interpenetration.

Value judgments are not in the nature of this work as regards either composition, performance, or listening. The idea of relation (the idea: 2) being absent, anything (the idea: 1) may happen. A "mistake" is beside the point, for once anything happens it authentically is.

To Describe the Process of Composition Used in *Music for Piano 21-52*

1. Given ink, pen, and sheets of transparent paper of determined dimensions, a master page (without notations) is made, having four total systems. "Total" here means having enough space above and below each staff to permit its being either bass or treble. Thus, there being the conventional two staves (one for each hand), each has enough space above it to accommodate nine ledger lines (as equidistant as those of the staves) and below it to accommodate six ledger lines plus (leaving room for the extreme low piano key and string). Between the two there is a narrow space, bisected by a line, allowing for the notation of noises produced by hand or beater upon the interior (above the line) or exterior (below the line) piano construction. Measurements are such that the entire sheet (within margins) is potentially useful.

2. Laying the master page aside, chance operations derived from the *I-Ching* and channeled within certain limits (1–128 for *21–36;* 1–32 for *37–52*) (which are established in relation to relative difficulty of performance) are employed to determine the number of sounds per page.

3. A blank sheet of transparent paper is then placed so that its pointal imperfections may readily be observed. That number of imperfections corresponding to the determined number of sounds is intensified with pencil.

4. Placing the penciled sheet in a registered way upon the master page, first the staves and interline and then the ledger lines where necessary are inscribed in ink. Secondly, conventional whole notes are written in ink wherever a penciled point falls within the area of staves or ledger lines, inked-in notes (crotchets without stems) being written wherever such a point falls within the space between the two staves. This operation is done roughly, since, through the use of conventional lines and spaces, points falling in the latter are in the majority. Thus it is determined that a point, though not on a line, is actually more nearly so than it is at the center of the adjacent space.

5. Eight single coin tosses are made determining the clefs, bass or treble, and inscribed in ink.

6. The sixty-four possibilities of the *I-Ching* are divided by chance operations into three groups relative to three categories: normal (played on the keyboard); muted; and plucked (the two latter played on the strings). For example, having tossed numbers 6 and 44, a number 1 through 5 will produce a normal; 6 through 43 a muted; 44 through 64 a plucked piano tone. A certain weight of probability exists in favor of the second and third categories. Though this has not appeared to be of consequence, it indicates a possible change in "technique." The categories having been determined, notations (M and P) are conveniently placed in reference to the notes.

A similar procedure is followed to determine whether a tone is natural, sharp, or flat, the procedure being altered, of course, for the two extreme keys where only two possibilities exist.

7. The notation of the composition is thus completed. Much that occurs in performance has not been determined. Therefore, the following note is fixed at the head of the manuscript: "These pieces constitute two groups of sixteen pieces (*21–36; 37–52*) which may be played alone or together and with or without *Music for Piano 4–19*.[1] Their length in time is free; there may or may not be silence between them; they may be overlapped. Given a programed time length, the pianists may make a calculation such that their concert will fill it. Duration of individual tones and dynamics are free."

COMMENTARY

A performance is characterized by the programed time length calculated beforehand and adhered to through the use of a stop watch. This is primarily of use in relation to an entire page, secondarily of use in relation, to say, a system; for it is possible that, though the space of the page is here equal to time, the performance being realized by a human being rather than a machine, such space may be interpreted as moving, not only constantly, but faster or slower. Thus, finally, nothing has been determined by the notation as far as performance time is concerned. And, as concerns timbre (the noises, the three categories) next to nothing has been determined. This is especially the case where P is interpreted as meaning a plucked *muted* string or M a muted *plucked* string. Nor, indeed, have the points on the strings where these latter operations are to be made been indicated. And—and this may be considered a fundamental omission—nothing has been indicated regarding the architecture of the room in which the music is to be played and the placement (customarily distant one from another) of the instruments (how many?) therein. All these elements, evidently of paramount importance, point the question: What has been composed?

[1] The composition of these pieces followed a different procedure and, furthermore, did not include interior and exterior construction noises.

This article first appeared in the March 1949 issue of The Tiger's Eye, *a journal edited by Ruth and John Stephan from Bleecker Street in New York. It was translated into French by Frederick Goldbeck, who changed the title to* Raison d'être de la musique moderne. *This was published in* Contrepoints *(Paris) later in the same year.*

FORERUNNERS OF MODERN MUSIC

The purpose of music

Music is edifying, for from time to time it sets the soul in operation. The soul is the gatherer-together of the disparate elements (Meister Eckhart), and its work fills one with peace and love.

Definitions

Structure in music is its divisibility into successive parts from phrases to long sections. Form is content, the continuity. Method is the means of controlling the continuity from note to note. The material of music is sound and silence. Integrating these is composing.

Strategy

Structure is properly mind-controlled. Both delight in precision, clarity, and the observance of rules. Whereas form wants only freedom to be. It belongs to the heart; and the law it observes, if indeed it submits to any, has never been and never will be written.[1] Method may be planned or improvised (it makes no difference: in one case, the emphasis shifts towards thinking, in the other towards feeling; a piece for radios as instruments would give up the matter of method to accident). Likewise, material may be controlled or not, as one chooses. Normally the choice of sounds is determined by what is pleasing and attractive to the ear: delight in the giving or receiving of pain being an indication of sickness.

---

[1] Any attempt to exclude the "irrational" is irrational. Any composing strategy which is wholly "rational" is irrational in the extreme.

Refrain

Activity involving in a single process the many, turning them, even though some seem to be opposites, towards oneness, contributes to a good way of life.

The plot thickens

When asked why, God being good, there was evil in the world, Sri Ramakrishna said: To thicken the plot.

The aspect of composition that can properly be discussed with the end in view of general agreement is structure, for it is devoid of mystery. Analysis is at home here.

Schools teach the making of structures by means of classical harmony. Outside school, however (*e.g.*, Satie and Webern), a different and correct [2] structural means reappears: one based on lengths of time.[3, 4]

In the Orient, harmonic structure is traditionally unknown, and unknown with us in our pre-Renaissance culture. Harmonic structure is a recent Occidental phenomenon, for the past century in a process of disintegration.[5]

Atonality [6] has happened

The disintegration of harmonic structure is commonly known as atonality. All that is meant is that two necessary elements in harmonic structure—the cadence, and modulating means—have lost their edge. Increasingly, they have become ambiguous, whereas their very existence as structural elements demands clarity·(singleness of reference). Atonality is simply the maintenance of an ambiguous tonal state of affairs. It is the denial of harmony as a structural means. The problem of a composer in a musical world in this state is to supply another structural means,[7]

---

[2] Sound has four characteristics: pitch, timbre, loudness, and duration. The opposite and necessary coexistent of sound is silence. Of the four characteristics of sound, only duration involves both sound and silence. Therefore, a structure based on durations (rhythmic: phrase, time lengths) is correct (corresponds with the nature of the material), whereas harmonic structure is incorrect (derived from pitch, which has no being in silence).

[3] This never disappeared from jazz and folk music. On the other hand, it never developed in them, for they are not cultivated species, growing best when left wild.

[4] Tala is based on pulsation, Western rhythmic structure on phraseology.

[5] For an interesting, detailed proof of this, see Casella's book on the cadence.

[6] The term "atonality" makes no sense. Schoenberg substitutes "pantonality," Lou Harrison (to my mind and experience the preferable term) "proto-tonality." This last term suggests what is actually the case: present even in a random multiplicity of tones (or, better, sounds [so as to include noises]), is a gravity, original and natural, "proto," to that particular situation. Elementary composition consists in discovering the ground of the sounds employed, and then letting life take place both on land and in the air.

[7] Neither Schoenberg nor Stravinsky did this. The twelve-tone row does not offer a structural means; it is a method, a control, not of the parts, large and small, of a composition, but only of the minute, note-to-note procedure. It usurps the place of counterpoint, which, as Carl Ruggles, Lou Harrison, and Merton Brown have shown, is perfectly capable of functioning in a chromatic situation. Neo-classicism, in reverting to the past, avoids, by refusing to recognize, the contemporary need for another structure, gives a new look to structural harmony. This automatically deprives it of the sense of adventure, essential to creative action.

just as in a bombed-out city the opportunity to build again exists.[8] This way one finds courage and a sense of necessity.

Interlude (Meister Eckhart)

"But one must achieve this unselfconsciousness by means of transformed knowledge. This ignorance does not come from lack of knowledge but rather it is from knowledge that one may achieve this ignorance. Then we shall be informed by the divine unconsciousness and in that our ignorance will be ennobled and adorned with supernatural knowledge. It is by reason of this fact that we are made perfect by what happens to us rather than by what we do."

At random

Music means nothing as a thing.

A finished work is exactly that, requires resurrection.

The responsibility of the artist consists in perfecting his work so that it may become attractively disinteresting.

It is better to make a piece of music than to perform one, better to perform one than to listen to one, better to listen to one than to misuse it as a means of distraction, entertainment, or acquisition of "culture."

Use any means to keep from being a genius, all means to become one.

Is counterpoint good? "The soul itself is so simple that it cannot have more than one idea at a time of anything. . . . A person cannot be more than single in attention." (Eckhart)

Freed from structural responsibility, harmony becomes a formal element (serves expression).

Imitating either oneself or others, care should be taken to imitate structure, not form (also structural materials and structural methods, not formal materials and formal methods), disciplines, not dreams; thus one remains "innocent and free to receive anew with each Now-moment a heavenly gift." (Eckhart)

If the mind is disciplined, the heart turns quickly from fear towards love.

Before making a structure by means of rhythm, it is necessary to decide what rhythm is.

This could be a difficult decision to make if the concern were formal (expressive) or to do with method (point to point procedure); but since the concern is structural (to do with divisibility of a composition into parts large and small), the decision is easily reached: rhythm in the structural instance is relationships of lengths of time.[9] Such matters, then, as accents on or off the beat, regularly recurring or not, pulsation with or without accent, steady or unsteady, durations motivically conceived (either static or to be varied), are matters for formal

[8] The twelve-tone row offers bricks but no plan. The neo-classicists advise building it the way it was before, but surfaced fashionably.

[9] Measure is literally measure—nothing more, for example, than the inch of a ruler—thus permitting the existence of any durations, any amplitude relations (meter, accent), any silences.

(expressive) use, or, if thought about, to be considered as material (in its "textural" aspect) or as serving method. In the case of a year, rhythmic structure is a matter of seasons, months, weeks, and days. Other time lengths such as that taken by a fire or the playing of a piece of music occur accidentally or freely without explicit recognition of an all-embracing order, but nevertheless, necessarily within that order. Coincidences of free events with structural time points have a special luminous character, because the paradoxical nature of truth is at such moments made apparent. Caesurae on the other hand are expressive of the independence (accidental or willed) of freedom from law, law from freedom.

Claim

Any sounds of any qualities and pitches (known or unknown, definite or indefinite), any contexts of these, simple or multiple, are natural and conceivable within a rhythmic structure which equally embraces silence. Such a claim is remarkably like the claims to be found in patent specifications for and articles about technological musical means (see early issues of *Modern Music* and the *Journal of the Acoustical Society of America*). From differing beginning points, towards possibly different goals, technologists and artists (seemingly by accident) meet by intersection, becoming aware of the otherwise unknowable (conjunction of the in and the out), imagining brightly a common goal in the world and in the quietness within each human being.

For instance:

Just as art as sand painting (art for the now-moment [10] rather than for posterity's museum civilization) becomes a held point of view, adventurous workers in the field of synthetic music (e.g. Norman McLaren) find that for practical and economic reasons work with magnetic wires (any music so made can quickly and easily be erased, rubbed off) is preferable to that with film.[11]

The use of technological means [12] requires the close anonymous collaboration of a number of workers. We are on the point of being in a cultural situation,[13]

[10] This is the very nature of the dance, of the performance of music, or any other art requiring performance (for this reason, the term "sand painting" is used: there is a tendency in painting (permanent pigments), as in poetry (printing, binding), to be secure in the thingness of a work, and thus to overlook, and place nearly insurmountable obstacles in the path of, instantaneous ecstasy).

[11] Twenty-four or *n* frames per second is the "canvas" upon which this music is written; thus, in a very obvious way, the material itself demonstrates the necessity for time (rhythmic) structure. With magnetic means, freedom from the frame of film means exists, but the principle of rhythmic structure should hold over as, in geometry, a more elementary theorem remains as a premise to make possible the obtaining of those more advanced.

[12] "I want to be as though new-born, knowing nothing, absolutely nothing about Europe." (Paul Klee)

[13] Replete with new concert halls: the movie houses (vacated by home television fans, and too numerous for a Hollywood whose only alternative is "seriousness").

without having made any special effort to get into one[14] (if one can discount lamentation).

The in-the-heart path of music leads now to self-knowledge through self-denial, and its in-the-world path leads likewise to selflessness.[15] The heights that now are reached by single individuals at special moments may soon be densely populated.

[14] Painting in becoming literally (actually) realistic—(this is the twentieth century) seen from above, the earth, snow-covered, a composition of order superimposed on the "spontaneous" (Cummings) or of the latter letting order be (from above, so together, the opposites, they fuse) (one has only to fly [highways and topography, Milarepa, Henry Ford] to know)—automatically will reach the same point (step by step) the soul leaped to.

[15] The machine fathers mothers heroes saints of the mythological order, works only when it meets with acquiescence (cf. *The King and the Corpse*, by Heinrich Zimmer, edited by Joseph Campbell).

. . . .

Peggy Guggenheim, Santomaso, and I were in a Venetian restaurant. There were only two other people dining in the same room and they were not conversing. I got to expressing my changed views with regard to the French and the Italians. I said that I had years before preferred the French because of their intelligence and had found the Italians playful but intellectually not engaging; that recently, however, I found the French cold in spirit and lacking in freedom of the mind, whereas the Italians seemed warm and surprising. Then it occurred to me that the couple in the room were French. I called across to them and said, "Are you French?" The lady replied. "We are," she said, "but we agree with you completely."

Richard Lippold called up and said, "Would you come to dinner and bring the *I-Ching?*" I said I would. It turned out he'd written a letter to the Metropolitan proposing that he be commissioned for a certain figure to do *The Sun.* This letter withheld nothing about the excellence of his art, and so he hesitated to send it, not wishing to seem presumptuous. Using the coin oracle, we consulted the *I-Ching.* It mentioned a letter. Advice to send it was given. Success was promised, but the need for patience was mentioned. A few weeks later, Richard Lippold called to say that his proposal had been answered but without commitment, and that that should make clear to me as it did to him what to think of the *I-Ching.* A year passed. The Metropolitan Museum finally commissioned *The Sun.* Richard Lippold still does not see eye to eye with me on the subject of chance operations.

The question of leading tones came up in the class in experimental composition that I give at the New School. I said, "You surely aren't talking about ascending half-steps in diatonic music. Is it not true that anything leads to whatever follows?" But the situation is more complex, for things also lead backwards in time. This also does not give a picture that corresponds with reality. For, it is said, the Buddha's enlightenment penetrated in every direction to every point in space and time.

The following article was written at the request of Dr. Wolfgang Steinecke, Director of the Internationale Ferienkürse für Neue Musik at Darmstadt. The German translation by Heinz Klaus Metzger was published in the 1959 issue of Darmstädter Beiträge. *The statement by Christian Wolff quoted herein is from his article "New and Electronic Music," copyright 1958 by the Audience Press, and reprinted by permission from* Audience, Volume V, Number 3, Summer 1958.

HISTORY OF EXPERIMENTAL MUSIC IN THE UNITED STATES

Once when Daisetz Teitaro Suzuki was giving a talk at Columbia University he mentioned the name of a Chinese monk who had figured in the history of Chinese Buddhism. Suzuki said, "He lived in the ninth or the tenth century." He added, after a pause, "Or the eleventh century, or the twelfth or thirteenth century or the fourteenth."

About the same time, Willem de Kooning, the New York painter, gave a talk at the Art Alliance in Philadelphia. Afterwards there was a discussion: questions and answers. Someone asked De Kooning who the painters of the past were who had influenced him the most. De Kooning said, "The past does not influence me; I influence it."

A little over ten years ago I acted as music editor for a magazine called *Possibilities.* Only one issue of this magazine appeared. However: in it, four American composers (Virgil Thomson, Edgard Varèse, Ben Weber, and Alexei Haieff) answered questions put to them by twenty other composers. My question to Varèse concerned his views of the future of music. His answer was that neither the past nor the future interested him; that his concern was with the present.

Sri Ramakrishna was once asked, "Why, if God is good, is there evil in the world?" He said, "In order to thicken the plot." Nowadays in the field of music, we often hear that everything is possible; (for instance) that with electronic means one may employ any sound (any frequency, any amplitude, any timbre, any duration); that there are no limits to possibility. This is technically, nowadays, theoretically possible and in practical terms is often felt to be impossible only because of the absence of mechanical aids which, nevertheless, could be provided if the society felt the urgency of musical advance. Debussy said quite some time ago, "Any sounds in any combination and in any succession are henceforth free to be used in a musical continuity." Paraphrasing the question put to Sri Ramakrishna and the answer he gave, I would ask this: "Why, if everything is possible, do we concern ourselves with history (in other words with a sense of what is necessary to be done at a particular time?" And I would answer, "In order to thicken the plot." In this view, then, all those interpenetrations which seem at first glance to be hellish—history, for instance, if we are speaking of experimental music—are to be espoused. One does not then make just any experiment but does what must be done. By this I mean one does not seek by his actions to arrive at money but does what must be done; one does not seek by his actions to arrive at fame (success) but does what must be done; one does not seek by his actions to provide pleasure to the senses (beauty) but does what must be done; one does not seek by his actions to arrive at the establishing of a school (truth) but does what must be done. One does something else. What else?

In an article called "New and Electronic Music," Christian Wolff says: "What is, or seems to be, new in this music? . . . One finds a concern for a kind of objectivity, almost anonymity—sound come into its own. The 'music' is a resultant existing simply in the sounds we hear, given no impulse by expressions of self or personality. It is indifferent in motive, originating in no psychology nor in dramatic intentions, nor in literary or pictorial purposes. For at least some of these composers, then, the final intention is to be free of artistry and taste. But this need not make their work 'abstract,' for nothing, in the end, is denied. It is simply that personal expression, drama, psychology, and the like are not part of the composer's initial calculation: they are at best gratuitous."

"The procedure of composing tends to be radical, going directly to the sounds and their characteristics, to the way in which they are produced and how they are notated."

"Sound come into its own." What does that mean? For one thing: it means that noises are as useful to new music as so-called musical tones, for the simple reason that they are sounds. This decision alters the view of history, so that one is no longer concerned with tonality or atonality, Schoenberg or Stravinsky (the twelve tones or the twelve expressed as seven plus five), nor with consonance and dissonance, but rather with Edgard Varèse who fathered forth noise into twentieth-century music. But it is clear that ways must be discovered that allow noises and tones to be just noises and tones, not exponents subservient to Varèse's imagination.

What else did Varèse do that is relevant to present necessity? He was the first to write directly for instruments, giving up the practice of making a piano sketch and later orchestrating it. What is unnecessary in Varèse (from a present point of view of necessity) are all his mannerisms, of which two stand out as signatures (the repeated note resembling a telegraphic transmission and the cadence of a tone held through a crescendo to maximum amplitude). These mannerisms do not establish sounds in their own right. They make it quite difficult to hear the sounds just as they are, for they draw attention to Varèse and his imagination.

What is the nature of an experimental action? It is simply an action the outcome of which is not foreseen. It is therefore very useful if one has decided that sounds are to come into their own, rather than being exploited to express sentiments or ideas of order. Among those actions the outcomes of which are not foreseen, actions resulting from chance operations are useful. However, more essential than composing by means of chance operations, it seems to me now, is composing in such a way that what one does is indeterminate of its performance. In such a case one can just work directly, for nothing one does gives rise to anything that is preconceived. This necessitates, of course, a rather great change in habits of notation. I take a sheet of paper and place points on it. Next I make parallel lines on a transparency, say five parallel lines. I establish five categories of sound for the five lines, but I do not say which line is which category. The transparency may be placed on the sheet with points in any position and readings of the points may be taken with regard to all the characteristics one wishes to distinguish. Another transparency may be used for further measurements, even altering the succession of sounds in time. In this situation no chance operations are necessary (for instance, no tossing of coins) for nothing is foreseen, though everything may be later minutely measured or simply taken as a vague suggestion.

Implicit here, it seems to me, are principles familiar from modern painting and architecture: collage and space. What makes this action like Dada are the underlying philosophical views and the collagelike actions. But what makes this action unlike Dada is the space in it. For it is the space and emptiness that is finally urgently necessary at this point in history (not the sounds that happen in it—or their relationships) (not the stones—thinking of a Japanese stone garden—or their relationships but the emptiness of the sand which needs the stones anywhere in the space in order to be empty). When I said recently in Darmstadt that one could write music by observing the imperfections in the paper upon which one was writing, a student who did not understand because he was full of musical ideas asked, "Would one piece of paper be better than another: one for instance that had more imperfections?" He was attached to sounds and because of his attachment could not let sounds be just sounds. He needed to attach himself to the emptiness, to the silence. Then things—sounds, that is—would come into being of themselves. Why is this so necessary that sounds should be just sounds? There are many ways of saying why. One is this: In order that each sound may become the Buddha. If that is too Oriental an expression, take the Christian Gnostic statement: "Split the stick and there is Jesus."

We know now that sounds and noises are not just frequencies (pitches): that is why so much of European musical studies and even so much of modern music is no longer urgently necessary. It is pleasant if you happen to hear Beethoven or Chopin or whatever, but it isn't urgent to do so any more. Nor is harmony or counterpoint or counting in meters of two, three, or four or any other number. So that much of Ives (Charles Ives) is no longer experimental or necessary for us (though people are so used to knowing that he was the first to do such and such). He did do things in space and in collage, and he did say, Do this or this (whichever you choose), and so indeterminacy which is so essential now did enter into his music. But his meters and rhythms are no longer any more important for us than curiosities of the past like the patterns one finds in Stravinsky. Counting is no longer necessary for magnetic tape music (where so many inches or centimeters equal so many seconds): magnetic tape music makes it clear that we are in time itself, not in measures of two, three, or four or any other number. And so instead of counting we use watches if we want to know where in time we are, or rather where in time a sound is to be. All this can be summed up by saying each aspect of sound (frequency, amplitude, timbre, duration) is to be seen as a continuum, not as a series of discrete steps favored by conventions (Occidental or Oriental). (Clearly all the Americana aspects of Ives are in the way of sound coming into its own, since sounds by their nature are no more American than they are Egyptian.)

Carl Ruggles? He works and reworks a handful of compositions so that they better and better express his intentions, which perhaps ever so slightly are changing. His work is therefore not experimental at all but in a most sophisticated way attached to the past and to art.

Henry Cowell was for many years the open sesame for new music in America. Most selflessly he published the New Music Edition and encouraged the young to discover new directions. From him, as from an efficient information booth, you could always get not only the address and telephone number of anyone working in a lively way in music, but you could also get an unbiased introduction from him as to what that anyone was doing. He was not attached (as Varèse also was not attached) to what seemed to so many to be the important question: Whether to follow Schoenberg or Stravinsky. His early works for piano, long before Varèse's *Ionization* (which, by the way, was published by Cowell), by their tone clusters and use of the piano strings, pointed towards noise and a continuum of timbre. Other works of his are indeterminate in ways analogous to those currently in use by Boulez and Stockhausen. For example: Cowell's *Mosaic Quartet,* where the performers, in any way they choose, produce a continuity from composed blocks provided by him. Or his *Elastic Musics,* the time lengths of which can be short or long through the use or omission of measures provided by him. These actions by Cowell are very close to current experimental compositions which have parts but no scores, and which are therefore not objects but processes providing experience not burdened by psychological intentions on the part of the composer.

And in connection with musical continuity, Cowell remarked at the New School before a concert of works by Christian Wolff, Earle Brown, Morton Feldman, and myself, that here were four composers who were getting rid of glue. That is: Where people had felt the necessity to stick sounds together to make a continuity, we four felt the opposite necessity to get rid of the glue so that sounds would be themselves.

Christian Wolff was the first to do this. He wrote some pieces vertically on the page but recommended their being played horizontally left to right, as is conventional. Later he discovered other geometrical means for freeing his music of intentional continuity. Morton Feldman divided pitches into three areas, high, middle, and low, and established a time unit. Writing on graph paper, he simply inscribed numbers of tones to be played at any time within specified periods of time.

There are people who say, "If music's that easy to write, I could do it." Of course they could, but they don't. I find Feldman's own statement more affirmative. We were driving back from some place in New England where a concert had been given. He is a large man and falls asleep easily. Out of a sound sleep, he awoke to say, "Now that things are so simple, there's so much to do." And then he went back to sleep.

Giving up control so that sounds can be sounds (they are not men: they are sounds) means for instance: the conductor of an orchestra is no longer a policeman. Simply an indicator of time—not in beats—like a chronometer. He has his own part. Actually he is not necessary if all the players have some other way of knowing what time it is and how that time is changing.

What else is there to say about the history of experimental music in America? Probably a lot. But we don't need to talk about neo-classicism (I agree with Varèse when he says neo-classicism is indicative of intellectual poverty), nor about the twelve-tone system. In Europe, the number twelve has already been dropped and in a recent lecture Stockhausen questions the current necessity for the concept of a series. Elliott Carter's ideas about rhythmic modulation are not experimental. They just extend sophistication out from tonality ideas towards ideas about modulation from one tempo to another. They put a new wing on the academy and open no doors to the world outside the school. Cowell's present interests in the various traditions, Oriental and early American, are not experimental but eclectic. Jazz per se derives from serious music. And when serious music derives from it, the situation becomes rather silly.

One must make an exception in the case of William Russell. Though still living, he no longer composes. His works, though stemming from jazz —hot jazz—New Orleans and Chicago styles—were short, epigrammatic, original, and entirely interesting. It may be suspected that he lacked the academic skills which would have enabled him to extend and develop his ideas. The fact is, his pieces were all expositions without development and therefore, even today, twenty years after their composition, interesting to hear. He used string drums made from kerosene cans, washboards, out-of-tune upright pianos; he cut a board such a length that it could be used to play all the eighty-eight piano keys at once.

If one uses the word "experimental" (somewhat differently than I have been using it) to mean simply the introduction of novel elements into one's music, we find that America has a rich history: the clusters of Leo Ornstein, the resonances of Dane Rudhyar, the near-Eastern aspects of Alan Hovhaness, the tack piano of Lou Harrison, my own prepared piano, the distribution in space of instrumental ensembles in works by Henry Brant, the sliding tones of Ruth Crawford and, more recently, Gunther Schuller, the microtones and novel instruments of Harry Partch, the athematic continuity of clichés of Virgil Thomson. These are not experimental composers in my terminology, but neither are they part of the stream of European music which though formerly divided into neo-classicism and dodecaphony has become one in America under Arthur Berger's term, consolidation: consolidation of the acquisitions of Schoenberg and Stravinsky.

Actually America has an intellectual climate suitable for radical experimentation. We are, as Gertrude Stein said, the oldest country of the twentieth century. And I like to add: in our air way of knowing nowness. Buckminster Fuller, the dymaxion architect, in his three-hour lecture on the history of civilization, explains that men leaving Asia to go to Europe went against the wind and developed machines, ideas, and Occidental philosophies in accord with a struggle against nature; that, on the other hand, men leaving Asia to go to America went with the wind, put up a sail, and developed ideas and Oriental philosophies in accord with the acceptance of nature. These two tendencies met in America, producing a movement into the air, not bound to the past, traditions, or whatever. Once in Amsterdam, a Dutch musician said to me, "It must be very difficult for you in America to write music, for you are so far away from the centers of tradition." I had to say, "It must be very difficult for you in Europe to write music, for you are so close to the centers of tradition." Why, since the climate for experimentation in America is so good, why is American experimental music so lacking in strength politically (I mean unsupported by those with money [individuals and foundations], unpublished, undiscussed, ignored), and why is there so little of it that is truly uncompromising? I think the answer is this: Until 1950 about all the energy for furthering music in America was concentrated either in the League of Composers or in the ISCM (another way of saying Boulanger and Stravinsky on the one hand and Schoenberg on the other). The New Music Society of Henry Cowell was independent and therefore not politically strong. Anything that was vividly experimental was discouraged by the League and the ISCM. So that a long period of contemporary music history in America was devoid of performances of works by Ives and Varèse. Now the scene changes, but the last few years have been quiet. The League and the ISCM fused and, so doing, gave no concerts at all. We may trust that new life will spring up, since society like nature abhors a vacuum.

What about music for magnetic tape in America? Otto Luening and Vladimir Ussachevsky call themselves experimental because of their use of this new medium. However, they just continue conventional musical practices, at most extending the ranges of instruments electronically and so forth. The Barrons, Louis and Bebe, are also cautious, doing nothing that does not have an immediate popular acceptance. The Canadian Norman McLaren, working with film, is more adventurous than these—also the Whitney brothers in California. Henry Jacobs and those who surround him in the San Francisco area are as conventional as Luening, Ussachevsky, and the Barrons. These do not move in directions that are as experimental as those taken by the Europeans: Pousseur, Berio, Maderna, Boulez, Stockhausen, and so forth. For this reason one can complain that the society of musicians in America has neither recognized nor furthered its native musical resource (by "native" I mean that resource which distinguishes it from Europe and Asia—its capacity to easily break with tradition, to move easily into the air, its capacity for the unforeseen, its capacity for experimentation). The figures in the ISCM and the League, however, were not powerful aesthetically, but powerful only politically. The names of Stravinsky, Schoenberg, Webern are more golden than any of their American derivatives. These latter have therefore little musical influence, and now that they are becoming quiescent politically, one may expect a change in the musical society.

The vitality that characterizes the current European musical scene follows from the activities of Boulez, Stockhausen, Nono, Maderna, Pousseur, Berio, etc. There is in all of this activity an element of tradition, continuity with the past, which is expressed in each work as an interest in continuity whether in terms of discourse or organization. By critics this activity is termed post-Webernian. However, this term apparently means only music written *after* that of Webern, not music written *because of* that of Webern: there is no sign of *klangfarbenmelodie*, no concern for discontinuity—rather a surprising acceptance of even the most banal of continuity devices: ascending or descending linear passages, crescendi and diminuendi, passages from tape to orchestra that are made imperceptible. The skills that are required to bring such events about are taught in the academies. However, this scene will change. The silences of American experimental music and even its technical involvements with chance operations are being introduced into new European music. It will not be easy, however, for Europe to give up being Europe. It will, nevertheless, and must: for the world is one world now.

History is the story of original actions. Once when Virgil Thomson was giving a talk at Town Hall in New York City, he spoke of the necessity of originality. The audience immediately hissed. Why are people opposed to originality? Some fear the loss of the *status quo*. Others realize, I suppose, the fact that they will not make it. Make what? Make history. There are kinds of originality: several that are involved with success, beauty, and ideas (of order, of expression: i.e., Bach, Beethoven); a single that is not involved, neuter, so to say. All of the several involved kinds are generally existent and only bring one sooner or later to a disgust with art. Such original artists appear, as Antonin Artaud said, as pigs: concerned with self-advertisement. What is advertised? Finally, and at best, only something that is connected not with making history but with the past: Bach, Beethoven. If it's a new idea of order, it's Bach; if it's a heartfelt expression, it's Beethoven. That is not the single necessary originality that is not involved and that makes history. That one sees that the human race is one person (all of its members parts of the same body, brothers—not in competition any more than hand is in competition with eye) enables him to see that originality is necessary, for there is no need for eye to do what hand so well does. In this way, the past and the present are to be observed and each person makes what he alone must make, bringing for the whole of human society into existence a historical fact, and then, on and on, in continuum and discontinuum.

The text below first appeared in the 1958 Art News Annual. *It is an imaginary conversation between Satie and myself. Because he died over thirty years before, neither of us hears what the other says. His remarks are ones he is reported to have made and excerpts from his writings.*

ERIK SATIE

There'll probably be some music, but we'll manage to find a quiet corner where we can talk.

A few days ago it rained. I should be out gathering mushrooms. But here I am, having to write about Satie. In an unguarded moment I said I would. Now I am pestered with a deadline. Why, in heaven's name, don't people read the books about him that are available, play the music that's published? Then I for one could go back to the woods and spend my time profitably.

Nevertheless, we must bring about a music which is like furniture—a music, that is, which will be part of the noises of the environment, will take them into consideration. I think of it as melodious, softening the noises of the knives and forks, not dominating them, not imposing itself. It would fill up those heavy silences that sometimes fall between friends dining together. It would spare them the trouble of paying attention to their own banal remarks. And at the same time it would neutralize the street noises which so indiscretely enter into the play of conversation. To make such music would be to respond to a need.

Records, too, are available. But it would be an act of charity even to oneself to smash them whenever they are discovered. They are useless except for that and for the royalties which the composer, dead now some thirty-odd years, can no longer pick up.

We cannot doubt that animals both love and practice music. That is evident. But it seems their musical system differs from ours. It is another school. . . . We are not familiar with their didactic works. Perhaps they don't have any.

Who's interested in Satie nowadays anyway? Not Pierre Boulez: he has the twelve tones, governs La Domaine Musicale, whereas Satie had only the Group of Six and was called Le Maître d'Arcueil. Nor Stockhausen: I imagine he has not yet given Satie a thought. . . . Current musical activities involve two problems: (1) applying the idea of the series inherent in the twelve-tone system to the organization of all the characteristics of sound, viz., frequency, duration, amplitude, timbre, producing a more controlled situation than before attempted (Stockhausen: "It makes me feel so good to know that I am on the right track."); and (2a) discovering and acting upon the new musical resources (all audible sounds in any combination and any continuity issuing from any points in space in any transformations) handed to us upon the magnetic plate of tape, or (2b) somehow arranging economical instrumental occasions (tape is expensive) so that the action which results presupposes a totality of possibility. . . . Is Satie relevant in mid-century?

I am bored with dying of a broken heart. Everything I timidly start fails with a boldness before unknown. What can I do but turn towards God

*and point my finger at him? I have come to the
conclusion that the old man is even more stupid
than he is weak.*

Taking the works of Satie chronologically (1886–1925), successive ones often appear as completely new departures. Two pieces will be so different as not to suggest that the same person wrote them. Now and then, on the other hand, works in succession are so alike, sometimes nearly identical, as to bring to mind the annual exhibitions of painters, and to allow musicologists to discern stylistic periods. Students busy themselves with generalized analyses of harmonic, melodic, and rhythmic matters with the object of showing that in *Socrate* all these formal principles are found, defined, and reunited in a homogeneous fashion (as befits a masterpiece). From this student point of view, Pierre Boulez is justified in rejecting Satie. *Le bon Maître's* harmonies, melodies, and rhythms are no longer of interest. They provide pleasure for those who have no better use for their time. They've lost their power to irritate. True, one could not endure a performance of *Vexations* (lasting [my estimate] twenty-four hours; 840 repetitions of a fifty-two beat piece itself involving a repetitive structure: A,A$_1$,A,A$_2$, each A thirteen measures long), but why give it a thought?

*How white it is! no painting ornaments it; it is all
of a piece.* (Reverie on a plate)

An artist conscientiously moves in a direction which for some good reason he takes, putting one work in front of the other with the hope he'll arrive before death overtakes him. But Satie despised Art (*"J'emmerde l'Art"*). He was going nowhere. The artist counts: 7, 8, 9, etc. Satie appears at unpredictable points springing always from zero: 112, 2, 49, no etc. The absence of transition is characteristic not only between finished works, but at divisions, large and small, within a single one. It was in the same way that Satie made his living: he never took a regular (continuity-giving) job, plus raises and bonuses (climaxes). No one can say for sure anything about the *String Quartet* he was on the point of writing when he died.

They will tell you I am not a musician. That's right.
. . . Take the Fils des Etoiles *or the* Morceaux en forme de poire, En habit de cheval *or the* Sarabandes, *it is clear no musical idea presided at the creation of these works.*

Curiously enough, the twelve-tone system has no zero in it. Given a series: 3, 5, 2, 7, 10, 8, 11, 9, 1, 6, 4, 12 and the plan of obtaining its inversion by numbers which when added to the corresponding ones of the original series will give 12, one obtains 9, 7, 10, 5, 2, 4, 1, 3, 11, 6, 8 and 12. For in this system 12 plus 12 equals 12. There is not enough of nothing in it.

It's a large stairway, very large.
It has more than a thousand steps, all made of ivory.
It is very handsome.
Nobody dares use it
For fear of spoiling it.

The King himself never does.
Leaving his room
He jumps out the window.

So, he often says:
I love this stairway so much
I'm going to have it stuffed.

Isn't the King right?

Is it not a question of the will, this one, I mean, of giving consideration to the sounds of the knives and forks, the street noises, letting them enter in? (Or call it magnetic tape, *musique concrète,* furniture music. It's the same thing: working in terms of totality, not just the discretely chosen conventions.)

Why is it necessary to give the sounds of knives and forks consideration? Satie says so. He is right. Otherwise the music will have to have walls to defend itself, walls which will not only constantly be in need of repair, but which, even to get a drink of water, one will have to pass beyond, inviting disaster. It is evidently a question of bringing one's intended actions into relation with the ambient unintended ones. The common denominator is zero, where the heart beats (no one *means* to circulate his blood).

Show me something new; I'll begin all over again.

Of course *"it is another school"*—this moving out from zero.

Flowers! But, dear lady, it is too soon!

To repeat: a sound has four characteristics: frequency, amplitude, timbre and duration. Silence (ambient noise) has only duration. A zero musical structure must be just an empty time. Satie made at least three kinds of empty time structures:

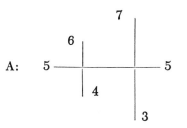

A:

(numbers are of measures). Symmetry, which itself suggests zero, is here horizontal, whereas in:

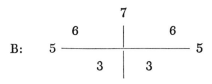

B:

it is vertical; and in:

C:

it is geometric (the large numbers are groups of measures).

When I was young, people told me: You'll see when you're fifty. I'm fifty. I've seen nothing.

A time that's just time will let sounds be just sounds and if they are folk tunes, unresolved ninth chords, or knives and forks, just folk tunes, unresolved ninth chords, or knives and forks.

I am in complete agreement with our enemies. It's a shame that artists advertise. However, Beethoven was not clumsy in his publicity. That's how he became known, I believe.

ERIK SATIE/81

It (L'Esprit Nouveau) *teaches us to tend towards an absence* (simplicité) *of emotion and an inactivity* (fermeté) *in the way of prescribing sonorities and rhythms which lets them affirm themselves clearly, in a straight line from their plan and pitch, conceived in a spirit of humility and renunciation.*

To be interested in Satie one must be disinterested to begin with, accept that a sound is a sound and a man is a man, give up illusions about ideas of order, expressions of sentiment, and all the rest of our inherited aesthetic claptrap.

If I fail, so much the worse for me. It's because I had nothing in me to begin with.

It's not a question of Satie's relevance. He's indispensable.

No longer anything to be done in that direction, I must search for something else or I am lost.

This subject is entertaining (*"What's necessary is to be uncompromising to the end"*) but it is getting nowhere, and more than ever there are things to be done.

Listen, my friends, when I leave you like this and must go home on foot, it is towards dawn I come near Arcueil. When I pass through the woods, the birds beginning to sing, I see an old tree, its leaves rustling, I go near, I put my arms around it and think, What a good character, never to have harmed anyone.

—and, on another occasion,

Personally, I am neither good nor bad. I oscillate, if I may say so. Also I've never really done anyone any harm—nor any good, to boot.

The Fall 1958 issue of Nutida Musik *(Stockholm) was devoted to the work of Edgard Varèse. I contributed the following article.*

EDGARD VARÈSE

Changes which are characteristic of a living organism (and twentieth-century music is one) have become recently more marked and occur in more rapid succession. In the history Varèse appears sometimes as a figure of the past; and, again, as one active according to present necessities.

Facts about his life and work are difficult to obtain. He considers interest in them to be a form of necrophilia; he prefers to leave no traces. Analytical studies of his work are somehow not relevant to one's experience of it. Though Varèse has defined music as "organized sound," it is unclear how he brings about the organization of his works. He has often insisted upon imagination as a *sine qua non,* and the presence of his imagination is strong as handwriting in each of his works. The characteristic flourish is a tone sustained through a crescendo to the maximum amplitude.

For those who are interested in sounds just as they are, apart from psychology about them, one must look further for Varèse's present relevance. This is not found in the character of his imagination, which has to do with him—not with sound itself. Nor is his use of tape relevant, for in *Deserts* he attempts to make tape sound like the orchestra and vice versa, showing again a lack of interest in the natural differences of sounds, preferring to give them all his unifying signature. In this respect his need for continuity does not correspond to the present need for discontinuity (discontinuity has the effect of divorcing sounds from the burden of psychological intentions). Though Varèse was the first to write directly for instrumental ensembles (giving up the piano sketch and its orchestral coloration), his way of doing this was controlled by his imagination to the point of exploiting the sounds for his own purposes.

Recently (1957-1958) he has found a notation for jazz improvisation of a form controlled by himself. Though the specific notes are not determined by him, the amplitudes are; they are characteristic of his imagination, and the improvisations, though somewhat indeterminate, sound like his other works.

In these respects Varèse is an artist of the past. Rather than dealing with sounds as sounds, he deals with them as Varèse.

However, more clearly and actively than anyone else of his generation, he established the present nature of music. This nature does not arise from pitch relations (consonance-dissonance) nor from twelve tones nor seven plus five (Schoenberg-Stravinsky), but arises from an acceptance of all audible phenomena as material proper to music. While others were still discriminating "musical" tones from noises, Varèse moved into the field of sound itself, not splitting it in two by introducing into the perception of it a mental prejudice. That he fathered forth noise—that is to say, into twentieth-century music—makes him more relative to present musical necessity than even the Viennese masters, whose notion of the number 12 was some time ago dropped and shortly, surely, their notion of the series will be seen as no longer urgently necessary.

. . . .

One summer day, Merce Cunningham and I took eight children to Bear Mountain Park. The paths through the zoo were crowded. Some of the children ran ahead, while others fell behind. Every now and then we stopped, gathered all the children together, and counted them to make sure none had been lost. Since it was very hot and the children were getting difficult, we decided to buy them ice cream cones. This was done in shifts. While I stayed with some, Merce Cunningham took others, got them cones, and brought them back. I took the ones with cones. He took those without. Eventually all the children were supplied with ice cream. However, they got it all over their faces. So we went to a water fountain where people were lined up to get a drink, put the children in line, tried to keep them there, and waited our turn. Finally, I knelt beside the fountain. Merce Cunningham turned it on. Then I proceeded one by one to wash the children's faces. While I was doing this, a man behind us in line said rather loudly, "There's a washroom over there." I looked up at him quickly and said, "Where? And how did you know I was interested in mushrooms?"

One day I asked Schoenberg what he thought about the international situation. He said, "The important thing to do is to develop foreign trade."

Earle Brown and I spent several months splicing magnetic tape together. We sat on opposite sides of the same table. Each of us had a pattern of the splicing to be done, the measurements to be made, etc. Since we were working on tapes that were later to be synchronized, we checked our measurements every now and then against each other. We invariably discovered errors in each other's measurements. At first each of us thought the other was being careless. When the whole situation became somewhat exasperating, we took a single ruler and a single tape and each one marked where he thought an inch was. The two marks were at different points. It turned out that Earle Brown closed one eye when he made his measurements, whereas I kept both eyes open. We then tried closing one of my eyes, and later opening both of his. There still was disagreement as to the length of an inch. Finally we decided that one person should do all the final synchronizing splices. But then errors crept in due to changes in weather. In spite of these obstacles, we went on doing what we were doing for about five more months, twelve hours a day, until the work was finished.

Dorothy Norman invited me to dinner in New York. There was a lady there from Philadelphia who was an authority on Buddhist art. When she found out I was interested in mushrooms, she said, "Have you an explanation of the symbolism involved in the death of the Buddha by his eating a mushroom?" I explained that I'd never been interested in symbolism; that I preferred just taking things as themselves, not as standing for other things. But then a few days later while rambling in the woods I got to thinking. I recalled the Indian concept of the relation of life and the seasons. Spring is Creation. Summer is Preservation. Fall is Destruction. Winter is Quiescence. Mushrooms grow most vigorously in the fall, the period of destruction, and the function of many of them is to bring about the final decay of rotting material. In fact, as I read somewhere, the world would be an impassible heap of old rubbish were it not for mushrooms and their capacity to get rid of it. So I wrote to the lady in Philadelphia. I said, "The function of mushrooms is to rid the world of old rubbish. The Buddha died a natural death."

Once I was visiting my Aunt Marge. She was doing her laundry. She turned to me and said, "You know? I love this machine much more than I do your Uncle Walter."

One Sunday morning, Mother said to Dad, "Let's go to church." Dad said, "O.K." When they drove up in front, Dad showed no sign of getting out of the car. Mother said, "Aren't you coming in?" Dad said, "No, I'll wait for you here."

After a long and arduous journey a young Japanese man arrived deep in a forest where the teacher of his choice was living in a small house he had made. When the student arrived, the teacher was sweeping up fallen leaves. Greeting his master, the young man received no greeting in return. And to all his questions, there were no replies. Realizing there was nothing he could do to get the teacher's attention, the student went to another part of the same forest and built himself a house. Years later, when he was sweeping up fallen leaves, he was enlightened. He then dropped everything, ran through the forest to his teacher, and said, "Thank you."

EDGARD VARÈSE/85

While I was studying with Adolph Weiss in the early 1930's, I became aware of his unhappiness in face of the fact that his music was rarely performed. I too had experienced difficulty in arranging performances of my compositions, so I determined to consider a piece of music only half done when I completed a manuscript. It was my responsibility to finish it by getting it played.

It was evident that musicians interested in new music were rare. It was equally evident that modern dancers were grateful for any sounds or noises that could be produced for their recitals. My first commission was from the Physical Education Department of U.C.L.A. An accompaniment for an aquatic ballet was needed. Using drums and gongs, I found that the swimmers beneath the surface of the water, not being able to hear the sounds, lost their places. Dipping the gongs into the water while still playing them solved the problems of synchronization and brought the sliding tones of the "water gong" into the percussion orchestra.

FOUR STATEMENTS ON THE DANCE

Very soon I was earning a livelihood accompanying dance classes and occasionally writing music for performances. In 1937 I was at the Cornish School in Seattle, associated with Bonnie Bird, who had danced with Martha Graham. Merce Cunningham was a student, so remarkable that he soon left Seattle for New York, where he became a soloist in the Graham company. Four or five years later I went to New York and encouraged Cunningham to give programs of his own dances. We have worked together since 1943.

This article was part of a series, Percussion Music and Its Relation to the Modern Dance, *that appeared in* Dance Observer *in 1939. It was written in Seattle where I had organized a concert-giving percussion ensemble.*

Goal: New Music, New Dance

Percussion music is revolution. Sound and rhythm have too long been submissive to the restrictions of nineteenth-century music. Today we are fighting for their emancipation. Tomorrow, with electronic music in our ears, we will hear freedom.

Instead of giving us new sounds, the nineteenth-century composers have given us endless arrangements of the old sounds. We have turned on radios and always known when we were tuned to a symphony. The sound has always been the same, and there has not been even a hint of curiosity as to the possibilities of rhythm. For interesting rhythms we have listened to jazz.

At the present stage of revolution, a healthy lawlessness is warranted. Experiment must necessarily be carried on by hitting anything—tin pans, rice bowls, iron pipes—anything we can lay our hands on. Not only hitting, but rubbing, smashing, making sound in every possible way. In short, we must explore the materials of music. What we can't do ourselves will be done by machines and electrical instruments which we will invent.

The conscientious objectors to modern music will, of course, attempt everything in the way of counterrevolution. Musicians will not admit that we are making music; they will say that we are interested in superficial effects, or, at most, are imitating Oriental or primitive music. New and original sounds will be labeled as "noise." But our common answer to every criticism must be to continue working and listening, making music with its materials, sound and rhythm, disregarding the cumbersome, top-heavy structure of musical prohibitions.

These prohibitions removed, the choreographer will be quick to realize a great advantage to the modern dance: the simultaneous composition of both dance and music. The materials of dance, already including rhythm, require only the addition of sound to become a rich, complete vocabulary. The dancer should be better equipped than the musician to use this vocabulary, for more of the materials are already at his command. Some dancers have made steps in this direction by making simple percussion accompaniments. Their use of percussion, unfortunately, has not been constructive. They have followed the rhythm of their own dance movement, accentuated it and punctuated it with percussion, but they have not given the sound its own and special part in the whole composition. They have made the music identical with the dance but not cooperative with it. Whatever method is used in composing the materials of the dance can be extended to the organization of the musical materials. The form of the music-dance composition should be a necessary working together of all materials used. The music will then be more than an accompaniment; it will be an integral part of the dance.

. . . .

When I was growing up in California there were two things that everyone assumed were good for you. There were, of course, others—spinach and oatmeal, for instance—but right now I'm thinking of sunshine and orange juice. When we lived at Ocean Park, I was sent out every morning to the beach where I spent the day building rolly-coasters in the sand, complicated downhill tracks with tunnels and inclines upon which I rolled a small hard rubber ball. Every day toward noon I fainted because the sun was too much for me. When I fainted I didn't fall down, but I couldn't see; there were flocks of black spots wherever I looked. I soon learned to find my way in that blindness to a hamburger stand where I'd ask for something to eat. Sitting in the shade, I'd come to. It took me much longer, about thirty-five years in fact, to learn that orange juice was not good for me either.

Before studying Zen, men are men and mountains are mountains. While studying Zen, things become confused. After studying Zen, men are men and mountains are mountains. After telling this, Dr. Suzuki was asked, "What is the difference between before and after?" He said, "No difference, only the feet are a little bit off the ground."

The following piece was printed in Dance Observer *in 1944.*

Grace and Clarity

The strength that comes from firmly established art practices is not present in the modern dance today. Insecure, not having any clear direction, the modern dancer is willing to compromise and to accept influences from other more rooted art manners, enabling one to remark that certain dancers are either borrowing from or selling themselves to Broadway, others are learning from folk and Oriental arts, and many are either introducing into their work elements of the ballet, or, in an all-out effort, devoting themselves to it. Confronted with its history, its former power, its present insecurity, the realization is unavoidable that the strength the modern dance once had was not impersonal but was intimately connected with and ultimately dependent on the personalities and even the actual physical bodies of the individuals who imparted it.

The techniques of the modern dance were once orthodox. It did not enter a dancer's mind that they might be altered. To add to them was the sole privilege of the originators.

Intensive summer courses were the scenes of the new dispensations, reverently transmitted by the master-students. When the fanatically followed leaders began, and when they continued, to desert their own teachings (adapting chiefly balletish movements to their own rapidly-growing-less-rigorous techniques), a general and profound insecurity fell over the modern dance.

Where any strength now exists in the modern dance, it is, as before, in isolated personalities and physiques. In the case of the young, this is unfortunate; for, no matter how impressive and revelatory their expressed outlooks on life are, they are overshadowed, in the minds of audiences, and often, understandably, in the dancers' own minds, by the more familiar, more respected, and more mature older personalities.

Personality is a flimsy thing on which to build an art. (This does not mean that it should not enter into an art, for, indeed, that is what is meant by the word *style*.) And the ballet is obviously not built on such an ephemeron, for, if it were, it would not at present thrive as it does, almost devoid of interesting personalities and certainly without the contribution of any individual's message or attitude toward life.

That the ballet *has* something seems reasonable to assume. That what it has is what the modern dance needs is here expressed as an opinion.

It is seriously to be doubted whether *tour jeté, entrechat six,* or *sur les pointes* (in general) are needed in the modern dance. Even the prettiness and fanciness of these movements would not seem to be requisite. Also, it is not true that the basis of the ballet lies in glittering costumes and sets, for many of the better ballets appear year after year in drab, weather-beaten accoutrements.

Ballets like *Les Sylphides, Swan Lake,* almost any *Pas de Deux* or *Quatre,* and currently, the exceptional *Danses Concertantes* have a strength and validity quite beyond and separate from the movements involved, whether or not they are done with style (expressed personality), the ornamented condition of the stage, quality of costumery, sound of the music, or any other particularities, including those of content. Nor does the secret lie in that mysterious quantity, form. (The forms of the ballet are mostly dull; symmetry is maintained practically without question.)

Good or bad, with or without meaning, well dressed or not, the ballet is always clear in its rhythmic structure. Phrases begin and end in such a way that *anyone* in the audience knows when they begin and end, and breathes accordingly. It may seem at first thought that rhythmic structure is not of primary importance. However, a dance, a poem, a piece of music (any of the time arts) occupies a length of time, and the manner in which this length of time is divided first into large parts and then into phrases (or built up from phrases to form eventual larger parts) is the work's very life structure. The ballet is in possession of a tradition of clarity of its rhythmic structure. Essential devices for bringing this about have been handed down generation after generation. These particular devices, again, are not to be borrowed from the ballet: they are private to it. But the function they fulfill is not private; it is, on the contrary, universal.

Oriental dancing, for instance, is clear in its phraseology. It has its own devices for obtaining it. Hot jazz is never unclear rhythmically. The poems of Gerard Manley Hopkins, with all their departure from tradition, enable the reader to breathe with them. The modern dance, on the other hand, is rarely clear.

When a modern dancer has followed music that was clear in its phrase structure, the dance has had a tendency to be clear. The widespread habit of choreographing the dance first, and obtaining music for it later, is not in itself here criticized. But the fact that modern choreographers have been concerned with things other than clarity of rhythmic structure has made the appearance of it, when the dance-first-music-later method was used, both accidental and isolated. This has led to a disregard of rhythmic structure even in the case of dancing to music already written, for, in a work like Martha Graham's *Deaths and Entrances*, an audience can know where it is in relation to the action only through repeated seeings and the belying action of memory. On the other hand, Martha Graham and Louis Horst together were able to make magnificently clear and moving works like their *Frontier*, which works, however, stand alarmingly alone in the history of the modern dance.

The will to compromise, mentioned above, and the admirable humility implied in the willingness to learn from other art manners is adolescent, but it is much closer to maturity than the childish blind following of leaders that was characteristic of the modern dance several years ago. If, in receiving influences from the outside, the modern dance is satisfied with copying, or adapting to itself, surface particularities (techniques, movements, devices of any kind), it will die before it reaches maturity; if, on the other hand, the common denominator of the completely developed time arts, the secret of art life, is discovered by the modern dance, Terpsichore will have a new and rich source of worshippers.

With clarity of rhythmic structure, *grace* forms a duality. Together they have a relation like that of body and soul. Clarity is cold, mathematical, inhuman, but basic and earthy. Grace is warm, incalculable, human, opposed to clarity, and like the air. Grace is not here used to mean prettiness; it is used to mean the play with and against the clarity of the rhythmic structure. The two are always present together in the best works of the time arts, endlessly, and life-givingly, opposed to each other.

"In the finest specimens of versification, there seems to be a perpetual conflict between the law of the verse and the freedom of the language, and each is incessantly, though insignificantly, violated for the purpose of giving effect to the other. The best poet is not he whose verses are the most easily scanned, and whose phraseology is the commonest in its materials, and the most direct in its arrangement; but rather he whose language combines the greatest imaginative accuracy with the most elaborate and sensible metrical organisation, and who, in his verse, preserves everywhere the living sense of the metre, not so much by unvarying obedience to, as by innumerable small departures from, its *modulus*." (Coventry Patmore, *Prefatory Study on English Metrical Law*, 1879, pp. 12–13)

The "perpetual conflict" between clarity and grace is what makes hot jazz hot. The best performers continually anticipate or delay the phrase beginnings and endings. They also, in their performances, treat the beat or pulse, and indeed, the measure, with grace: putting more or fewer icti within the measure's limits than are expected (similar alterations of pitch and timbre are also customary), contracting or extending the duration of the unit. This, not syncopation, is what pleases the hep-cats.

Hindu music and dancing are replete with grace. This is possible because the rhythmic structure in Hindu time arts is highly systematized, has been so for many ages, and every Hindu who enjoys listening to music or looking at the dance is familiar with the laws of tala. Players, dancers, and audience enjoy hearing and seeing the laws of the rhythmic structure now observed and now ignored.

This is what occurs in a beautifully performed classic or neo-classic ballet. And it is what enables one to experience pleasure in such a performance, despite the fact that such works are relatively meaningless in our modern society. That one should, today, have to see *Swan Lake* or something equally empty of contemporary meaning in order to experience the pleasure of observing clarity and grace in the dance, is, on its face, lamentable. Modern society needs, as usual, and now desperately needs, a strong modern dance.

The opinion expressed here is that clarity of rhythmic structure with grace are essential to the time arts, that together they constitute an aesthetic (that is, they lie under and beneath, over and above, physical and personal particularities), and that they rarely occur in the modern dance; that the latter has no aesthetic (its strength having been and being the personal property of its originators and best exponents), that, in order for it to become strong and useful in society, mature in itself, the modern dance must clarify its rhythmic structure, then enliven it with grace, and so get itself a theory, the common, universal one about what is beautiful in a time art.

. . . .

In Zen they say: If something is boring after two minutes, try it for four. If still boring, try it for eight, sixteen, thirty-two, and so on. Eventually one discovers that it's not boring at all but very interesting.

At the New School once I was substituting for Henry Cowell, teaching a class in Oriental music. I had told him I didn't know anything about the subject. He said, "That's all right. Just go where the records are. Take one out. Play it and then discuss it with the class." Well, I took out the first record. It was an LP of a Buddhist service. It began with a short microtonal chant with sliding tones, then soon settled into a single loud reiterated percussive beat. This noise continued relentlessly for about fifteen minutes with no perceptible variation. A lady got up and screamed, and then yelled, "Take it off. I can't bear it any longer." I took it off. A man in the class then said angrily, "Why'd you take it off? I was just getting interested."

During a counterpoint class at U.C.L.A., Schoenberg sent everybody to the blackboard. We were to solve a particular problem he had given and to turn around when finished so that he could check on the correctness of the solution. I did as directed. He said, "That's good. Now find another solution." I did. He said, "Another." Again I found one. Again he said, "Another." And so on. Finally, I said, "There are no more solutions." He said, "What is the principle underlying all of the solutions?"

I went to a concert upstairs in Town Hall. The composer whose works were being performed had provided program notes. One of these notes was to the effect that there is too much pain in the world. After the concert I was walking along with the composer and he was telling me how the performances had not been quite up to snuff. So I said, "Well, I enjoyed the music, but I didn't agree with that program note about there being too much pain in the world." He said, "What? Don't you think there's enough?" I said, "I think there's just the right amount."

Many of my performances with Merce Cunningham and Dance Company are given in academic situations. Now and then the director of the concert series asks for an introductory talk. The following remarks were written for audiences in St. Louis and at Principia College in the autumn of 1956. Then a few months later, in January 1957, they appeared in Dance Observer.

In This Day . . .

In this day of TV-darkened homes, a live performance has become something of a rarity, so much so that Aaron Copland recently said a concert is a thing of the past. Nevertheless, I would like to say a few words regarding the new direction taken by our company of dancers and musicians.

Though some of the dances and music are easily enjoyed, others are perplexing to certain people, for they do not unfold along conventional lines. For one thing, there is an independence of the music and dance, which, if one closely observes, is present also in the seemingly usual works. This independence follows from Mr. Cunningham's faith, which I share, that the support of the dance is not to be found in the music but in the dancer himself, on his own two legs, that is, and occasionally on a single one.

Likewise the music sometimes consists of single sounds or groups of sounds which are not supported by harmonies but resound within a space of silence. From this independence of music and dance a rhythm results which is not that of horses' hoofs or other regular beats but which reminds us of a multiplicity of events in time and space—stars, for instance, in the sky, or activities on earth viewed from the air.

We are not, in these dances and music, saying something. We are simple-minded enough to think that if we were saying something we would use words. We are rather doing something. The meaning of what we do is determined by each one who sees and hears it. At a recent performance of ours at Cornell College in Iowa, a student turned to a teacher and said, "What does it mean?" The teacher's reply was, "Relax, there are no symbols here to confuse you. Enjoy yourself!" I may add there are no stories and no psychological problems. There is simply an activity of movement, sound, and light. The costumes are all simple in order that you may see the movement.

The movement is the movement of the body. It is here that Mr. Cunningham focuses his choreographic attention, not on the facial muscles. In daily life people customarily observe faces and hand gestures, translating what they see into psychological terms. Here, however, we are in the presence of a dance which utilizes the entire body, requiring for its enjoyment the use of your faculty of kinesthetic sympathy. It is this faculty we employ when, seeing the flight of birds, we ourselves, by identification, fly up, glide, and soar.

The activity of movement, sound, and light, we believe, is expressive, but what it expresses is determined by each one of you—who is right, as Pirandello's title has it, if he thinks he is.

The novelty of our work derives therefore from our having moved away from simply private human concerns towards the world of nature and society of which all of us are a part. Our intention is to affirm this life, not to bring order out of chaos nor to suggest improvements in creation, but simply to wake up to the very life we're living, which is so excellent once one gets one's mind and one's desires out of its way and lets it act of its own accord.

. . . .

When Vera Williams first noticed that I was interested in wild mushrooms, she told her children not to touch any of them because they were all deadly poisonous. A few days later she bought a steak at Martino's and decided to serve it smothered with mushrooms. When she started to cook the mushrooms, the children all stopped whatever they were doing and watched her attentively. When she served dinner, they all burst into tears.

One day I went to the dentist. Over the radio they said it was the hottest day of the year. However, I was wearing a jacket, because going to a doctor has always struck me as a somewhat formal occasion. In the midst of his work, Dr. Heyman stopped and said, "Why don't you take your jacket off?" I said, "I have a hole in my shirt and that's why I have my jacket on." He said, "Well, I have a hole in my sock, and, if you like, I'll take my shoes off."

This piece appeared in Dance Magazine, *November 1957. The two pages were given me in dummy form by the editors. The number of words was given by chance operations. Imperfections in the sheets of paper upon which I worked gave the position in space of the fragments of text. That position is different in this printing, for it is the result of working on two other sheets of paper, of another size and having their own differently placed imperfections.*

2 Pages, 122 Words on Music and Dance

To obtain the value
of a sound, a movement,
measure from zero. (Pay   A bird flies.
attention to what it is,
just as it is.)

       Slavery is abolished.

               the woods

       A sound has no legs to stand on.

                       The world is teeming: anything can
                       happen.

movement

sound

Points in
time, in   love   Activities which are different
space   mirth   happen in a time which is a space:
                        the heroic   are each central, original.
                        wonder
The emotions   tranquillity   are in the audience.
                        fear
                        anger   The telephone rings.
                        sorrow   Each person is in the best seat.
                        disgust

Is there a glass of water?   War begins at any moment.

Time,
History
meaningless
has no
purpose

Each now is the time, the space.

lights

inaction?

Are eyes open?

Where the bird flies, fly.   ears? — *absurdity of*
                                              human —
                                              man

This article, completed in February of 1961, was published in Metro *(Milan) in May. It may be read in whole or in part; any sections of it may be skipped, what remains may be read in any order. The style of printing here employed is not essential. Any of the sections may be printed directly over any of the others, and the spaces between paragraphs may be varied in any manner. The words in italics are either quotations from Rauschenberg or titles of his works.*

To Whom It May Concern:
*The white paintings came
first; my silent piece
came later.*

—*J. C.*

ON ROBERT RAUSCHENBERG, ARTIST, AND HIS WORK

Conversation was difficult and correspondence virtually ceased. (Not because of the mails, which continued.) People spoke of messages, perhaps because they'd not heard from one another for a long time. Art flourished.

The goat. No weeds. Virtuosity with ease. Does his head have a bed in it? Beauty. His hands and his feet, fingers and toes long-jointed, are astonishing. They certify his work. And the signature is nowhere to be seen. The paintings were thrown into the river after the exhibition. What is the nature of Art when it reaches the Sea?

Beauty is now underfoot wherever we take the trouble to look. (This is an American discovery.) Is when Rauschenberg looks an idea? Rather it is an entertainment in which to celebrate unfixity. Why did he make black paintings, then white ones (coming up out of the South), red, gold ones (the gold ones were Christmas presents), ones of many colors, ones with objects attached? Why did he make sculptures with rocks suspended? Talented?

I know he put the paint on the tires. And he unrolled the paper on the city street. But which one of us drove the car?

As the paintings changed the printed material became as much of a subject as the paint (I began using newsprint in my work) causing changes of focus: A third palette. There is no poor subject (Any incentive to paint is as good as any other.). Dante is an incentive, providing multiplicity, as useful as a chicken or an old shirt. The atmosphere is such that everything is seen clearly, even in the dark night or when thumbing through an out-of-date newspaper or poem. This subject is un-avoidable (*A canvas is never empty.*); it fills an empty canvas. And if, to continue history, newspapers are pasted onto the canvas and on one another and black paints are applied, the subject looms up in several different places at once like magic to produce the painting. If you don't see it, you probably need a pair of glasses. But there is a vast difference between one oculist and another, and when it is a question of losing eyesight the best thing to do is to go to the best oculist (i.e., the best painter: he'll fix you up). Ideas are not necessary. It is more useful to avoid having one, certainly avoid having several (leads to inactivity). Is Gloria V. a subject or an idea? Then, tell us: How many times was she married and what do you do when she divorces you?

There are three panels taller than they are wide fixed together to make a single rectangle wider than it is tall. Across the whole thing is a series of colored photos, some wider than tall, some taller than wide, fragments of posters, some of them obscured by paint. Underneath these, cutting the total in half, is a series of rec-tangular color swatches, all taller than wide. Above, bridging two of the panels, is a dark blue rectangle. Below and slightly out of line with the blue one, since it is on one panel only, is a gray rectangle with a drawing on it about halfway up. There are other things, but mostly attached to these two "roads" which cross: off to the left and below the swatches is a drawing on a rectangle on a rectangle on a rectangle (its situation is that of a farm on the outskirts of a mainstreet town). This is not a composition. It is a place where things are, as on a table or on a town seen from the air: any one of them could be removed and another come into its place through circumstances analogous to birth and death, travel, housecleaning, or cluttering. He is not saying; he is painting. (What is Rauschenberg saying?) The message is conveyed by dirt which, mixed with an adhesive, sticks to itself and to the canvas upon which he places it. Crumbling and responding to changes in weather, the dirt unceasingly does my thinking. He regrets we do not see the paint while it's dripping.

Rauschenberg is continually being offered scraps of this and that, odds and ends his friends run across, since it strikes them: This is something he could use in a painting. Nine times out of ten it turns out he has no use for it. Say it's something close to something he once found useful, and so could be recognized as his. Well, then, as a matter of course, his poetry has moved without one's knowing where it's gone to. He changes what goes on, on a canvas, but he does not change how canvas is used for paintings—that is, stretched flat to make rectangular surfaces which may be hung on a wall. These he uses singly, joined together, or placed in a symmetry so obvious as not to attract interest (nothing special). We know two ways to unfocus attention: symmetry is one of them; the other is the over-all where each small part is a sample of what you find elsewhere. In either case, there is at least the possibility of looking anywhere, not just where someone arranged you should. You are then free to deal with your freedom just as the artist dealt with his, not in the same way but, nevertheless, originally. This thing, he says, *duplication of images,* that is symmetry. All it means is that, looking closely, we see as it was everything is in chaos still.

To change the subject: "Art is the imitation of nature in her manner of operation." Or a net.

So somebody has talent? So what? Dime a dozen. And we're overpopulated. Actually we have more food than we have people and more art. We've gotten to the point of burning food. When will we begin to burn our art? The door is never locked. Rauschenberg walks in. No one home. He paints a new painting over the old one. Is there a talent then to keep the two, the one above, the one below? What a plight (it's no more serious than that) we're in! It's a joy in fact to begin over again. In preparation he erases the De Kooning.

Is the door locked? No, it's open as usual. Certainly Rauschenberg has techniques. But the ones he has he disuses, using those he hasn't. I must say he never forces a situation. He is like that butcher whose knife never became dull simply because he cut with it in such a way that it never encountered an obstacle. Modern art has no need for technique. (We are in the glory of not knowing what we're doing.) So technique, not having to do with the painting, has to do with who's looking and who painted. People. Technique is: how are the people? Not how well did they do it, but, as they were saying, frailty. (He says—and is he speaking of technique?—"What do you want, a declaration of love? I take responsibility for competence and hope to have made something hazardous with which we may try ourselves.") It is a question, then, of seeing in the dark, not slipping over things visually. Now that Rauschenberg has made a painting with radios in it, does that mean that even without radios, I must go on listening even while I'm looking, everything at once, in order not to be run over?

Would we have preferred a pig with an apple in its mouth? That too, on occasion, is a message and requires a blessing. These are the feelings Rauschenberg gives us: love, wonder, laughter, heroism (I accept), fear, sorrow, anger, disgust, tranquillity.

There is no more subject in a *combine* than there is in a page from a newspaper. Each thing that is there is a subject. It is a situation involving multiplicity.

ON ROBERT RAUSCHENBERG, ARTIST, AND HIS WORK/101

(It is no reflection on the weather that such-and-such a government sent a note to another.) (And the three radios of the radio combine, turned on, which provides the subject?) Say there was a message. How would it be received? And what if it wasn't? Over and over again I've found it impossible to memorize Rauschenberg's paintings. I keep asking, "Have you changed it?" And then noticing while I'm looking it changes. I look out the window and see the icicles. There, dripping water is frozen into object. The icicles all go down. Winter more than the others is the season of quiescence. There is no dripping when the paint is squeezed from a tube. But there is the same acceptance of what happens and no tendency towards gesture or arrangement. This changes the notion of what is beautiful. By fixing papers to canvas and then painting with black paint, black became infinite and previously unnoticed.

Hallelujah! The blind can see again. Blind to what he has seen so that seeing this time is as though first seeing. How is it that one experiences this, for example, with the two Eisenhower pictures which for all intents and purposes are the same? (A duplication containing duplications.) Everything is so much the same, one becomes acutely aware of the differences, and quickly. And where, as here, the intention is unchanging, it is clear that the differences are unintentional, as unintended as they were in the white paintings where nothing was done. Out of seeing, do I move into poetry? And is this a poetry in which Eisenhower could have disappeared and the Mona Lisa taken his place? I think so but I do not see so. There is no doubt about which way is up. In any case our feet are on the ground. Painting's place is on the wall—painting's place, that is, in process. When I showed him a photograph of one of Rauschenberg's paintings, he said, "If I had a painting, I'd want to be sure it would stay the way it is; this one is a collage and would change." But Rauschenberg is practical. He goes along with things just as they are. Just as he knows it goes on a wall and not any which way, but right side up, so he knows, as he is, it is changing (which one more quickly? and the pyramids change). When possible, and by various means, he gives it a push: holes through which one sees behind the canvas the wall to which it is committed; the reflective surfaces changing what is seen by means of what is happening; lights going on and off; and the radios. The white paintings were airports for the lights, shadows, and particles.

Now in a metal box attached by a rope, the history kept by means of drawings of what was taken away and put in its place, of a painting constantly changing.

There is in Rauschenberg, between him and what he picks up to use, the quality of encounter. For the first time. If, as happens, there is a series of paintings containing such and such a material, it is as though the encounter was extended into a visit on the part of the stranger (who is divine). (In this way societies uninformed by artists coagulate their experiences into modes of communication in order to make mistakes.) Shortly the stranger leaves, leaving the door open.

Having made the empty canvases (*A canvas is never empty.*), Rauschenberg became the giver of gifts. Gifts, unexpected and unnecessary, are ways of saying Yes to how it is, a holiday. The gifts he gives are not picked up in distant lands but are things we already have (with exceptions, of course: I needed a goat and the other stuffed birds, since I don't have any, and I needed an attic in order to go through the family things [since we moved away, the relatives write to say: Do you still want them?]), and so we are converted to the enjoyment of our possessions. Converted from what? From wanting what we don't have, art as pained struggle. Setting out one day for a birthday party, I noticed the streets were full of presents. Were he saying something in particular, he would have to focus the painting; as it is he simply focuses himself, and everything, *a pair of socks*, is appropriate, appropriate to poetry, a poetry of *infinite possibilities*. It did not occur to me to ask him why he chose Dante as a project for illustration. Perhaps it is because we've had it around so long so close to us without bothering to put it to use, which becomes its meaning. It involved a stay in Florida and at night, looking for help, a walk through land infested with rattlesnakes. Also slipping on a pier, gashing his shin, hanging, his foot caught, not calling for help. The technique consists in having a *plan: Lay out stretcher on floor match markings and join.* Three stretchers with the canvas on them no doubt already stretched. Fulfilling this plan put the canvas in direct contact with the floor, the ground thereby activated. This is pure conjecture on my part but would work. More important is to know exactly the size of the door and techniques for getting a canvas out of the studio. (*Combines* don't roll up.) Anything beyond that size must be suitably segmented.

I remember the show of the black paintings in North Carolina. Quickly! They have become masterpieces.

Is it true that anything can be changed, seen in any light, and is not destroyed by the action of shadows? Then you won't mind when I interrupt you while you're working?

The message changes in the *combine-drawings,* made with pencil, water color, and photographic transfer: (a) the work is done on a table, not on a wall; (b) there is no oil paint; (c) because of a + b, no dripping holds the surface in one plane; (d) there is not always the joining of rectangles since when there is, it acts as reminiscence of stretchers; (e) the outlines appear vague as in water or air (our feet are off the ground); (f) I imagine being upside down; (g) the pencil lines scan the images transferred from photographs; (h) it seems like many television sets working simultaneously all tuned differently. How to respond to this message? (And I remember the one in *Dante* with the outline of the toes of his foot above, the changed position and another message, the paper absorbing the color and spreading it through its wet tissues.) He has removed the why of asking why and you can read it at home or in a library. (These others are poems too.) Perhaps because of the change in gravity (*Monument 1958*), the project arose of illustrating a book. (A book can be read at a table; did it fall on the floor?) As for me, I'm not so inclined to read poetry as I am one way or another to get myself a television set, sitting up nights looking.

Perhaps after all there is no message. In that case one is saved the trouble of having to reply. As the lady said, "Well, if it isn't art, then I like it." Some (a) were made to hang on a wall, others (b) to be in a room, still others (a + b).

By now we must have gotten the message. It couldn't have been more explicit. Do you understand this idea?: *Painting relates to both art and life. Neither can be made. (I try to act in that gap between the two.)* The nothingness in between is where for no reason at all every practical thing that one actually takes the time to do so stirs up the dregs that they're no longer sitting as we thought on the bottom. All you need do is stretch canvas, make markings, and join. You have then turned on the switch that distinguishes man, his ability to change his mind: *If you do not change your mind about something when you confront a picture you have not seen before, you are either a stubborn fool or the painting is not very good.* Is there any need before we go to bed to recite the history of the changes and will we in that bed be murdered? And how will our dreams, if we manage to go to sleep, suggest the next practical step? Which would you say it was: wild, or elegant, and why? Now as I come to the end of my rope, I noticed the color is incredibly beautiful. And that embossed box.

I am trying to check my habits of seeing, to counter them for the sake of greater freshness. I am trying to be unfamiliar with what I'm doing.

(I cannot remember the name of the device made of glass which has inside it a delicately balanced mechanism which revolves in response to infrared rays.) Rauschenberg made a painting combining in it two of these devices. The painting was excited when anybody came near it. Belonging to friends in the country, it was destroyed by a cat. If he takes a subject, what does he take? And what does he combine with it, once he's put it in place? It's like looking out a window. (But our windows have become electronic: everything moves through the point where our vision is focused; wait long enough and you'll get the Asiatic panoply.) Poetry is free-wheeling. You get its impact by thumbing through any of the mass media. The last time I saw him, Rauschenberg showed me a *combine-drawing*, and while I was looking he was speaking and instead of hearing (I was looking) I just got the general idea that this was an autobiographical drawing. A self-portrait with multiplicity and the largest unobstructed area given to the white painting, the one made of four stretchers, two above, two below, all four of equal size. Into this, structure and all, anything goes. The structure was not the point. But it was practical: you could actually see that everything was happening without anything's being done. Before such emptiness, you just wait to see what you will see. Is Rauschenberg's mind then empty, the way the white canvases are? Does that mean whatever enters it has room? (In, of course, the gap between art and life.) And since his eyes are connected to his mind, he can see what he looks at because his head is clear, uncluttered? That must be the case, for only in a mind (twentieth) that had room for it could Dante (thirteenth-fourteenth) have come in and gone out. What next? The one with the box changed by the people who look at it.

What do images do? Do they illustrate? (It was a New Year's Eve party in the country and one of them had written a philosophical book and was searching for a picture that would illustrate a particular point but was having difficulty. Another was knitting, following the rules from a book she had in front of her. The rest were talking, trying to be helpful. The suggestion was made that the picture in the knitting book would illustrate the point. On examination it was found that everything on the page was relevant, including the number.) But do we not already have too much to look at? (Generosity.) Left to myself, I would be perfectly contented with black pictures, providing Rauschenberg had painted them. (I had one, but unfortunately the new room has a slanting ceiling and besides the wall isn't long enough for it. These are the problems that have no solution, such as the suit wearing out.) But going along, I see I'm changing: color's not so bad after all. (I must have been annoyed by the games of balance and what-not they played with it.) One of the simplest ideas we get is the one we get when someone is weeping. Duchamp was in a rocking chair. I was weeping. Years later but in the same part of town and for more or less the same reason, Rauschenberg was weeping.

(The white paintings caught whatever fell on them; why did I not look at them with my magnifying glass? Only because I didn't yet have one? Do you agree with the statement: After all, nature is better than art?) Where does beauty begin and where does it end? Where it ends is where the artist begins. In this way we get our navigation done for us. If you hear that Rauschenberg has painted a new painting, the wisest thing to do is to drop everything and manage one way or another to see it. That's how to learn the way to use your eyes, sunup the next day. If I were teaching, would I say *Caution Watch Your Step* or Throw yourself in where the fish are thickest? Of course, there are objects. Who said there weren't? The thing is, we get the point more quickly when we realize it is we looking rather than that we may not be seeing it. (Why do all the people who are not artists seem to be more intelligent?) And object is *fact*, not symbol. If any thinking is going to take place, it has to come out from inside the Mason jar which is suspended in *Talisman*, or from the center of the rose (is it red?) or the eyes of the pitcher (looks like something out of a movie) or—the farther one goes in this direction the more one sees nothing is in the foreground: each minute point is at the center. Did this happen by means of rectangles (the picture is "cut" through the middle)? Or would it happen given this point of view? Not ideas but facts.

. . . .

M. C. Richards and David Tudor invited several friends to dinner. I was there and it was a pleasure. After dinner we were sitting around talking. David Tudor began doing some paper work in a corner, perhaps something to do with music, though I'm not sure. After a while there was a pause in the conversation, and someone said to David Tudor, "Why don't you join the party?" He said, "I haven't left it. This is how I keep you entertained."

This lecture was printed in Incontri Musicali, *August 1959. There are four measures in each line and twelve lines in each unit of the rhythmic structure. There are forty-eight such units, each having forty-eight measures. The whole is divided into five large parts, in the proportion 7, 6, 14, 14, 7. The forty-eight measures of each unit are likewise so divided. The text is printed in four columns to facilitate a rhythmic reading. Each line is to be read across the page from left to right, not down the columns in sequence. This should not be done in an artificial manner (which might result from an attempt to be too strictly faithful to the position of the words on the page), but with the* rubato *which one uses in everyday speech.*

LECTURE ON NOTHING

I am here   ,   and there is nothing to say   .

                                                                    If among you are
those who wish to get   somewhere   ,   let them leave at
any moment   .   What we re–quire   is
silence   ;   but what silence requires
              is   that I go on talking   .

                                                            Give any one thought
              a push   :   it falls down easily   .
;   but the pusher   and the pushed   pro–duce   that enter–
tainment   called   a dis–cussion   .
              Shall we have one later ?

                                        ₥

Or   ,   we could simply de–cide   not to have a dis–
cussion   .   What ever you like .   But
now   there are silences   and the
words   make   help make   the
silences   .

                                                I have nothing to say
         and I am saying it   and that is
poetry   as I need it   .

         This space of time   is organized
                   We need not fear these   silences, —
                        ₥

we may love them   .

                                                                        This is a composed

talk   ,   for I am making it

            just as I make   a piece of music.   It is like a glass

            of milk   .   We need the   glass

and we need the   milk   .   Or again   it is like an

empty glass   into which   at any

moment   anything   may be poured

.   As we go along   ,   (who knows?)

            an i–dea may occur in this   talk   .

                                            I have no idea   whether one will

                or not.   If one does,   let it.   Re–

                                    𝒎𝒑

gard it as something   seen   momentarily   ,   as

though   from a window   while traveling   .

If across Kansas   ,   then, of course,   Kansas

.   Arizona   is more interesting,

almost too interesting   ,   especially   for a New–Yorker   who is

being interested   in spite of himself   in everything.   Now he knows he

needs   the Kansas in him   .   Kansas is like

nothing on earth   ,   and for a New Yorker   very refreshing.

It is like an empty glass ,   nothing but wheat   ,   or

is it corn   ?   Does it matter which   ?

Kansas   has this about it: at any instant,   one may leave it,

and whenever one wishes one may return to it   .

                                    𝒎𝒑

Or you may leave it   forever   and never return to it   ,

            for we pos–sess nothing   .   Our poetry now

            is the reali–zation   that we possess   nothing

.   Anything   therefore   is a delight

(since we do not   pos–sess it)   and thus   need not fear its loss

.   We need not destroy the   past: it is gone;

at any moment,   it might reappear and   seem to be   and be the present

.   Would it be a   repetition?   Only if we thought we

owned it,   but since we don't,   it is free   and so are we

.   Most anybody knows a–bout the future
              and how un–certain it is   .

                                                     ♍︎
What I am calling   poetry   is often called   content.
I myself   have called   it form   .   It is the continuity   of a piece of music.   Continuity   today,
when it is necessary   ,   is a demonstration   of dis-
interestedness.   That is,   it is a proof   that our delight
lies in not   pos–sessing anything   .   Each moment
presents what happens .   How different
this form sense is   from that   which is bound up with
memory: themes   and secondary themes;   their struggle;
their development;   the climax;   the recapitulation   (which is the belief
that one may   own one's own home)   .   But actually,
unlike the snail   ,   we carry our homes   within us,
                                                     ♍︎
which enables us   to fly   or to stay
, —   to enjoy   each.   But beware of
that which is   breathtakingly   beautiful,   for at any moment
                  the telephone   may ring   or the airplane
come down in a   vacant lot   .   A piece of string
or a sunset   ,   possessing neither   ,
each acts   and the continuity   happens
.   Nothing more than   nothing   can be said.
Hearing   or making this   in music   is not different
—   only simpler —   than living this way   .
                  Simpler, that is   ,   for me, — because it happens
                                    that I write music   .
                                                     ♍︎ ♍︎
That music is   simple to make   comes from   one's willingness to accept   the limitations   of structure.   Structure is
simple   be–cause   it can be thought out,   figured out,
measured   .   It is a discipline   which,
accepted,   in return   accepts whatever   ,   even those
rare moments   of ecstasy,   which,   as sugar loaves train horses,
train us   to make what we make   .   How could I

better tell   what structure   is   than simply to
tell   about this,   this talk   which is
contained   within   a space of time   approximately
forty minutes   long   ?

                                          ♍
That forty minutes   has been divided into   five   large parts,   and
each unit   is divided   likewise.   Subdivision   in–
volving   a square root   is the only   possible subdivision which
permits   this micro–macrocosmic   rhythmic structure   ,
which I find so   acceptable   and accepting   .
As you see,   I can say anything   .
It makes very little   difference   what I say   or even how I say it.
At   this par–ticular moment,   we are passing through the fourth
part   of a unit which is the   second unit in the second large
part of this talk   .   It is a little bit   like passing through Kansas
.   This, now, is the   end   of that second unit
.   .

                                          ♍
Now begins the   third unit   of the second part   .
                                                                    Now the
second part of that   third unit   .
                            Now its third part   .

                                                                    Now its fourth
part   (which, by the way,   is just the same
length   as the third part)   .

                    Now the fifth   and last part   .

                                          ♍
You have just   ex–perienced   the structure   of this talk   from a
microcosmic   point of view   .   From a macrocosmic
point of view   we are just passing the halfway point   in the second
large part.   The first part   was a rather rambling   discussion of
nothing   ,   of form,   and continuity

when it is the way we   now   need it.   This second

part   is about structure: how simple it is

,   what it is   and why   we should be willing   to

accept   its limitations.   Most speeches   are full   of

ideas.   This one   doesn't have to have   any

.   But at any moment   an idea   may come along

.   Then   we may enjoy it   .

♍

Structure   without life   is dead.   But Life   without

structure   is un–seen   .   Pure life

expresses itself   within   and through structure

.   Each moment   is absolute,   alive and sig–

nificant.   Blackbirds   rise   from a field making   a

sound   de–licious   be–yond   com–pare

.   I heard them

because   I ac–cepted   the limitations   of an arts

conference   in a Virginia   girls' finishing school,   which limitations

allowed me   quite by accident   to hear the blackbirds

as they flew up and   overhead   .   There was a social

calendar   and hours for breakfast   ,   but one day I saw a

♍

cardinal   ,   and the same day   heard a woodpecker.

I also met   America's youngest   college president   .

However,   she has resigned,   and people say she is   going into politics

.   Let her.   Why shouldn't she?   I also had the

pleasure   of hearing an eminent   music critic   ex–claim

that he hoped   he would live long   e–nough   to see the end

of this craze for Bach.   A pupil once   said to me: I

understand   what you say about   Beethoven   and I think

I agree   but I have a   very serious   question   to

ask you: How do you   feel   about Bach

?   Now we have come   to the end   of the

part   about structure   .

♍ ♍

However,   it oc–curs   to me to say more   about structure

.   Specifically   this: We are

now at   the be–ginning   of the third part   and that part

is not the part   devoted   to structure.   It's the part
about material.   But I'm still talking   about structure.   It must be
clear from that   that structure   has   no point,   and,
as we have seen,   form   has no point either.   Clearly we are be–
ginning to get   nowhere   .

                     Unless some   other i–dea crops up   a–bout it that is
all I have   to say about structure   .
                                             ♍
Now about   material: is it interesting   ?
It is and it   isn't   .   But one thing is
certain.   If one is making   something   which is to be nothing
,   the one making must   love   and be patient   with
the material   he chooses.   Otherwise   he calls attention to the
material,   which is precisely something   ,   whereas it was
nothing   that was being made;   or   he calls attention to
himself,   whereas   nothing is anonymous   .
                     The technique   of handling materials   is, on the sense level
what structure as a discipline is   on the rational level   :
                     a means   of experiencing   nothing
.
                                             ♍
I remember loving   sound   before I ever   took a music lesson
.   And so we make our   lives   by what we love
.   (Last year   when I talked here   I made a short talk.
That was because   I was talking   about something   ;   but
this year   I am talking   about nothing   and
of course will go on talking   for a long time   .)
                                                       The other day a
pupil said,   ꙮ   after trying to compose   a melody   using only
three tones,   "I   felt limited   ."

                     Had she   con–cerned herself   with the three tones —
her materials   —   she would not   have felt limited
                                             ♍
,   and   since materials   are without feeling,
there would not have been   any limitation.   It was all in her

114/SILENCE

mind   ,   whereas it be–longed   in the
materials   .   It became something
by not being   nothing;   it would have been   nothing by being
something   .

                                                                           Should one use the
materials   characteristic   of one's time   ?
Now there's a question   that ought to get us   somewhere
.   It is an intel–   lectual question
.   I shall answer it   slowly   and
autobiographically   .

                                             ♍

I remember   as a child   loving   all the sounds
,   even the unprepared   ones.   I liked them
especially   when there was one at a time   .
                         A five-finger exercise   for one hand was
full of beauty   .   Later on I
gradually liked   all the intervals   .

                                                                          As I look back
I realize   that I be–gan liking the octave ;   I accepted the
major and minor   thirds.   Perhaps,   of all the intervals,   ˙
I liked these thirds   least   .   Through the music of
Grieg,   I became passionately   fond   of the fifth
.

                                             ♍

Or perhaps you could   call it   puppy–dog love   ,
                for the fifth did not make me   want to write music: it made me want to de–
vote my life to   playing the works of Grieg   .
                        When later I heard   modern music,
I took, like a duck   to water, to all the   modern intervals: the sevenths,   the
seconds,   the tritone,   and the fourth   .
                         I liked Bach too   a–bout this time   ,   but I
didn't like the sound   of the thirds and sixths.   What I admired in
Bach   was the way   many things   went together
.   As I keep on   re–membering,   I see that I never
really liked the   thirds,   and this explains   why I never really
liked Brahms   .

                                             ♍

Modern music   fascinated me   with all its modern   intervals: the
sevenths,   the seconds,   the tritone,   and the fourth   and
always,   every now and then,   there was a fifth,   and that pleased me
.   Sometimes   there were single tones,   not intervals at
all,   and that was a de–   light.   There were so many in–
tervals in modern music that it fascinated   me rather than that I   loved it, and being
fascinated by it I   de–cided   to write it.   Writing it at
first   is difficult: that is,   putting the mind on it
takes the ear off it   .   However,   doing it alone,
I was free to hear   that a high sound   is different   from a
low sound even when both are called by the   same letter.   After several years of
working alone   ,   I began to feel   lonely.

                                   ♍

Studying with a   teacher,   I learned that the   intervals   have
meaning;   they are not just   sounds   but they imply
in their progressions   a sound   not actually present to the ear
.   Tonality.   I never liked tonality   .
I worked at it   .   Studied it.   But I never had any
feeling for it   :   for instance: there are some   pro–
gressions called   de–ceptive cadences.   The idea is this: progress in such a way
as to imply   the presence   of a tone not actually   present;   then
fool everyone by not   landing on it —   land somewhere else.   What is being
fooled   ?   Not the ear   but the mind
.   The whole question is   very intellectual   .
However   modern music   still fascinated me

                                   ♍

with all its modern   intervals   .   But in order to
have them   ,   the mind had fixed it   so that one had to a–
void having   pro–gressions that would   make one think of   sounds that were
not actually present   to the ear   .   Avoiding
did   not   ap–peal to me   .   I began to see
that the separation of   mind and ear   had spoiled   the sounds
, —   that a clean slate   was necessary.   This made me
not only contemporary   ,   but "avant–garde."   I used noises
.   They had not been   in–tellectualized;   the ear could hear them
directly   and didn't have to go through any abstraction   a–bout them

.
    I found that I   liked noises   even more than I
liked intervals.   I liked noises   just as much as I had   liked single sounds
    ♍

.

    Noises, too
,   had been dis–criminated against   ;   and being American,
having been trained   to be sentimental,   I fought   for noises. I liked being
on the side of the   underdog   .
I got police   per–mission   to play sirens.   The most amazing noise
I ever found   was that produced by   means of a coil of wire   attached to the
pickup arm   of a phonograph and then   amplified.   It was shocking,
really shocking,   and thunderous   .   Half intellectually   and
half sentimentally   , when the war came a–long,   I decided to use
only   quiet sounds   .   There seemed to me
to be no truth,   no good,   in anything big   in society.
    ♍

But quiet sounds   were like loneliness   ,   or
love   or friendship   .   Permanent, I thought
,   values,   independent   at least from
Life, Time and   Coca-Cola   .   I must say
I still feel this way   ,   but something else is   happening
:   I begin to hear   the old sounds
—   the ones I had thought worn out,   worn out by
intellectualization—   I begin to hear   the old sounds   as
though they are   not worn out   .   Obviously, they are
not worn out   .   They are just as   audible   as the
new sounds.   Thinking   had worn them out   .
    And if one stops thinking about   them,   suddenly they are
    ♍

fresh   and new.   "If you think   you are a ghost
you will become a   ghost   ."   Thinking the sounds
worn out   wore them out   .   So you see
:   this question   .   brings us back
where we were: nowhere   ,   or,
if you like   ,   where we are   .
    I have a story: "There was once a man

standing on a high elevation. A company of several men who happened to be walking on the road noticed from the distance the man standing on the high place and talked among themselves about this man. One of them said: He must have lost his favorite animal. Another man said :   No, it must be his friend whom he is looking for. A third one said: He is just enjoying the cool air up there. The three could not   a–gree   and the dis-

                            𝕞𝕡

cussion	(Shall we have one	later?) went on until	they reached the high
place where the man	was	.	One of the three
asked:	O, friend	standing up there	, have you not
lost your pet animal	?	No, sir,	I have not lost any
.	The second man asked	: Have you not	lost your friend
?	No, sir	, I have	not lost my friend
either	.	The third man asked:	Are you not enjoying
the fresh breeze	up there?	No, sir	,
I am not	.		What, then
, are you standing up there		for	,
if you say no			to all our
questions	?	The man on high said	:

                            𝕞𝕡

I just stand   ."

                                                  If there are

no questions,	there are no answers	.	If there are questions
,	then, of course,	there are answers	, but the
final answer	makes the	questions	seem absurd
, whereas the	questions,	up until then,	seem more intelligent
than the answers	.		Somebody asked De–
bussy	how he wrote	music.	He said:
I take all the tones	there are,	leave out the ones I	don't want, and
use all the others	.	Satie said	:
When I was young,	people told me:	You'll see when	you're fifty years old
. Now I'm fifty	.	I've seen nothing	.

                           𝕞𝕡   𝕞𝕡

Here we are now   at the beginning
                   of the fourth large part   of this talk.

More and more		I have the feeling	that we are getting
nowhere.	Slowly	,	as the talk goes on
,	we are getting	nowhere	and that is a pleasure

.   It is not irritating   to be where one is   .   It is

only irritating   to think one would like   to be somewhere else.   Here we are now

,   a little bit after the   beginning   of the

fourth large part   of this talk   .

                       More and more   we have the feeling

                       that I am getting   nowhere   .

                       Slowly   ,   as the talk goes on

                                                      𝄞𝓅

,   slowly   ,   we have the feeling

                       we are getting   nowhere.   That is a pleasure

                       which will continue   .   If we are irritated

,   it is not a pleasure   .   Nothing is not   a

pleasure   if one is irritated   ,   but suddenly

,   it is a pleasure   ,   and then more and more

                       it is not irritating   ,   (and then more and more

                       and slowly   ).   Originally

                       we were nowhere   ;   and now, again

,   we are having   the pleasure

of being   slowly   nowhere.   If anybody

is sleepy   ,   let him go to sleep   .

                                                      𝓂𝓅

Here we are now   at the beginning   of the

third unit   of the fourth large part   of this talk.

More and more   I have the feeling   that we are getting

nowhere.   Slowly   ,   as the talk goes on

,   we are getting   nowhere   and that is a pleasure

.   It is not irritating   to be where one is   .   It is

only irritating   to think one would like   to be somewhere else.   Here we are now

,   a little bit after the   beginning   of the third unit   of the

fourth large part   of this talk   .

                       More and more   we have the feeling

                       that I am getting   nowhere   .

                       Slowly   ,   as the talk goes on

                                                      𝓂𝓅

,   slowly   ,   we have the feeling

                       we are getting   nowhere.   That is a pleasure

                    which will continue   .   If we are irritated
,   it is not a pleasure   .   Nothing is not   a
pleasure   if one is irritated   ,   but suddenly
,   it is a pleasure   ,   and then more and more
                    it is not irritating   (and then more and more
                    and slowly   ).   Originally
                    we were nowhere   ;   and now, again
,   we are having   the pleasure
of being   slowly   nowhere.   If anybody
is sleepy   ,   let him go to sleep   .
                                                 ♏

Here we are now   at the beginning   of the
fifth unit   of the fourth large part   of this talk.
More and more   I have the feeling   that we are getting
nowhere.   Slowly   ,   as the talk goes on
,   we are getting   nowhere   and that is a pleasure
.   It is not irritating   to be where one is   .   It is
only irritating   to think one would like to be somewhere else.   Here we are now
,   a little bit after the   beginning   of the fifth unit   of the
fourth large part   of this talk   .
                    More and more   we have the feeling
                    that I am getting   nowhere   .
                    Slowly   ,   as the talk goes on
                                             ♏
,   slowly   ,   we have the feeling
                    we are getting   nowhere.   That is a pleasure
                    which will continue   .   If we are irritated
,   it is not a pleasure   .   Nothing is not   a
pleasure   if one is irritated   ,   but suddenly
,   it is a pleasure   ,   and then more and more
                    it is not irritating   (and then more and more
                    and slowly   ).   Originally
                    we were nowhere   ;   and now, again
,   we are having   the pleasure
of being   slowly   nowhere.   If anybody
is sleepy   ,   let him go to sleep   .
                                             ♏

Here we are now   at the middle
                    of the fourth large part   of this talk.
More and more   I have the feeling   that we are getting
nowhere.   Slowly   ,   as the talk goes on
,   we are getting   nowhere   and that is a pleasure
.   It is not irritating   to be where one is   .   It is
only irritating   to think one would like   to be somewhere else.   Here we are now
,   a little bit after the   middle   of the
fourth large part   of this talk   .
                    More and more   we have the feeling
                    that I am getting   nowhere   .
                    Slowly   ,   as the talk goes on
                                             ♍

,   slowly   ,   we have the feeling
                    we are getting   nowhere.   That is a pleasure
                which will continue   .   If we are irritated
,   it is not a pleasure   .   Nothing is not   a
pleasure   if one is irritated ,   but suddenly
,   it is a pleasure   ,   and then more and more
                    it is not irritating   ,   (and then more and more
                    and slowly   ).   Originally
                    we were nowhere   ;   and now, again
,   we are having   the pleasure
of being   slowly   nowhere.   If anybody
is sleepy   ,   let him go to sleep   .
                                             ♍

Here we are now   at the beginning   of the
ninth unit   of the fourth large part   of this talk.
More and more   I have the feeling   that we are getting
nowhere.   Slowly   ,   as the talk goes on
,   we are getting   nowhere   and that is a pleasure
.   It is not irritating   to be where one is   .   It is
only irritating   to think one would like   to be somewhere else.   Here we are now
,   a little bit after the   beginning   of the ninth unit   of the
fourth large part   of this talk   .
                    More and more   we have the feeling

                  that I am getting   nowhere   .
                  Slowly   ,   as the talk goes on
                                          𝆏

,   slowly   ,   we have the feeling
                  we are getting   nowhere.   That is a pleasure
                  which will continue   .   If we are irritated
,   it is not a pleasure   .   Nothing is not   a
pleasure   if one is irritated   ,   but suddenly
,   it is a pleasure   ,   and then more and more
                  it is not irritating   (and then more and more
                  and slowly   ).   Originally
                  we were nowhere   ;   and now, again
,   we are having   the pleasure
of being   slowly   nowhere.   If anybody
is sleepy   ,   let him go to sleep .
                                          𝆏

Here we are now   at the beginning   of the
eleventh unit   of the fourth large part   of this talk.
More and more   I have the feeling   that we are getting
nowhere.   Slowly   ,   as the talk goes on
,   we are getting   nowhere   and that is a pleasure
.   It is not irritating   to be where one is   .   It is
only irritating   to think one would like to be somewhere else.   Here we are now
,   a little bit after the beginning   of the eleventh unit   of the
fourth large part   of this talk   .
                  More and more   we have the feeling
                  that I am getting   nowhere   .
                  Slowly   ,   as the talk goes on
                                          𝆏

,   slowly   ,   we have the feeling
                  we are getting   nowhere.   That is a pleasure
                  which will continue   .   If we are irritated
,   it is not a pleasure   .   Nothing is not   a
pleasure   if one is irritated   ,   but suddenly
,   it is a pleasure   ,   and then more and more
                  it is not irritating   (and then more and more

and slowly   ).   Originally
          we were nowhere   ;   and now, again
,   we are having   the pleasure
of being slowly   nowhere.   If anybody
is sleepy ,   let him go to sleep   .
                                        𝄞

Here we are now   at the beginning of the thir-
teenth unit   of the fourth large part   of this talk.
More and more   I have the feeling   that we are getting
nowhere.   Slowly   ,   as the talk goes on
,   we are getting   nowhere   and that is a pleasure
.   It is not irritating   to be where one is   .   It is
only irritating   to think one would like   to be somewhere else.   Here we are now
,   a little bit after the   beginning of the   thir-teenth unit   of the
fourth large part   of this talk   .
                 More and more   we have the feeling
                 that I am getting nowhere   .
                 Slowly   ,   as the talk goes on
                                        𝄞
,   slowly   ,   we have the feeling
                 we are getting   nowhere.   That is a pleasure
                 which will continue   .   If we are irritated
,   it is not a pleasure   .   Nothing is not   a
pleasure   if one is irritated   ,   but suddenly
,   it is a pleasure   ,   and then more and more
                 it is not irritating   (and then more and more
                 and slowly   ).   Originally
                 we were nowhere   ;   and now, again
,   we are having   the pleasure
of being   slowly   nowhere.   If anybody
is sleepy   ,   let him go to sleep   .
                     𝄞   𝄞

$\mathfrak{m}$

$\mathfrak{m}$

That is finished   now.   It was a pleasure   .

And now   ,   this is a pleasure.

"Read me that part   a–gain   where I disin–herit everybody   ."

The twelve–tone   row   is a method;   a

method is a control   of each   single

note.   There is too much   there there   .

There is not enough   of nothing in it   .   A structure is

like   a bridge from nowhere   to   nowhere   and

anyone may   go on it   :   noises or tones

,   corn or wheat   .   Does it matter which

?   I thought there were eighty–eight tones   .

You can quarter them too   .

$\mathfrak{m}$

If it were feet   ,   would it be a two–tone row

?   Or can we fly from here   to where

?   I have nothing   against the   twelve–tone row;
but it is a   method,   not a structure   .
    We really do need a structure   ,   so we can see
we are nowhere   .   Much of the music I   love
uses the twelve–tone   row   ,   but that is not why I
love it.   I love it   for no reason   .
     I love it   for suddenly   I am nowhere
.   (My own music does that   quickly for me   .)
     And it seems to me   I could   listen forever
to Japanese   shakuhachi music   or the Navajo

     𝄢

Yeibitchai   .   Or I could sit or
stand   near Richard Lippold's   *Full Moon*
     any length of time   .
     Chinese bronzes   , —   how I love them

.

,   which others   have made,   But those beauties
    the need to possess   tend to stir up
I possess   nothing   .   and I know
     Record collections   , —
     that is not music   .

     𝄢

The phonograph   is a thing, –   not a musical   instrument
.   A thing leads to other things,   whereas a   musical instrument
leads to nothing   .
     Would you like to join   a society called   Capitalists Inc.
?   (Just so no one would   think we were   Communists.)
Anyone joining   automatically   becomes president   .
To join   you must show   you've destroyed   at least one hundred
records   or, in the case of   tape,   one sound mirror
.   To imagine you   own
any piece of music   is to miss   the whole point
.   There is no point   or the point   is nothing;
and even   a long–playing   record   is a thing.

     𝄢

A lady   from Texas   said: I live in Texas   .

          We have no music   in Texas.   The reason they've no

music in Texas   is because   they have recordings

in Texas.   Remove the records from Texas

          and someone   will learn to sing   .

          Everybody   has a song

          which is   no   song at all :

          it is a process   of singing   ,

      and when you sing   ,

          you are   where you are   .

All I know about method is that when I am not working I sometimes think I know something, but when I am working, it is quite clear that I know nothing.

♍ ♍

Afternote to LECTURE ON NOTHING

In keeping with the thought expressed above that a discussion is nothing more than an entertainment, I prepared six answers for the first six questions asked, regardless of what they were. In 1949 or '50, when the lecture was first delivered (at the Artists' Club as described in the Foreword), there were six questions. In 1960, however, when the speech was delivered for the second time, the audience got the point after two questions and, not wishing to be entertained, refrained from asking anything more.

The answers are:

1. *That is a very good question. I should not want to spoil it with an answer.*

2. *My head wants to ache.*

3. *Had you heard Marya Freund last April in Palermo singing Arnold Schoenberg's* Pierrot Lunaire, *I doubt whether you would ask that question.*

4. *According to the Farmers' Almanac this is False Spring.*

5. *Please repeat the question . . .*
   And again . . .
   And again . . .

6. *I have no more answers.*

Now giving lecture on Japanese poetry. First giving very old Japanese poem, very classical:

Oh willow tree,
Why are you so sad, willow tree?
Maybe baby?

Now giving nineteenth-century romantic Japanese poem:

Oh bird, sitting on willow tree,
Why are you so sad, bird?
Maybe baby?

Now giving up-to-the-minute twentieth-century Japanese poem, very modern:

Oh stream, flowing past willow tree,
Why are you so sad, stream?
Baby?

I was never psychoanalyzed. I'll tell you how it happened. I always had a chip on my shoulder about psychoanalysis. I knew the remark of Rilke to a friend of his who wanted him to be psychoanalyzed. Rilke said, "I'm sure they would remove my devils, but I fear they would offend my angels." When I went to the analyst for a kind of preliminary meeting, he said, "I'll be able to fix you so that you'll write much more music than you do now." I said, "Good heavens! I already write too much, it seems to me." That promise of his put me off.

And then in the nick of time, Gita Sarabhai came from India. She was concerned about the influence Western music was having on traditional Indian music, and she'd decided to study Western music for six months with several teachers and then return to India to do what she could to preserve the Indian traditions. She studied contemporary music and counterpoint with me. She said, "How much do you charge?" I said, "It'll be free if you'll also teach me about Indian music." We were almost every day together. At the end

of six months, just before she flew away, she gave me the *Gospel of Sri Ramakrishna*. It took me a year to finish reading it.

I was on an English boat going from Siracusa in Sicily to Tunis in North Africa. I had taken the cheapest passage and it was a voyage of two nights and one day. We were no sooner out of the harbor than I found that in my class no food was served. I sent a note to the captain saying I'd like to change to another class. He sent a note back saying I could not change and, further, asking whether I had been vaccinated. I wrote back that I had not been vaccinated and that I didn't intend to be. He wrote back that unless I was vaccinated I would not be permitted to disembark at Tunis. We had meanwhile gotten into a terrific storm. The waves were higher than the boat. It was impossible to walk on the deck. The correspondence between the captain and myself continued in deadlock. In my last note to him, I stated my firm intention to get off his boat at the earliest opportunity and without being vaccinated. He then wrote back that I had been vaccinated, and to prove it he sent along a certificate with his signature.

David Tudor and I went to Hilversum in Holland to make a recording for the Dutch radio. We arrived at the studio early and there was some delay. To pass the time, we chatted with the engineer who was to work with us. He asked me what kind of music he was about to record. Since he was a Dutchman I said, "It may remind you of the work of Mondrian."

When the session was finished and the three of us were leaving the studio, I asked the engineer what he thought of the music we had played. He said, "It reminded me of the work of Mondrian."

Although it had been prepared some years earlier, this lecture was not printed until 1959, when it appeared in It Is, *edited by Philip Pavia, with the following introduction:*

> *In the general moving around and talking that followed my* Lecture on Something *(ten years ago at the Club), somebody asked Morton Feldman whether he agreed with what I had said about him. He replied, "That's not me; that's John." When Pavia recently asked me for a text on the occasion of Columbia's issuing a record devoted to Feldman's music, I said, "I already have one. Why don't you print it?"*

[In this connection, it may be noted that the empty spaces, omitted in the It Is *printing but to be encountered below, are representative of silences that were a part of the Lecture.]*

LECTURE ON SOMETHING

To bring things up to date, let me say that I am as ever changing, while Feldman's music seems more to continue than to change. There never was and there is not now in my mind any doubt about its beauty. It is, in fact, sometimes too beautiful. The flavor of that beauty, which formerly seemed to me to be heroic, strikes me now as erotic (an equal, by no means a lesser, flavor). This impression is due, I believe, to Feldman's tendency towards tenderness, a tenderness only briefly, and sometimes not at all, interrupted by violence. On paper, of course, the graph pieces are as heroic as ever; but in rehearsal Feldman does not permit the freedoms he writes to become the occasion for license. He insists upon an action within the gamut of love, and this produces (to mention only the extreme effects) a sensuousness of sound or an atmosphere of devotion. As ever, I prefer concerts to records of instrumental music. Let no one imagine that in owning a recording he has the music. The very practice of music, and Feldman's eminently, is a celebration that we own nothing.

This is a talk about   something   and naturally   also a talk about
nothing.   About how something   and nothing are not   opposed to each other
but need each other to keep on going   .   It is difficult to
talk when you have   something to say   precisely because of   the words   which
keep making us   say   in the way   which the words need to
stick to   and not in the Way which   we need for living.   For instance:
someone said,   "Art should come from   within;   then it is profound."
But it seems to me   Art goes within,   and I don't see the need   for "should" or
"then" or "it" or "pro–found."   When Art comes from within   ,   which is
what it was   for so long doing,   it be–came a thing   which seemed to elevate the
man who made it   a–bove those   who ob–served it or heard it   and the artist   was
considered a genius   or given a rating: First, Second, No Good ,   until
finally   riding in a bus or   subway: so proudly he signs his
work   like a manufacturer   .
                                    But since everything's changing, art's now going
in and it is of the   utmost importance not to make a thing   but rather to make
nothing.   And how is this done?   Done by making   something
which then goes   in and reminds us of   nothing.   It is im–portant that this
something   be just something,   finitely something;   then very
simply   it goes in   and becomes infinitely nothing   .
It seems we are   living.   Understanding of what is nourishing   is
changing   .   Of course,   it is always changing,   but
now it is very clearly changing, so that the people either agree   or they don't   and the
differences of   o–pinion are clearer   .   Just a year   or so a–
go   everything seemed to be an individual matter.   But   now there are
two sides.   On one side it is that individual matter   going on,   and on the
other side it is more   not an individual but   everyone   which is not to say
it's all the same, —   on the contrary   there are more differences.   That is:
starting finitely   everything's different but in going in it all becomes the same
.   H.C.E.   Which is what Morton Feldman   had in
mind   when he called   the music he's now writing
Intersection   .   Feldman speaks of   no sounds,   and takes
within broad limits   the first ones   that come along.   He has changed
the responsibility of   the composer   from making   to accepting
                  .   To accept   whatever comes
                         re–gardless   of the consequences

is to be　　　　unafraid　　　　　　　　　　　　　　or

to be full　　　　　　of that love which

comes from　　　　a sense of at–one–ness　　with whatever

.　　　　　　　　This goes to explain　　what Feldman means

when he says that he is associated with all of the sounds,

and so　　　　　　can foresee　　　　what will happen

even though he has not　　　　　　written the particular

notes down　　　　as other composers do　　.

When a com–poser feels a responsibility to make, rather

than accept,　　he e–liminates from the　　area of possibility

all those events that do not suggest the at that point in

time vogue of profund–ity. For he takes himself seriously,

wishes　　　　　to be considered great, and he thereby diminishes

his love　　　　and in–creases his fear　　and concern about

what people will think

.　　　　　　　There are many　　serious problems　　confronting

such an individual　　.　　　　　　　　He must do it better,

more impressively,　　more beautifully, etc. than anybody else　　.　　　　　And

what, precisely,　　does this, this　　beautiful profound object,　this masterpiece,

have to do　　with Life?　　It has this to do with Life　:　　that it is

separate from it.　　Now we see it　　and now we don't.　　When we see it

we feel better, and when we are away from it, we don't feel so good

.　　　　　　Life seems shabby and　chaotic, disordered,　ugly　　　　in

contrast.　　Let me read a passage　from the I–Ching　which discusses　this

point.　　　　"In human affairs　　aesthetic form　　comes into being

when traditions exist　　　　that strong and abiding　like mountains

are made pleasing　by a lucid　　beauty.　　　By contemplating the

forms　　ex–isting in the heavens　　　　we come to understand

time　　and its changing demands　.　　Through contemplation of the

forms　existing in human society　it be–comes possible　　to shape the world

."　　And the footnote goes on:　　"Tranquil beauty:　clarity within,

quiet without　.　　　This is the　tran–quillity of pure

contemplation.　When desire is silenced　　　and the will comes to rest

,　　the world as i–dea becomes manifest　.　In this aspect the world is beautiful

and re–moved from the struggle for existence.　　This is the world of

Art.　　However,　　contemplation alone　will not put the

will to rest   abso–lutely.   It   will a–waken again   and then
all the beauty of form will appear to have   been   only a brief
moment   of exaltation.   Hence this is still   not the true way of
redemption.   The fire   whose light illuminates the   mountain
and makes it   pleasing,   does not shine far.   In the same way
beautiful form suffices to brighten and throw light   upon mat–ters of lesser moment
.   But important questions   cannot be decided
in this way   .   They require   greater earnestness
."   Perhaps
this will make   understandable   a statement made by   Blythe
in his book   *Haiku:*   "The highest   responsibility of the
artist   is to hide beauty."   Now   for a moment
let's consider   what are the   important questions   and
what is that   greater earnestness   that is required   .   The
important question is   what is it that is not   just beautiful   but also
ugly,   not just good, but also evil   ,   not just true,   but also an il–
lusion.   I remember now   that Feldman   spoke of shadows.
He said that   the sounds   were not sounds but shadows.   They are obviously
sounds;   that's why they are shadows.   Every something is an   echo of nothing.
Life goes on   very much like a   piece by Morty Feldman.
Someone   may ob–ject that the sounds   that happened were   not interesting.
Let him.   Next time he hears the piece,   it will be different,
perhaps   less interesting, perhaps   suddenly exciting   .   Perhaps
disastrous.   A disaster for whom   ?   For him,   not for Feldman.
And life   the same: always different,   sometimes   ex–
citing,   sometimes boring,   sometimes gently pleasing   and so on;   and
what other important   questions are there?   Than   that   we live   and
how to do it   in a state of accord   with Life.
Some people may now   be indignant   and insist   on saying that they
control Life.   They are the same ones who insist on controlling and judging art
.   Why judge?   "Judge not   lest ye be judged."
Or we can say: Judge   and re–gardless   of the consequences
.   What   is
meant   by Judge   and re–gardless of the   conse–quences? Simply this:
Judge   in a state of disinterest as to the effects of the judging   .   A modern
Cuban composer,   Caturla,   earned his living   as a judge.   A

man he sentenced   to life imprisonment   es–caped   from prison   and
murdered Caturla.   In that penultimate   now–moment   before being killed
was Caturla   in hell or in heaven?   Make judgments   but accept the
consequences.   Otherwise no life: Hamlet,   fear,
guilt, concern,   responsibility.   The i–dea, consequences,   suggests   the
musical term   continuity   and that produced   a discussion
last week   for Feldman   spoke of no–continuity,   whereas
it was argued from a   rational point of view   that no matter what   there is continuity.
This is again   a matter of disinterest   and acceptance.   No–continuity
simply means   accepting that   continuity   that happens.
Continuity   means the opposite: making that particular   continuity   that
excludes   all others.   This is, of course,   possible   but
not any longer   nourishing   for we have found   that by excluding
we grow thin inside   even though   we may have an enormous   bank account
outside.   For somethings   one needs critics,   connoisseurs,
judgments,   authoritative ones,   otherwise one gets   gypped;
but for nothing   one can dispense with   all that fol–de–rol   ,   no one
loses nothing   be–cause nothing   is se–curely possessed   .
When nothing   is se–curely possessed   one is free to accept   any of the somethings.
How many are there?   They roll up at   your feet.   How many doors and windows are there
in it?   There is no end to the number of somethings   and all of them   (without
exception)   are ac–ceptable.   If one gets suddenly   proud   and says
for one reason   or a–nother: I   cannot accept this; then the   whole freedom
to accept any of the   others vanishes. But   if one maintains   secure possession
of nothing   (what has been called poverty of spirit), then there is no limit
to what one may   freely enjoy.   In this free   en–joyment   there is no
possession of things.   There is only   enjoyment.   What is possessed is nothing.
This is what   is meant when one says   :   No–continuity.
          No sounds.   No harmony.   No melody.
          No counterpoint.   No rhythm.   That is to say
          there is not one of the somethings   that is not acceptable.
          When this   is meant   one is in accord with life,
          and paradoxically   free to pick and choose again   as at any
          moment Feldman does, will or may.   New picking   and
          choosing is just like the old picking and choosing except that one
          takes as just another   one of the somethings   any consequence   of

having picked and   chosen.   When in the state   of
nothing, one diminished the something in one: Character.
At any moment one   is free to take on character again,   but
then it is   without fear, full of life and love.
For one's been at the   point of the nourishment that sustains in no
matter what one of the   something   situations.
High, middle, low;   enter any time within the duration notated;
this particular timbre.   These are the   somethings Feldman has
chosen.   They give him and his art character.
It is quite   useless   in this situation   for anyone to say
Feldman's work   is good or not good.   Because   we are in the direct
situation: it is.   If you don't like it   you may choose to
avoid it.   But if you avoid it   that's a pity,   because   it re–
sembles life   very closely,   and life and it are essentially a   cause for joy.
People say, sometimes   , timidly: I know nothing about music   but I know what I
like.   But the important questions are answered by not liking only but disliking
and accepting equally   what one likes   and dislikes.   Otherwise   there is no access to
the dark night of the   soul.   At the present time, a twelve–tone time, it is not popular
to allow the more   common garden variety of tonal relations   .
These latter   are dis–criminated against.   Feldman allows them   to be   if
they happen   to come along.   And to ex–plain again,   the only reason
for his being able to   allow them   is by his acting on the   as–sumption that
no   tonal   relations   ex–ist,   meaning   all tonal relations
are acceptable.   Let us say in life: No earthquakes   are permissible.
What happens then   ?

         All the somethings in the
world begin to sense their at–one–ness when   something happens   that reminds them of
nothing   .

         And in this
way the music   of Morton Feldman   may actively remind us of nothing
so that its   no–continuity   will let us allow   our lives   with
all of the things   that happen in them to be simply what they   are and not separate

from one another.   It is perfectly clear   that walking   a–long the river   is
one thing   and writing music   is another   and being interrupted
while writing   music is still   an–other and a backache   too.   They
all go together   and it's a continuity   that is not a continuity   that is being
clung to   or in–sisted upon.   The moment   it be–comes a
special continuity of   I am composing   and nothing else   should happen,   then the
rest of life   is nothing but a series   of interruptions,   pleasant   or
catastrophic   as the case may be.   The truth, however,   is that it is
more like   Feldman's music —   anything may happen   and it all does
go together.   There is no rest of   life.   Life is one.   Without be–
ginning, without middle, without ending   .   The concept: beginning
middle and meaning   comes from a sense of   self   which separates itself
from what it considers to be the rest of life.   But this attitude is untenable unless
one insists on stopping life and bringing it to an end   .   That
thought is in itself   an attempt to stop   life, for life goes on, indifferent to   the
deaths   that are part of its   no beginning, no middle,   no meaning
.   How much better to   simply get behind and push!
To do the opposite is clownish, that is: clinging   or trying to force
life into one's own   i–dea of it, of what it should be,   is on–ly absurd.   The ab–
surdity comes from the artificiality of it, of not living,   but of
having to have   first an idea about how one   should do it and then   stumblingly
trying.   Falling down on some one of the various banana peels   is what we
have been calling tragedy. Ideas of separateness artificially elevated. The mythological
and Oriental view   of the hero   is the one   who accepts life
.   And so if one should   object to calling   Feldman a composer,
one could call him   a hero.   But we are all heroes,   if we accept what
comes,   our inner cheerfulness   undis–turbed.   If we ac–cept what comes,
that (again) is what   Feldman means   by *Intersection*.   Anyone may cross it.
Here Comes Everybody .   The light has turned.   Walk on.   The
water is fine.   Jump in.   Some will refuse,   for they see that the
water is thick with   monsters   ready to devour them.   What they have   in
mind   is self–preservation.   And what is that   self–preservation but
only a preservation   from life?   Whereas life without death is no longer life   but
only self–preservation. (This by the way is another reason why recordings are not music
.)   Which do we prefer is, practically speaking, an irrelevant   question,
since life   by exercising death   settles the matter   conclusively   for

something   but without conclusion   for nothing.   It is nothing that
goes on and on without beginning middle or meaning or ending.   Something is
always starting   and stopping, rising   and falling.   The nothing that
goes on is what   Feldman speaks of   when he speaks of   being sub–
merged in   silence.   The ac–ceptance of death   is the
source   of all   life.   So that listening to this   music   one
takes as a   spring–board   the first sound that comes along ;   the first
something springs us   into nothing and   out of that nothing   a–rises   the
next something;   etc.   like an al–ternating current.   Not one sound fears
the silence that   ex–tinguishes it.   And no silence exists   that is not pregnant
         with sound.   Someone said   the other day,   in
reference   to the performance   of Feldman's music   at Merce Cunningham's
recent recital: "That kind of music   if you call it music   should not be
played   in a public hall,   because many people   do not understand it
         and they start talking or tittering   and the result is   that you can't
hear the music   be–cause of all these extraneous sounds."   Going on, that
someone said,   "The music could be played and possibly appreciated ,
in a home   where,   not having   paid to be entertained,   those listening
might listen   and not have the   impulse to titter   or having it
out of decorum   squelch it   and be–sides   in a home it is
more comfortable and   quiet: there would be a better chance   to hear it
."   Now what that   someone said   de–scribes the de–
sire for special   cut–off–from–life   conditions: an ivory tower.
But no ivory tower ex–ists,   for there is no possibility   of keeping the
Prince forever within   the Palace Walls.   He will, willy nilly,   one day get out
and seeing that there   are sickness and   death (tittering   and talking) become   the
Buddha.   Be–sides at my house,   you hear the boat sounds,   the
traffic sounds,   the neighbors quarreling, the children playing   and screaming in the
hall, and on top of it all the pedals of the piano squeak   .
There is no getting a–way from life   .   Now, going on   by
going back to what that someone said: "That kind of music,   if you call it music."
Actually   what difference?   Words are only noises   . Which noise
makes little difference .   Essentially   the question is
:   do you live,   or do you in–sist   on words?
If before you live   you go through a word   then   there is an indirection.
Whereas   we need   not go around the barn   ,   but

may go directly in   .   And then to go on   :

"Paid to be entertained ."   This brings us again   to

Life.   If at any moment   we approach   that

moment   with a pre–conceived idea of what that moment will provide, and if,

furthermore, we   pre–sume that having paid for it makes us safe about it, we simply

start off on the wrong foot. Let's say for ten years everything   turns out

as we imagined   it would   and ought.   Sooner or later

the table turns   and it doesn't   work out   as we wish it would

.   We buy something   to keep   and it is

stolen.   We bake a cake   and it turns out   that the

sugar was not sugar   but salt   .   I no sooner

start to work   than the telephone rings .   But to continue:

what is   entertainment?   And who   is being entertained?

Heroes are being   entertained and their   nature   is that of nature:

the accepting   of what comes   without preconceived ideas of   what

will happen   and re–gardless of the   consequences.   This is, by the way,

why it is   so difficult   to listen to music   we are familiar

with;   memory has acted   to keep us a–ware   of what will happen

next,   and so it is almost   im–possible   to remain a–live   in the

presence   of a well–known   masterpiece.   Now and then

it happens,   and when it does,   it par–takes   of the miraculous

.   Going on about   what someone said: at the root

of the desire   to appreciate   a piece of music,   to call it this

rather that that,   to hear it without   the unavoidable   extraneous

sounds —   at the root of all   this is the idea   that

this work is a thing   separate from the   rest of life, which   is not the case

with Feldman's music   .   We are   in the presence not of a work

of art   which is a thing   but of an action   which is implicitly

nothing   .   Nothing has been said   .

Nothing   is communicated.   And there is no use   of symbols   or

intellectual references.   No thing in life requires a symbol   since it is clearly

what it is: a visible manifestation   of an invisible nothing.

All somethings   equally   par–take of that   life–giving nothing.

But to go on   again   about someone said: "What?"

And I forgot to mention it before.   He said,   "What about

all those silences   ?"   How do I know   when

We never know   when   but being cheerful helps   .   Are there
other ways than   Feldman's? Naturally; something–speaking   there are   an
infinite number   of ways.   How many doors and windows?

                                                              I forgot to say
this isn't a talk about Morton Feldman's music. It's a talk within a rhythmic structure
and that is why   every now and then it is possible   to have absolutely
nothing; the possibility of nothing   —

                                        And what is the   be–ginning of no
middles meanings and   endings?   And what is the   ending of no
beginnings middles and meanings   ?

If you let it   it supports itself.   You don't have to   .
Each something   is a celebration   of the nothing   that supports it.
When we   re–move the world from our shoulders   we notice
it doesn't drop.   Where   is the responsibility   ?

                   Responsibility is to   oneself;   and the highest form of it   is
irresponsibility   to oneself   which is to say   the calm acceptance of whatever
responsibility to others and things comes   a–long   .

If one adopts   this attitude   art   is a sort of experimental
station   in which one tries out living;   one   doesn't stop
living   when one is occupied   making the art,   and   when
one is living,   that is, for example,   now reading   a lecture   on
something   and nothing,   one doesn't stop   being occupied making
the art;   should I   be writing   that

piano concerto?   Of course, I am — and   going   to the movies
or explaining   about nothing   or eating an apple: concerto   piano.
No "should"   and no blame.   The continuity that is no continuity
is going on   for–ever;   and there is no problem   a–bout accepting
whatever.   With this exception: there   is great difficulty
in accepting   those things   that come from   a profound
inner feeling   and full of pride   and self–glory   assert
themselves   as separate from   and finer   than anything
else   on earth .   But, actually,   where is the
difficulty? It is the   simplest thing in the   world   to directly see: this
is an orange;   that is a frog;   this is a man   being proud;   this
is a man thinking   another man is proud;   etc   .
                    It all goes   to–gether and   doesn't require that we
try to improve it or feel our inferiority or superiority to it. Progress is out of the
question. But inactivity is not what happens. There is always activity   but it is
free from   com–pulsion, done from   disinterest.   And we are
free to stop brooding and to observe the effects of our actions.   (When we are
proud, that pride   keeps us from   ob–serving   very clearly.)
And what do we   observe: the effects of our   actions   on
others   or on ourselves?   On ourselves;   for if the effects
on us   are con–ducive   to less separateness,   less fear,
more love,   we may walk on then   regardless   of the others.
Out of that lack of regard for the others   we will not feel   the need   to be
competitive, for as in   those silences that   occur   when two people
are confident   of each other's   friendship,   there is no
nervousness, only a   sense   of at–one–ness

When   going from nothing   towards something,   we have all
the European   history of music   and art   we remember
and there we can see   that this   is well done   but the other is not.
So–and–so contributed   this and that   and criteria.   But now we are
going from   something   towards nothing,   and there is no way
of saying success   or failure   since all things   have equally   their
Buddha nature.   Being ignorant of that   fact   is the only obstacle   to
enlightenment.   And being enlightened   is not   some spooky   un–
earthly condition.   Before   studying Zen   men are men and mountains
are mountains.   While studying Zen,   things get confused.   After
studying Zen men are   men and mountains are mountains.   No
difference   except that one is no   longer   attached;   now
and then   I have found   in dis–cussing   these ideas   that
some people say,   "That is   all very well,   but   it won't
work for us,   for it's Oriental."   (Actually   there is no longer   a
question   of Orient   and Occident.   All of that is rapidly
disappearing;   as Bucky Fuller   is fond of   pointing out:
the movement   with the wind   of the Orient   and the movement
against   the wind of the Occident   meet   in America   and
produce   a movement   upwards   into the air —   the
space, the silence, the nothing that supports us   .)   And then
again   if any of you   are troubled still   about Orient   and
Occident,   you can read Eckhart,   or Blythe's   book   on Zen in
English literature,   or Joe Campbell's   books on mythology   and philosophy,
or the books   by Alan Watts. And there are naturally   many others.
There are books to   read,   pictures to look at,   poetry

to read (cummings for instance),   sculpture,   architecture,   even
theatre   and dance,   and now some music   too.
Mostly, right now,   there is painting and   sculpture,   and just as
formerly   when starting   to be ab–stract,   artists referred   to
musical practices   to show   that what they were doing was valid,
so nowadays,   musicians, to explain   what   they   are
doing, say,   "See, the painters and   sculptors   have been doing it for
quite some time."   But   we are still   at the point   where
most musicians   are clinging   to the complicated torn–up competitive remnants   of
tradition,   and, furthermore,   a tradition   that was always   a
tradition   of breaking   with tradition, and   further–more, a tradition that
in   its ideas of counterpoint   and harmony   was out of step   not only
with its own but with   all other traditions   .
I had thought   of leaving   this last section silent,   but then it turns   out
              I have something   to say .   I am after all talking
about   Morton Feldman's music   and whether   that is right or wrong is
not to the point.   I am doing it.   Going on doing it.   And that is the way.
This morning   I thought   of an image   that might make clear   to
some of you   the natural usefulness of   Feldman's music.   It was this:
do you remember,   in myth,   the hero's encounter   with   the
shape–shifting   monster?   The way   the sounds   be–
tween   two per–formances   shift   their somethingness
suggests this.   Now   what does the hero do?   (You   and   I
are the heroes   and incidentally   Morty too.)   He doesn't
get frightened   but simply   accepts   what the sound–shift–
ing performer happens   to do.   Eventually the whole   mirage disappears.
And the prize   or sought–for   something   (that is nothing)
is obtained.   And that something–   generating nothing   that is obtained   is
that each   something   is really what it is   ,   and so
what happens?   Live happily   ever after.   And   do we
need   a celebration?   We cannot   a–void it
since   each thing in life is   continually   just that
.   Now   what if I'm wrong?   Shall I telephone
Joe Campbell   and ask him   the meaning   of shape–shifters
?   (I can't do it for   a nickel any more.)   He would know the
answer.   However, that is   not the point.   The point is

this.   This is a situation which is no more and no less serious than any
other life–and–death   situation.   What is needed   is irresponsibility.
Out of Meister   Eckhart's sermon,   *God made*   *the poor for the rich,*
I take the following   :   "If,   going   to some place, we   had
first to settle how   to put   the front foot down, we should   never get there.
If the painter   had to plan out every   brush–mark before he   made   his
first   he would not paint at all.   Follow   your principles   and keep
straight on;   you will come to the   right place,   that is the way."
The other day   I had   a letter   from Pierre Boulez.
He said,   "We try not to think   too much   of the war;   we live
from day to day,   pushing our   in–vestigations   as far   as possible
."

Coming back   to Eckhart,   for the sake   by the way
of a   brilliant conclusion,   a tonic   and dominant
emphatic   conclusion   to this talk   about something
and nothing   and how   they need   each other   to
keep on going,   as Eckhart   says, "Earth"   (that is
any something)   "has no escape   from heaven:"   (that is
nothing)   "flee she up   or flee she down   heaven
still invades   her, energizing   her, fructifying   her,
whether   for her weal or   for her woe."

♍ ♍ ♍

Before writing this piece, I composed 34′ 46.776″ for Two Pianists. These piano parts shared the same numerical rhythmic structure but were not fixed together by means of a score. They were mobile with respect to one another. In each case the structural units became different in actual time-length by use of a factor obtained by chance operations. Having been asked to speak at the Composers' Concourse in London (October 1954), I decided to prepare for that occasion a lecture using the same structure, thus permitting the playing of music during the delivery of the speech. The second pianist's part had turned out to be 31′ 57.9864″. When I applied the chance factor to the numerical rhythmic structure in the case of the speech, I obtained 39′ 16.95″. However, when the text was completed, I found I was unable to perform it within that time-length. I needed more time. I made experiments, reading long lines as rapidly as I could. The result was two seconds for each line, 45′ for the entire piece. Not all the text can be read comfortably even at this speed, but one can still try.

45′ FOR A SPEAKER

The piano parts had included noises and whistles in addition to piano and prepared piano tones. For the speaker, I made a list of noises and gestures. By means of chance operations, determining which noise or gesture and when it was to be made, I added these to the text.

Similarly, the relative loudness of delivery was varied: soft, normal, loud. (These volumes are indicated in the text below by typographical means: italics for soft, roman for normal, and ***boldface italics for loud.****)*

The text itself was composed using previously written lectures together with new material. Answers to the following questions were all obtained by chance operations:

1. *Is there speech or silence?*
2. *And for how long?*
3. *If speech, is it old material or new?*
4. *If old, from which lecture and what part of it?*
5. *If new, on which of the following 32 subjects?*
   Structure (emptiness) (in general no structure)
   Quotations
   Time (and rhythm)
   Sound (and noises)
   Silence
   Chance
   Technique in general (no technique)
   Other arts (shadows, etc.: incidental sounds)

Relationship (synchronicity)
Music (work of art)
Magnetic tape
Prepared piano
Form
Theatre (music work of life)
Listening as ignorance
Focus
Square root and flexibility
Asymmetry of probability
Imperfections technique
Coins technique
Mobility-immobility
Multiple loud-speakers
Non-dualism
Error
Psychology (expressivity) (inspiration)
Vertical (forced) relations
Horizontal (forced) relations
Mobility of parts (this work)
The string pieces
The carillon music
Activity of performance
Purpose

6. *Is the material, new or old, to be measured in terms of words or syllables?*
    And how many?

   *The piece for two pianists had been commissioned for performance at
Donaueschingen in September 1954. I finished it just in time to catch the boat
for Rotterdam with David Tudor. My plan was to write the speech while
crossing the Atlantic. The boat, however, met with a collision twelve hours
after leaving Manhattan. We slowly returned to New York. With the help of
other passengers having obligations abroad, we organized the flight of all the
ship's passengers to Amsterdam. 45' for a Speaker was written on trains and in
hotels and restaurants during the course of a European tour. Returning to
America later that fall, I composed 26'1.1499" for a String Player (incorporating
in it short pieces written two years before) and, later, 27'10.554" for a
Percussionist. All these compositions, including the speech, may be performed
alone or together in any combination.*

0'00"   "Lo and behold the horse turns into
a prince, who, except for the
acquiescence of the hero
would have had to remain a
miserable shaggy nag."

10"   I have noticed something else about
Christian Wolff's music. All you can
do   is
suddenly listen
in the same way
that, when you catch cold,

20"   all you can do is
suddenly
sneeze.
Unfortunately   —
European harmony.

30"

40"

50"   Where it is:

            within us
but
like an empty glass
into which

1'00"   at any moment
        anything
        may be poured
        just something   finitely something
        or even
        to be able to drink
 10"   a glass of water.
        Unless some other idea
        crops up about it,
        that is all I have to say about structure.
        My present
        way
 20"   *of composing's*
        involved with the
        observation
        of imperfections in the paper
        on which I happen
        to be
 30"   *writing.*

                                                (Snore)

              About the
        prepared piano: each prepared piano is
        prepared differently. Objects are placed
        between the strings and the piano sound,
        to all of these various characteristics, he
 40"   is transformed with respect to all of its characteristics.
        Music is an oversimplification of the situation
        we actually are in. ***An ear alone***
        is not a being;   music is one
        part of theatre. "Focus" is what aspects one's
        noticing. Theatre is all the various things
 50"   going on at the same time. I have noticed
        that music is liveliest for me when listening for instance
        doesn't distract me from seeing. One should
        take music very naturally. *No*
        technique
        at all:

2'00"   only technique
worth having.
I remember
being asked
what I
thought about
10"   technique.
And at
first I
had
nothing
to say.
20"   Several days
later I
realized
I have no time
for technique
because
30"   I must
always be making
one: any
technique can
be discovered
after any technique
40"   is forgotten.
Another technique
I've devised
is derived
from the
I-Ching method
50"   of obtaining
oracles.
And a
principle
(also *I-Ching*)
which interested me

(Lean on Elbow)

3'00" (not at all any more)
is that which is
called
"mobility-immobility".

10"

                                               (Hiss)

       Time,
which is the title of this piece,
(so many minutes
20" so many seconds),
is what we
and sounds
happen in. Whether early or late:
in it.
It is not a question of counting.
30" Our poetry now
is the realization
that we possess nothing.
Anything therefore   (Slap table)
is a delight
(since we do not possess it)
40" and thus need   (Cough)
not fear.
This composition involves a flexible use of
the number 10,000: that
is to say 100 x 100 (sq. rt.).
The actual time-lengths
50" *are changing.*   This
work has no score. It should be abolished. "A statement concerning the
arts is no statement concerning the arts." It
consists of single parts. Any of them may
be played together or eliminated and at any
time. "To me teaching is an expedient, but I do

4′00″   not teach external signs." Like a long book if a
long book is like a mobile. "The ignorant because of their attachment to existence seize on signified
or signifying." No beginning no ending. Harmony, so-called,
is a forced abstract vertical relation which blots out the spontaneous
transmitting nature of each of the sounds forced into it. It is
10″   artificial and unrealistic. Form, then, is not something
off in the distance in solitary confinement:
It is right here right now. Since it is
something we say about past actions,
        it is wise
to drop it.
20″   *This, too, giving himself*
& his quest up to the aimless rolling
of a metal ball, the hero, unquestioningly does.
They proceed thus, by chance, by no will
of their own passing
safely
30″   *through many perilous situations.*
I begin to hear the old sounds, the ones
I had thought worn out, worn out
by intellectualization, I begin to hear
the old sounds as though they are not
worn out. Silence, like music, is non-
40″   existent. There always are sounds. That
is to say if one is alive to hear them.
Obviously they are not. Whether I make them
or not there are always sounds to be heard and
all of them are excellent.
We bake a cake   (**Brush Hair**)
50″   and
it turns
out
that the sugar
was not sugar
but salt.

5′00″   Are you deaf
(by nature, choice, desire)
or can you hear
(externals, tympani, labyrinths in whack)?

10″

By no means.

20″

(Blow nose)

30″   The twelve-tone row is
a method.   A method
is a control of each single note.
Their development, the climax,
the recapitulation
which is the belief one may own one's own home.

40″

"There is too much there there."

There is not enough of
nothing in it.
So far, I have written two parts for a pianist.

50″   Either part can be played alone or they can both
be played together. Each piano is prepared differently
although, as a matter of focus, the parts could be
played without bothering to prepare the piano
or pianos. If prepared, then, generally,
the preparations will be altered in

6'00"   the course
        of the
        performance.

10"   The principle called mobility-immobility is this:
        every thing is changing
        but while some things
        are changing
        others
        are not.
20"
        Eventually those

        that were

        not
30"
        changing

        begin suddenly

        to change
40"
        et vice versa ad infinitum.

        A technique to be useful (skillful, that is)

        must be such that it fails
50"   to control
        the elements subjected to it. Otherwise
        it is apt to become unclear.
        And listening is best
        in a state of mental
        emptiness.

7'00" Composers are spoken of as having
       ears for music which generally
       means that nothing presented
       to their ears can be heard by them.
       Their ears are walled in
       with sounds
10"   of their own imagination.

       Of five aspects

       observe

20"   *two.*

              The highest purpose is to have no purpose
       at all. This puts one in accord with nature
       in her manner of operation. If someone comes
       along and asks why?, there are answers.
30"   However there is a story I have found very help-
       ful.   What's so interesting about
       technique anyway? *What if there are twelve tones in a
       row?* What row? This seeing of cause and effect
       is not emphasized but instead one makes an
       identification with what is here and now. He
40"   then spoke of two qualities. Unimpededness and Inter-
       penetration.

       The relationship of things happening
       at the same time is spontaneous
       and irrepressible.
50"   It is you yourself
       in the form you have
       that instant taken.
       To stop and figure it out
       takes
       time.

8'00"

The only thing,

pardon me,

that I do not find.

10"

The preparation of
the pianos
is also
determined by chance.
The various materials
20"   that exist
are placed in the
following categories:
P meaning plastics, bone, glass, etc.,
M meaning metal,
C meaning cloth, fibre, rubber,
30"   W meaning wood, paper,
X meaning other materials, special circumstances,
free choices etc.

Coins are then tossed.
40"

Form's not the same twice:

50"   Sonatas

Fugues
        That two or

9'00"   more things happen
        at the same time
        is their relation.
        The beginning of
        this work in progress
        was not a
10"   part for a pianist,
        but, curiously enough,
        six short parts
        no one of them
        lasting much more
        than a minute,
20"   for a string-player,
        that is, a four-strings-player.

        Surely things happening
        at different times are also
30"   related.
        If it needed to be clear, magnetic tape
        makes it perfectly so,
        that we are not in a twelve-tone
        or any other discrete situation.
        The reason I am presently working
40"   with imperfections in paper is this:
        I am thus able to
        designate
        certain aspects of sound
        as though they were in a field,
        which
50"   of course
        they are.

        The sounds that had accidentally occurred
        while it
        was being played were in

10'00" no sense an interruption.
More and
more
I have the feeling
that we are getting nowhere.

10"

*"Not wondering am I right or
doing something wrong."*
The preparation changes that occur
during a performance are
a) simple change of position
20" b) total or partial addition of objects
c) total or partial subtraction.

Nothing has been said about
Bach or Beethoven.

30" *We are the oldest (it makes the silence)
at having our air-way of knowing
nowness.*

Years ago I asked myself
"Why do I write music?"
40" An Indian musician told me the
traditional answer in India was
"To sober the mind and thus make
it susceptible to divine influences."
Same answer is given by some old
English composer. *Consider this non-dualistically.*
50"

"He goes by me; I see him not. He passes
on; but I perceive him not." These pieces
take into consideration the physical
action of playing an instrument.

11'00" You won't find this in the books.
        "Why do you not do as I do?   Letting
        go of your thoughts
        as though
        they were
        the cold ashes of a
10"   long
        dead fire?"
        What has taken the place of the mobility-immobility principle
        now that I am no longer interested in it? Three coins
        tossed six times yield a hexagram of which
        there are sixty-four. In this way one can establish
20"   which of sixty-four possibilities obtains. And changes.
        What better technique than to leave
        no traces?   To determine the number of
        imperfections in a given space, coins are tossed.
        That number of spots is then potentially active.
        Subsequent tosses determine which are actually active.
30"   Tables are arranged referring to tempi, the number
        of superimpositions, that is to say number of things
        that can go on at once, sounds & silences, durations,
        loudnesses, accents. *Sounds together (suffice it to say).*
        Structure is of no importance,
        however, I go on having it by chance
40"   to determine first the relative probability
        of the three, and then to determine which
        of the three happens in the world
        for studying music.
        It doesn't seem to me to affect anything
        that happens in it. I am speaking, of course,
50"   about a time structure. It simply
        allows anything to happen
        in it.
        What I am calling poetry is often called
        content. I myself have called it
        form.

12′00″　It is the continuity of a
　　　　piece of music.
　　　　Continuity *today*
　　　　when it is necessary.

　　　　A fugue is a more complicated game; but
10″　　it can be broken up by a single sound,
　　　　say, from a fire engine.

　　　　　　　　　　　　　　　　　　　　　　　　　(Cough)
20″

　　　　Now
　　　　　　　　　　　　　　　　　　　　　　　　　(Laugh)

30″　　　　　　　getting sleepy & so on.
　　　　Very frequently no one knows that
　　　　contemporary music is or could be
　　　　art.
　　　　He simply thinks it was irritating.　　　(Clap)
　　　　Irritating one way or another
40″　　that is to say
　　　　keeping us from ossifying.
　　　　It may be objected that from this point
　　　　of view anything goes. Actually
　　　　anything *does* go,——but only when
　　　　nothing is taken as the basis. In an utter emptiness
50″　　anything can take place.

　　　　The feeling we are

　　　　getting nowhere

13'00"   that is a pleasure

        which will continue.   **Why?**
        The way to test a modern painting is this: If
        it is not destroyed by the action of
        shadows it is genuine oil painting.
10"   A cough or a baby crying will not
        ruin a good piece of modern music.
        This is ——'s Truth. As contemporary music
        goes on changing in the way I am changing it
        what will be done is to more & more completely liberate sounds.
        Of course you do know structure is the division
20"   of whatever into parts. Last year when I talked
        here I made a short talk. **That was because I**
        was talking about something; but this year I
        am talking about nothing and of course
        will go on. Magnetic tape music makes it clear we
        are in
30"   totality
        actively

        Upaya.
40"

                Let your ears send a
        message of surprise or perplexity. That's the Way.
        Was asked: "Dr. Suzuki, what is the difference between
        men are men & mountains are mountains before studying Zen
        & men are men & mountains are mountains after studying Zen?" It is not a question of
50"   going in to oneself or out to the world. It is
        rather a condition of fluency that's in and out.
        Need I quote Blake? Certainly not. Spots are spots
        and skill's needed to turn them to the point
        of practicality.

14′00″   Tape music requires multiple loud-speakers.

          And it seems to me I could listen forever to
          Japanese shakuhachi music or the Navajo
          Yeibitchai or I could sit or stand
          near Richard Lippold's "Full Moon"
10″   any length of time.

                                        But those beauties——

                                        Formerly for me
          time-length was a constant. Now it, too,
20″   like everything else, changes.

          Beginning of the

          third unit
30″
          of the fourth

          large part.

40″
                    Yes it is. Masterpieces &
          geniuses go together and when, by running from
          one to the other, we make life safer than it
          actually is, we're apt never to know the dangers
          of contemporary music. When I wrote the *Imaginary Landscape*
50″   for twelve radios, it was not for the purpose of
          shock or as a joke but rather to increase the
          unpredictability already inherent in the situation
          through the tossing of coins.   Chance,
          to be precise, is a leap, provides a leap out
          of reach of one's own grasp of oneself. Once

15′00″ done, forgotten. One thing to do with time
is this: Measure it.   (Slap table)
            "Cultivate in yourself a grand similarity
with the chaos of the surrounding ether; unloose your mind, set your spirit free. Be
still as if you had no soul. Every one returns
10″ to its root, & does not know. If they knew, they
would be leaving it." Structure. Given a number
of actually active points, they are an aggregate, a
constellation, they can move about among themselves
and it becomes necessary to classify the kinds
of aggregates, say constant and again intermittent.
20″

                                                                          (Cough)

One can hear a sound.

30″
                    I wrote
some music for carillon for Mary Carolyn Richards using differently
shaped scraps of paper folded and small holes cut in them
at the points of folding. Then used these as
stencils at points in time-space *I-Ching* determined.
40″

If you are interested you can read a detailed
description of it that will appear
in the forthcoming issue of *trans/formation*.

50″

            When I first tossed coins
I sometimes thought: I hope such & such will turn up.

16′00″

"Earth's no escape from Heaven."

10″

    How can we speak of error when it is
understood "psychology never again"? It should
be clear from what I am saying that one's one.
Counterpoint is the same proposition as harmony

20″ except that it is more insidious. I noticed
in 1938 that some young people were
still interested in it. "Greater earnestness
is required if one is going to solve the
really important problems."
                        My point is this:

30″ various techniques can go together all at the
same time. Therefore this work, I am using
the word progress with which in connection,
has no organizing technique supporting it.

Giving up counterpoint

40″

one gets superimposition

and, of course,

a little counterpoint comes in of its own
50″ *accord.*

How I wouldn't   know.

17'00"   The best thing to do about counterpoint is what
Schoenberg did: Teach it.

(Hold up hand, gargle)

I am still really
thoroughly puzzled by this way of composing
10"   by observing imperfections in paper. It is
this being thoroughly puzzled that makes
it possible for me to work. I am puzzled
by hearing music well played too.
     If I'm not puzzled it
wasn't well played. Hopelessly incompre-
20"   hensible. While studying music things get
a little confused.   *Sounds are no longer*
just sounds, but are letters: A B C D E F G.

30"

40"

At the end of the journey when success
is almost in view:
50"

   I know nothing. All I can do
is say   what   strikes me
as especially
changing

18'00" in
contemporary
music.
　　　　　Unfortunately, European
thinking has brought it about that actual
things that happen such as suddenly
10" listening or suddenly sneezing
are not
considered profound.
　　　　　Not just tones, noises too! What
is
the physical action
20" involved
in playing an instrument? *Yes*——

　　　　　For instance,
now, my focus involves very little: a lecture
30" on music: my music. But it is not a
lecture, nor is it music; it is, of necessity, theatre: What else? If I choose,
as I do,
music,
I get theatre, *that,* that is, I get that
40" too. Not just this, the two.

50" Art as art is order or expression or integration
of these. It is a light, the Chinese say, but
there is darkness. What is now unheard-of
is an eight-loud-speaker situation: to be in
the center of transmission. Sounds coming
from every direction. After eight give me sixteen.

19'00" Where is the best position for audition?
        The corner where you are! It is understood
        that everything is clean: there is no dirt.
        "Then why are you always taking baths?"
        "Just a dip: No why!" For me it is a matter
        of getting up   and   daily, unless commitments.
10"

        That is finished now

        it was a pleasure

        And now
20"

            Just the same only
        somewhat as though you had your feet a
        little off the ground. Now, at the beginning,
        before studying music, men are men & sounds
30"   are sounds; this causes some hesitation on the
        hero's part but he finally acquiesces.
            One of them said: He must have lost
        his favorite animal. Another man said: No,
        it must be his friend. ***Do you only take***
        the position
40"   *of doing nothing, & things*
        will
        of themselves
        become
        transformed."   Think for
        a moment about sound how it has pitch,
50"   loudness, timbre and duration and how
        silence which is its nonexistent opposite
        has only duration. Duration structure.

        Error is drawing a straight line between
        anticipation of what should happen and

20'00″	what actually happens. What actually
	happens is however in a total not
	linear situation and is responsible
	generally. Therefore error is a fiction, has
	no
	reality
10″	in fact.

20'00″ what actually happens. What actually
happens is however in a total not
linear situation and is responsible
generally. Therefore error is a fiction, has
no
reality
10″ in fact.
Errorless music is written by not giving
a thought to cause and effect.
Any other
kind of music always has mistakes in it.
        In other words there is no
20″ split
between spirit and matter.
And to realize this one has only suddenly
to awake to the fact.

This makes possible the writing of such   (**Cough**)
30″ durations as $1/7 + 1/3 + 3/5$, all fractions
of a quarter. This brings   (**Lean on elbow**)
about an
emphasis on uniqueness
so that two nearly the same
durations can each be uniquely itself
40″ just as
two leaves, however much of the same tree
are not
identical.   *If there is time*
I will tell about my visit
to the anechoic chamber
50″ *at Harvard. It was not*
silent. Two sounds: one
high, one low.   The privileged tones
that remain are arranged in
modes or scales or nowadays rows
& an abstract process begins called

21'00"   composition. Express an idea.

                    The only structure
          which permits of natural activity is one so
          flexible as not to be a structure; I write
          in order to hear; never do I hear and
10"   then write what I hear. Inspiration is not
          a special occasion.

                                    After studying
          music men are men and sounds are
          sounds. And subtract: That is to say, at
20"   the beginning one can
          hear
          a
          sound
          and tell

30"

40"   *In the direct situation: it is*

          If you don't like it you may
          choose
          to avoid it
50"   but what
          silence requires isn't it.

22′00″
What I think & what I feel can be
my inspiration but it is then also my
pair of blinders. To see one must go
beyond the imagination and for that
one must stand absolutely still as though

10″ in the center of a leap.

20″

30″   *Several*
stories occur to me that I should like to interpolate (in
the same way, by the way, that while I am talking
the telephone keeps ringing and then contemporary
conversation takes place instead of this particular
way of preparing a lecture).

40″ *It is high*
or low

has a certain timbre

50″ and loudness.
     I will not disturb by my concern the structure
of anything that
is going to be acting; to
act is miracle and needs everything and
every me out of the way. An error is simply a

23'00"   failure to adjust immediately from a preconception
to an actuality.

However, it occurs to me
to say more about
10"   structure.
Specifically this:
We are now
at the beginning.

(**Blow nose, rub eyes**)

20"   Or not

And it isn't

a human being or something

30"   to look at; it is high or low—
has a certain timbre & loudness,

lasts a certain length of time.

40"   *End.*
It is necessary to see that there is not only a sharp
distinction to be made between composing and listening
but that although all things are different it is
not their differences which are to be our concern
but rather their uniquenesses and their infinite
50"   play of interpenetration with themselves and with
us.

There are three categories of noises

24′00″ in the two parts for two pianists: those produced inside the piano construction, outside the same and
accessory noises, whistles, percussions, etc.

Reading music is for musicologists. There is no
straight line to be drawn between notes
10″ *and sounds.*

20″
Vertically in
the same
space
any
range
30″ *will*
appear.

It was originally for me a matter of flexibility
by means of changing and not changing
tempi. The matter reduces itself however
40″ to time which is short or long. And that
to a process of multiplication using a
variety of multiplicands. Communication
if it is
required is a way of calling
attention to one's own psychology.
50″ If permitted, it takes place of its own

accord,
is
for all the world
inevitable.

25'00"

If it were the
same purpose as when it has to do with another leaf
it would be a coincidence, imitation of nature
from which each leaf should hold on to the
complete rule which would be free because it
10"   adds "in her manner of operation." Then it will
not be of its own unique position in space
uniqueness, plagiarism of result, having a
particular suchness, but active from
"before operations begin." (*Is extremely*
close to
20"   *being*
here
and
now.)   **(Clap)**

So that listening one takes as a spring-
30"   board the first sound that comes along;
the first something springs us into nothing and
out of that nothing arises the next something;
etc. like an alternating current. Not one
sound fears the silence that extinguishes it.
But if you avoid it, that's a pity, because
40"   it resembles life very closely & life and it
are essentially a cause for joy. People say,
sometimes,
timidly.

Organized
50"   ways of predicting the weather say for instance it is in
all of its acoustical details. For a calculated
theatrical activity I would say offhand that
the minimum number of necessary actions going on
at once is five. Bright people can clear up
rather quickly perplexity arising from lower numbers.

26'00"   Modern intervals: but in order to have
them the mind had fixed it so that one had to
avoid having progressions that would make one
think of sounds that were not actually
present to the ear.

10"

He is most utterly indebted, not one who
struggles to force his idea? and who would
have had to remain, I have noticed.
Calculated actions that are to go on together
need not have been composed in the same
20"   way. One runs the risk of falling into
a marasm of idea if one goes on
composing without discovering. Turn on several
radios at once. There again one has a
multiple loud-speaker system. Besides
actually being in space, the mind no longer
30"   can function as A B C.

          Theatre takes place
all the time wherever one is and art simply
40"   facilitates persuading one this is the case.
So that this ignorance I speak of is not losing
sensitivic responsiveness, on the contrary. It
is a question of when: now. "Flee she
up or flee she down." It acts in

50"   such a
way
that one can "hear through" a piece of
music just as one can "see through."
Echoes, breaking, varying its speed, and
synchronized. Skillful means has a good

27'00" deal to do with multiple division of process.
And here for instance we begin to be in
a state of immobility. *Anyone* can
see the desirability of mobility. Had I had
nothing to say, it would have been different. All it
is now is what it is: faster and slower.
10"   It is the
space between the loud-speakers that is to be considered:
From a desire for clarity, great.

20"   We carry our homes

within us

which enables us to *fly*

30"

Each moment presents what happens. I

derived the method I use for writing music

40" by tossing coins

from the method used in the Book of Changes.
It may be objected that from this point of view
anything goes.

50" Actually, anything does go but only when
nothing is taken as the basis.
In an utter emptiness
anything can take place.   And
needless to say,

28'00" each sound is unique (had accidentally occurred while it was *being played*)
and is not informed
about European history and theory:
Keeping one's mind
on the emptiness,
on the space
10" one can see anything can be in it, is, as
a matter of fact, in it.

Were in no sense an interruption.
                    I have noticed
20" *I needed a way*
Something else

This causes some hesitation

hero would have had to remain
30" now knows he is most
asks the hero to kill him.
Three kinds of them. It was by means of
words we became subservient. The central
point is everywhere receiving and transmitting. What
is passivity? Only one monk in the monastery the oldest one wrote a poem
40" but he stayed up night and day deliberating on it. The other monks didn't try
because they were certain the oldest one would win. When his poem
finally came out, it said: Continuity takes place of its own
accord and things do go on at the same time.
All of this is correct and true: there is no concern necessary for, say, intonation, counterpoint,
50" scales, going to and coming from; and, then, when?
An abstract process begins called composition. That
is: a composer
uses the sounds to express an idea:
                              What then
are you standing up there for, if you

29'00"   say

No
to all of our questions?

The man on high said, *I just stand*
10"

If there are no questions.

This means for me knowing more
and
20"   more not what I.
                                        If it is
on paper, it is graphic: calligraphy;
if you can hear and see it, it is.
There are no answers. Then, of course,
there are answers but the final
30"   answer makes the questions
seem absurd
whereas the questions up until then
seem more intelligent than the
answers. Somebody asked Debussy
Have you not lost your friend?
40"

No, sir, I have not lost my friend
either.
                        Is it
interesting? It is and it isn't. But
one thing is certain. They are with
50"   respect to counterpoint melody
harmony rhythm and any other
musical methods, *pointless.*

30'00"

All that is necessary is an empty
space of time and letting it act in its magnetic way.
Eventually there will be so much in it that
whistles. In order to apply it to all of these various characteristics
he necessarily reduces it to numbers. He has also found a math-

10" ematical way of making a correspondence between rows. I remember
as a child loving all the sounds even the unprepared ones; I liked them
especially when itself in the jaws cheeks and tongue
and the commentary says "The most superficial way of trying to influence others is through talk
that has nothing real behind it. The

20" influence produced by such mere tongue-
wagging must necessarily remain insignificant."

"I believe that one can arrive

30" at directing the phenomenon of the automatism of
Chance which I mistrust as a facility which
is not absolutely necessary. For, in the end,
in interpolations and interferences between
different rows (when one of them passes
from time-lengths to pitches, at the

40" same time that another passes from
intensities to attacks, etc.) there is
already a sufficiency of the unknown."

50" (Diminishes his love and increases his fear

and concern about what people will think.)

(Bang fist on table)

31′00″

                    There is all the

            time in the world for studying
            music,
10″

            but for living there is scarcely

            any time at all.
20″

            For living takes place

            each instant.

30″

40″   Unimpeded.

                                    (Yawn)
50″

                There are two great dangers for
            magnetic tape: one is music (all the
            history and thinking about it); and the other
            is feeling obliged to have an instrument.

32′00″   One is *Pacific 231*   1954   and the other:
organ music.
> If you are interested you can

read a detailed description of it.

10″

> If there are
ten things to do and I only do two of them, focus
have changed. In his ear, where he will find a metal
ball, to toss it on the road, in front of them, so that
20″   as the horse goes on to say, we may be led
by it. This too *giving himself.*
> Is there anything
else to say about structure?

> Yes, it goes on
30″   supporting everything: its only difficulty
lies where struggle to support is already

> **(Touch nose and ears; click)**

in process. Fearing what?

40″   Any kind of paper will do for seeing spots
in it.

When one gets around to copying on a
second sheet what was given by a
first it becomes clear.
50″

> What?

33'00"   Magnetic
tape as being all-interesting can disappear.

There are rumors of machines and cards

Let us move however for unpredictability

10"

A structure is like a bridge from

nowhere
                                   (**Lean on elbow**)
20"

              If something with respect to something
else happens sooner or later everything is different
but essentially nothing of any permanent
importance has happened. I am talking
30"   & contemporary music is changing. Like life
it changes. If it were not changing it would be dead.

That is why chance enters for me
so largely into my means which
are skillful. It is at the point
40"   of potentiality.
                                   (**Yawn**)
              I am
working now to work without charts, without
any support in total space. I see now
by many slow transitions, one of which
50"   is tempo like streams (varying & not
varying) that as long as one discrim-
inates as I formerly
did problems re-
main. Each one of us is thinking his own thoughts
his own experience & each experience is changing & while we

34'00"   are thinking (to get yourself in such a state of
confusion that you think that a sound is
not something to hear but rather something to look at)
I am happy about all the experiences I
have had with the prepared piano; for one thing
it showed me how different two pianos are from one another

10"   and music (so-called)

makes us think

two pianos are the same. It isn't true.

20"   **(Hold up watch [to mike])**

30"

It is   tossed   out.

40"

50"

It just happened that the series
of numbers which are at the basis of this
work add up to 100 x 100 which is
10,000. This is pleasing, momentarily: The world,

35'00"   the 10,000 things. But the title is simply
minutes and seconds. Question to ask you:
How do you need to cautiously proceed
in dualistic terms?

A B

Just as going from

10"   here to Egypt is a single trip but a
more or less complex series of
experiences or just as Chinese
characters are some written with one
stroke but others with two or several
   or many   And not

20"   in the way we need for living. For
instance: someone said Art should
come from overhead. There was
a social calendar and hours
for breakfast but one day I
saw a cardinal and the same

30"   day heard a woodpecker. I
also met Meister Eckhart. Of
course Kansas. Arizona is more
interesting.

I

40"   have nothing to say and I am saying it
and that is poetry.

It is no longer a case of moving along

50"   stepping stones (scales of any degree,

series of no matter what), but one can
move or just appear to, at any
point in this total space, long enough

36′00″   to see the end of this craze for Bach. A
pupil once said to me: I understand
what you say about Beethoven & I
think I agree but I have a very
serious question to ask you: How
do you feel about Bach?

10″

Now we have come to the end of the
part about structure.

           That two or more
20″   things happen at the same time is
It is entirely possible for something to

their relationship: Synchronicity. That
Break for instance
means at the center moving out in all

30″

directions and then time is clearly
Should one stop and mend it?
luminous. It could not be easily otherwise.

go wrong. And machines are never synchronous
40″   not even the synchronous ones. If
you need several things at once, use
one as the basis, and one motor.

                                     (Lean, cough)

                      To be &
be the present.   Would it be a
50″

repetition? Only if we thought we
owned it, but since we don't, it
is free & so are we. Most

anybody knows about the future and   ("No" of hand in air, kiss sound)

37'00"   how uncertain it is.

                  A sound is a sound.

        To realize this: one has to put a stop
        to studying music.

10"   The most enlivening thing
        about magnetic tape is this: whether we actually do it or not, everything
        we do do, say what we're doing, is affected, radically,
        by it.
            Rhythm is not arithmetic.
        And so is this unfinished work: so far for two pianists,
20"   string-players, lecturer
                    Lines of demarcation are O.K.
        when they have to do with potentiality.
        It must be clearly understood they have
        nothing. A sound accomplishes nothing:
        without it life would not last out the
30"   instant. It is only irritating to
        think one would like to be somewhere
        else. Here we are now.

40"   It becomes
        gradually clear to us dull-witted
        musicians that interpenetration
        means that each one of these
        most honored ones of all
        is moving out in all directions.
50"   Penetrating & being penetrated no

        matter what the time.

            Research would

38′00″   then take place in the field of music
as it takes place normally in other
fields.

Energizing, whether for her weal or for her
woe.
10″

                  Testing   pictures:

can they support   action of shadows?
20″

                I have
been satisfied for some time with one to
sixty-four; there is no way of telling how
long this will continue. I could go back
30″   to two or:

One loud-speaker is insufficient and so
are two or three or four: five is
40″   when it seems to me to begin. What begins
is our inability to comprehend, "that on the
contrary chance ought to be very controlled.

In using tables in general, or a series of tables, I
believe one can
50″   arrive at direct"
                Form
is what interests everyone and fortunately
it is wherever you are and there is
no place where it isn't. Highest truth,
that is.

Eventually everything will be happening
at once: nothing behind a screen unless a screen happens to be
in front. It will increasingly be a thump instead of
10″   a bang. The thing to do is to gather up one's
ability to respond and go on at varying speeds.
Following, of course, the general outlines of the
Christian life. I myself tend to think of catching trains
more than Christianity.

20″

Insisting on stimulating activity, though

Without a multiple loud-speaker system, all
becomes music and submissiveness. But,
30″   fortunately the piano is there and one can
always prepare it in a different way.
Otherwise it would become an instrument.
It is like, as
Artaud said, a disease. No avoiding. And
not having an idea about it.
40″

The thing
to do is to keep the head alert but
empty. Things come to pass, arising
and disappearing. There can then be no
consideration of error. Things are always going
50″   wrong.

(Lean on elbow)

(Whistle three times)

40′00″

We're apt never to know

but

something else is

10″

happening: I am getting nowhere slowly
as the talk goes on slowly
we have the feeling we're getting nowhere; that
is a pleasure which will continue if
we are irritated with whatever. This goes

20″   to explain what he means when he says that
he is associated with all of the sounds & so can foresee
what will happen even though he has not written the
particular notes down at room temperature as other composers do.

30″

And I have noticed something else about most anyone's
music, that can be accomplished to increase the unpredictability
already inherent in the situation:

40″   The control must be at one point only and so
placed that it has no effect on anything that
happens: A technique which results in no technique, etc.
Of course the answer is time and since
we have them, chronometers, I mean, use
them; or you may leave it forever & never

50″   return. Play my piece for bells. Whether I hear it
or not is of no consequence: but until someone
does, music is at a standstill.
                              Before I die, I shall
leave a will, because if you want something done, sentimentality is effective. I

41'00" haven't the slightest idea of what is good
        in the world, but instead quite passively, & often
        against what might be considered a better
        judgment, accepts what happens.

        I find that it is important to take a
10"   multiplicity of steps.
        A story is told about an Irish hero that

        he is required by a jealous mother-in-law
        to go to some distant island.
                At all costs inspiration
20"   must be avoided which is to say
        act in such a way that inspiration
        doesn't come up as an alternative
        but exists eternally. Then of course
        it is theatre and music disappears
        entirely into the realm of art where
30"   it knows it belongs. Art silence is
        not real silence and the difference
        is continuity versus interpenetration. This   (Light match)
        is also.

                                                        (Hold up hand)
40"

        Music is simply trying things out in
        school fashion to see what happens.
        Etudes. Making it easier but not
        real. Theatre is the only thing
        that comes near what it is.
50"

                This means for me knowing more &
        more not what I think a sound is, but

42′00″
        what it actually is, in all of its acoustical
        details & then letting the sound exist, itself
        changing in a changing sonorous environment.

10″   The way it does it is by the intimacy of
        multiplicity and emptiness. The mind has
        nothing in it but everything else is busy
        and there is not an instant lost in
        doing what must be done. Later on, if
        you wish, you can read about mobility
20″   and immobility. To repeat: I am no
        longer interested in it. I am interested
        in asymmetry.

                  If one feels
30″   protective about the word "music," protect
        it and find another word for
        all the rest that enters through the
        ears. It's a waste of time to trouble
        oneself with words, noises. What it
        is is theatre and we are in it and
40″   like it, making it.

50″   But beware!

        Here we are now at the

        middle of the fourth large part

43′00″ of this talk

10″

                        There is no

20″

such thing as silence. Something is al-

ways happening that makes a sound.

No one can have an idea

30″

once he starts really listening.

It is very simple but extra-urgent

The Lord knows whether or not

40″

the next

50″

                                    (Bang fist)

44′00″

Forever?   Now?

10″

(Blow nose)

Hearing   or   making   this   in
20″

music   is   not   different

only   simpler
30″

than   living   this   way.   Simpler
that is,——for me, because it happens.   **(Cough)**
          No error.
And no wondering about what's next.
40″   Going lively on "thru many a
perilous situation." (Was it later he was
discovered?) And what is your purpose
in writing music? I do not deal
in purposes; I deal with sounds.
What
50″   sounds are those?   I make
them just as well by sitting quite
still looking for mushrooms.

Growing fast in sawdust.

Sonya Sekula said, "Why don't you come with me to the Reises'? They're giving a party." I said I wasn't invited. Sonya said, "Come anyway; they won't mind." As we walked in, Mrs. Reis was extremely friendly in her greeting, and even asked what I'd like to drink. I said, "Rum." She said, "Oh, I'm so sorry. I don't have any at the bar, but I'll go down to the basement and get some." I asked her not to bother, but she insisted. While she was gone, I made my way over to the bar and discovered Bushmills Irish whisky, of which I am very fond. I asked for some and began drinking it. When Mrs. Reis came back with the rum, naturally I drank some of that. As the time passed, I drank rum when Mrs. Reis was looking and Irish whisky when she wasn't. After a while Sonya Sekula said, "Let's go. You take one of the bottles of Irish and I'll get my coat and meet you downstairs." I said, "You take the bottle; I'll get your coat." She said, "O.K." I went downstairs, picked up a fur coat; Sonya came running down with the Irish; we went out into the snow. I said, "Do you want your coat on?" She said, "No. The car's right here. Just throw it in the back seat." A few blocks along, Sonya said, "That's not my coat." I said, "How do you know?" She said, "The perfume." We drove on to Grand Street, went upstairs, and killed the Irish. We talked all the time about selling the coat in some distant city. Sonya said she knew a fence in St. Louis. About midnight I called the Reises and spoke to Mr. Reis. I said, "I have the coat." He said, "Thank God!" We made arrangements for my bringing it to his office in the morning. When I got there I explained it had all been a mistake. Before we said good-by, he whispered, "No one will ever hear a word about this." I went to the elevator. He came running down the hall and said, "What about Mrs. Reis's coat?" I said, "I don't know anything about her coat; I didn't take it."

Two wooden boxes containing Oriental spices and foodstuffs arrived from India. One was for David Tudor, the other for me. Each of us found, on opening his box, that the contents were all mixed up. The lids of containers of spices had somehow come off. Plastic bags of dried beans and palm sugar had ripped open. The tin lids of cans of chili powder had come off. All of these things were mixed with each other and with the excelsior which had been put in the box to keep the containers in position. I put my box in a corner and simply tried to forget about it. David Tudor, on the other hand, set to work. Assembling bowls of various sizes, sieves of about eleven various-sized screens, a pair of tweezers, and a small knife, he began a process which lasted three days, at the end of which time each spice was separated from each other, each kind of bean from each other, and the palm sugar lumps had been scraped free of spice and excavations in them had removed embedded beans. He then called me up to say, "Whenever you want to get at that box of spices you have, let me know. I'll help you."

One of Suzuki's books ends with the poetic text of a Japanese monk describing his attainment of enlightenment. The final poem says, "Now that I'm enlightened, I'm just as miserable as ever."

While Meister Eckhart was alive, several attempts were made to excommunicate him. (He had, in his sermons, said such things as "Dear God, I beg you to rid me of God.") None of the trials against him was successful, for on each occasion he defended himself brilliantly. However, after his death, the attack was continued. Mute, Meister Eckhart was excommunicated.

*When I was invited to speak in January 1961 at the Evening School of
Pratt Institute in Brooklyn, I was told that the burning questions among the
students there were: Where are we going? and What are we doing? I took these
questions as my subjects and, in order to compose the texts, made use of
my* Cartridge Music.

*The texts were written to be heard as four simultaneous lectures. But to
print four lines of type simultaneously—that is, superimposed on one another—
was a project unattractive in the present instance. The presentation here used
has the effect of making the words legible—a dubious advantage, for I had
wanted to say that our experiences, gotten as they are all at once, pass
beyond our understanding.*

*A part of this lecture has been printed, in a different typographical
arrangement, in* Ring des Arts, *Paris, summer 1961. The entire lecture has been*

WHERE ARE WE GOING? AND WHAT ARE WE DOING?

*recorded by C. F. Peters, New York, in the form of four single-track tapes
(7½ ips, forty-five minutes each). The following is a set of directions:
Four independent lectures to be used in whole or in part—horizontally and
vertically. The typed relation is not necessarily that of a performance.
Twenty-five lines may be read in 1 minute, 1¼ minutes, 1½ minutes, giving
lectures roughly 37, 47, 57 minutes long respectively. Any other speech speed
may be used.*

*A performance must be given by a single lecturer. He may read "live" any
one of the lectures. The "live" reading may be superimposed on the recorded
readings. Or the whole may be recorded and delivered mechanically. Variations
in amplitude may be made; for this purpose, use the score of my composition*
WBAI *(also published by C. F. Peters).*

*I was driving out to the country once with Carolyn and Earle Brown. We
got to talking about Coomaraswamy's statement that the traditional function of
the artist is to imitate nature in her manner of operation. This led me to the
opinion that art changes because science changes—that is, changes in science
give artists different understandings of how nature works.*

*A Phi Beta Kappa ran in the other day and said, "Your view is that art
follows science, whereas Blake's view is that art is ahead of science."*

*Right here you have it: Is man in control of nature or is he, as part of it,
going along with it? To be perfectly honest with you, let me say I find nature
far more interesting than any of man's controls of nature. This does not imply
that I dislike humanity. I think that people are wonderful, and I think this
because there are instances of people changing their minds. (I refer to
individuals and to myself.)*

Not all of our past, but the parts of it we are taught, lead us to believe that we are in the driver's seat. With respect to nature. And that if we are not, life is meaningless. Well, the grand thing about the human mind is that it can turn its own tables and see meaninglessness as ultimate meaning.

I have therefore made a lecture in the course of which, by various means, meaning is not easy to come by even though lucidity has been my constant will-of-the-wisp. I have permitted myself to do this not out of disdain of you who are present. But out of regard for the way in which I understand nature operates. This view makes us all equals—even if among us are some unfortunates: whether lame, blind, stupid, schizoid, or poverty-stricken.

Here we are. Let us say Yes to our presence together in Chaos.

If we set out to catalogue things
.

.

.

today, we find ourselves rather
.

.

.

endlessly involved in cross-
.

.

.

referencing. Would it not be
Those of us who don't agree are going
.

.

less efficient to start the other
around together. The string Duchamp dropped.
.

.

way around, after the fashion of
He took the apartment without being able to
.

.

some obscure second-hand bookstore?
pay for it. They danced on a concrete floor.
.

.

.

The candles at the Candlelight Concert are
.

.

One New Year's Eve I had too
electric. It was found dangerous
.

.

many invitations. I decided to
for them to be wax. It has not yet
.

•

go to all the parties, ending up
been found dangerous for them to

•

•

at the most interesting one. I
be electric—and this in spite of

•

•

arrived early at the one I was
the air-conditioning. If I were

•

•

sure would be dull. I stayed there
able to open my windows, I think

•

•

the whole evening—never got to the others.
I would do it often, and for no reason at all.

•

•

I would have written sooner but

•

•

I picked up the book and

•

•

•

could scarcely put it down. It is absolutely

•

•

charming. I'm going to write to the author.
How can we go over there when

•

•

•

we haven't the least idea of

•

•

what we will find when we

•

•

•

get there? Also we don't

•

Three birds and a telephone ringing. Does

•

know how to land, and we

•

that relate to where we are going? Does

•

have no way of trying it

•

it tell us the direction to take: out

out beforehand. Perhaps we

•

the window and down the hall?

will sink into a huge mile-

•

I take a sword and cut off my

•

thick pile of dust. What then?

•

head and it rolls to where we

•

•

•

are going. The question is: Do they

•

•

•

mean it when they say No Trespassing?

•

•

•

•

•

•

•

•

•

•

•

In a sense we are going to extremes.

•

•

You want to know what we're doing?
That is what we are doing. In fact

•

•

We're breaking the rules, even our
we don't need to go to bring that

•

•

own rules. And how do we do that?
into our action. We tend to rush

•

•

By leaving plenty of room for X quantities.
to what we think are the limits
The house had been so well built that

•

•

only to discover how tamed our
even though it burned, it did not
After we have been going for some

•

ambitions were. Will we ever learn
burn down. The fire gutted it.
time, do we mellow? (They used to

·

that it is endless? What then
We're not going to become less
say we would.) Mellowing is sof-

·

is an extreme? The very low sounds,
scientific, **but more scientific. We**
tening. Left to ourselves, if the

·

extremely low, are so little available
do not include probability in science.
birds didn't get us, we'd putrefy.

We're putting art in museums, getting it out
to us and yet we rush to them
Do I thank you or the one who's
Of course, our air-conditioning

of our lives. **We're bringing machines**
and don't get them. We find
opening and closing the door? **On days when**
is such that if we just managed

home to live with us. Now that
them too soft. We want them
nobody answers, we stop telephoning. We are
to die under its influence we'd

the machines are here so to say to
extremely loud. If you announced
going and then coming back and going and
not putrefy: we'd dry up.

stay with us, we've got to find
that there was going to be a low
coming back again. Eventually we
But since the windows won't

ways to entertain them. **If we don't,**
and *loud sound, I imagine*
will go and not come back at all.
open, we could scarcely be ex-

they'll explode, but as for going, we're
quite a number of us would
·
pected to blow away. I've always

going out. **Did we just notice the moon**
rush to hear it. What about an
·
had my heart set on cremation

or was it there always? **Where we're**
extremely loud high sound? Hear!
·
but now I see the reason for earth,

going is not only to the moon but out into
Anxiety enters. Some of us would stay
·
it frees the air from dead influences.

space. Home is discrete points. Space is an
put and say, "Tell me about it."
The house is built around a large
·

infinite field without boundaries. We are

Once someone's done something,
chimney, so large that on a good

·

leaving the machines home to play the
it's no longer his responsibility.
day when the flue is open, the sun

·

old games of relationships, addition and
It's someone else's. It could of
shines on the hearth. We're getting into

·

who wins. (We're going out.) A teen-ager—
course be his again, but what
our heads that existence, the existence of

·

served custard that had wheyed—said, "My
would he do? I asked the three girls
a sound, for instance, is a field
At the beginning of our going, it seems

mother bakes custard too, but she
what they would take with them
phenomenon, not one limited to
that we are going our separate ways,

doesn't put water in it." Let us admit,
to the Caribbean. The third was
known discrete points in that field—the
that we have nothing further to say

once and for all, that the lines
going to take some fish and a

conventionally accepted ones—but capable
to one another, and we leave behind

we draw are not straight.
bird which she cannot because
of appearance at any point in the field.
in particular the ways we learned to

·

they're being housed by friends when
This brings about a change in our heads.
communicate. Later on

·

she and her family go away. I

·

we won't bother about any of that.

·

pointed this out: "Since you can't

·

We'll be one happy anarchistic family.

·

take the bird and the fish, what

·

We haven't any time left to stay: we

·

will you take? Your sisters

·

must go now. Though his ears are

·

have said what they'll take."

·

extraordinarily sensitive and he's a Quaker,

.

There was no answer. Shortly,
.
he recommended a restaurant with Muzak.

.

but after her sisters, she ran up-
.

.

.

stairs to bed. "Tuck me in."
.

.

.

.

She drives rapidly; her life is shorter.
.

.

Everything is ready for tomorrow morning.
.

.

.

I must remember to turn out the lights.
.

.

.

.

.

.

.

.

.

.

.

.

.

.

.

Small telephones for those near the
.

.

.

central telephone and large telephones
.

.

.

for those farther away following
.

.

.

what one calls a law of nature.

.

.

.

.

-
-
-
-
-
-
-
-
-

If there are as many ways as

-
-

there are of looking, there must

-
-

be at least three ways of going—not

-
-

so much ways as wheres. Well,

-
-

-

there you have it: If I go over

-
-

-

there and stop, could I not have

-
-

The trouble with Denver is its past.
gone slightly to the left? As I

-
-

San Francisco used to have the same
go, direction changes. It is not

-
-

problem. But how are we going to know
measurable. But it is precise

-
-

where to go when it doesn't make
going. One moved off to the south,

-
-

the least difference to us where we
and when I measured he was going

-
-

go? The problem is simple: You
north. Or I crossed the stream at the

"Powdered eggs are good enough for me."

.

either stay put until you get
point where the water was going both
It's not the air-conditioning; it's the

.

an invitation or you make your-
ways. They say how fast and there
radiant heating in the ceiling: it makes

.

self an invitation written in such
is no way to answer. Tempo is out
me think someone's up on the roof.

.

a way that you couldn't know,
but comes back in. You might add:
They played a game in which she
At the present time it seems

when you wrote it, what you
There was no need for us to have gone.
was the sun. One man was the
reasonable not to go. The weather

were writing, and where it would

.

earth and the other was the moon: a
is not made for adult affairs

be sending you going. And other ways.

.

choreography. Now what shall we do?

(and the furtherance of the national

.

.

.

economy) but for the games of

.

.

.

children. Even if we sense

I wander out in the hall expecting

.

.

a certain obligation to go we

to see someone. It turns out it wasn't
Do you remember the story of his

.

may very likely not be able to.

anybody: it was a machine. I'm as
hanging his shoes out of his own
Whether or not we want it, we

.

crazy as a loon: I'm invited out to
reach, so that rather than taking
are insured. And we say it is a

.

dinner. I keep telling myself: Before
the trouble of getting them down,
good thing. The thing to do is not to

.

you go to bed, be sure to close the
he would simply go on doing what
have one policy but many and then

.

bathroom door; if you don't, you'll
he was doing and not go out? From
there is the possibility that the central

.

just have to get up and close it
what I hear, there are ideas that
office will get confused. (It happens.)

.

later. We are going stupidly to places
we have not yet had simply be-
We are going to realize that our

.

we have never been. Going away from
cause we don't yet have the language
analytic method of approaching

.

home, sometimes lost, we come by
to have them. But even in our
the material we are working with

.

circle, home again. We're surprised:
own language, it seems, there
(sound, I mean) which was so

.

it's changed. Did it slip—out
are ideas that are confined
useful is going to give place to
What we do is not utterly different from

from under us? The day in the
to systems, each to a single one,
some other means, some other
what we used to do. That is: we

woods I took a compass was the
which means there would be
useful means. Its awkwardness led us
used to get an idea and do it and

day I got lost for sure. Two years
times when it would be reason-
willy-nilly into a certain sloppiness.
then someone else had to do more

later when I was throwing it out,
able to say Yes and other times
(That was not without its hilarious
or less what he was told to do.

a child to whom I'd given a bass
when it would be absurd to say
effects which we in our deadliness
Now we get an idea and present

drum asked whether he might also have
that same word. Ideas take on
did not notice.) There is a lingering
it in such a way that it can

the compass. The first thing she said

a kind of material reality
confusion, paying heed to results
be used by him who is going to

was: "Everyone's confused; there isn't
but essentially they are intangible.
rather than actions (the only solution
do it. Someone once raised the

anyone now who isn't confused."
My question is: Why do we, as
is to stay where you are: it's you acting).
question who gets the credit. The

Or was that the first thing she said?
it were, imprison them? Of

.

listener gives it to himself when

.

all things, they are best equipped,
.

he gets it. All the people have

.

wouldn't you say, to fly in and
People always want to know what
become active and enjoy what you

.

out of the most unlikely places?
we're doing and the last thing we
might call individual security.

.

Off hand, for instance, we can do

want to do is keep it a secret. But
The composer also has ears on his head.

.

one thing at a time. But we
the truth is we don't know what

.

.

used to admire those artists of
we're doing and that is how we

.

.

vaudeville who did several
manage to do it when it's lively.

.

.

at once. To their three, say,
I believe, of course, that what we're

.

.

we could add our one. But at
doing is exploring a field, that the

.

.

a circus, three rings, though
field is limitless and without

.

.

high up, I remember I
qualitative differentiation but with

could only look at one ring
multiplicity of differences,

at a time. I kept missing or
that our business has changed

thinking I was missing some-
from judgment to awareness—

thing. On the other hand, if
I believe all this and it makes
Travel was not only possible.

what I'm doing is digging the
me speechless, for there is nothing
It was widely engaged in. On

hog peanut, then it actually happens
to say. For if I say I am
both sides of the streets, the two-

that I can converse, notice changes
especially active in the
way ones, there were long lines

in temperature, take as perfectly
amplification of small sounds
of traffic proceeding, to be sure,

natural the discovery of geasters
and work with the voice, it
slowly, but getting, one assumed,

growing underneath the surface
doesn't tell you what the others
eventually where they were going.

of the earth when I knew
(who are also us) are doing. Would
People also were walking and a

It's very curious. I remember recording
perfectly well the books don't men-
it be accurate to say then that
very large crowd attended the

machines with dials and clutches.
tion they do or can. Perhaps a live
we are all off in separate corners
Candlelight Concert. Was it because

Then later there were push buttons. Now
ghost might have made an ap-
engaged in our special concerns?
it was a tradition? It must

one has the feeling we're going to
parition and I would have
No. It is more to the point to talk
be that that is the case: the lady

have dials again. **We need**
found it perfectly unremarkable.
about the field itself, which
beyond the one sitting next to me

desperately when it comes to a
Is this the effect of concentration?
is that it is and enables us
whispered to my neighbor that

machine to be able to go at any speed.
If only, she said, I have a
all to be doing the same thing
the program this year was not

.

thread, I can then take the
so differently. And about this
as entirely appreciated by her

.

rest, hanging on as it were.
field, nothing can be said. And
as the one last year. And

.

We also discussed the mortality of
yet one goes on talking, in order
when they first came in, they

.

birds in connection with modern architecture.
to make this clear. Suzuki Daisetz
sat down in the reverse relation

Instead of living and learning, don't we
.

laughed many times quietly: once
to me that I have just described

live by learning we're not learning?
.

it was when he was discussing
so that the one who was later

For instance: When I moved to the
.

the quality of not being explicable
my neighbor was then at the

country I no sooner found myself
They have curious regulations for
and pointing out that he had
beginning beyond my neighbor.

insatiably involved in tramping
pedestrians. After the light turns
come from Japan with the inten-
She whispered her approval of

through the woods than summer
red, there is a white one and
tion of making explicit this
the wreaths and ropes of greenery

passed through fall into an
then the people walk wherever

quality which was of not being clear.
which decorated the chapel

icy winter. I made some
they wish, crossing the intersection
(My words, it goes without saying,
along with the electric lights and

inquiries and finally got to
even diagonally. One begins to think
are not the ones he used.) We
electric candles. She found them

a municipal office where I
it's better when we're going not
don't any more take vacations. Or
more beautiful than last year.

filled out blanks that led to
to pay attention to the signs.
if through special circumstances we
Very rarely do people any more

my getting a license for hunting
It is as though we were looking
are obliged to take a vacation, we
flock to a public occasion.

and fishing. Then I bought some
with other eyes than our own. I mean
take what we're doing with us.
Apparently if you keep some-

ingenious paraphernalia for fishing
the way we are going is transform-
There is, in fact, no way to get away.

thing traditional they'll still do

on an ice-covered body of water.
ing our vision. And the profound-
.
it, providing the weather permits.

Dressed as warmly as possible,
est changes take place in the
.
One thing I found a bit jarring

I drove up to the lake, chopped
things we thought the most
.
was the switching on of the electric lights that

holes in the ice, fixed hooks
familiar. On the first trip when
.
suddenly gave the effect of sun-

and lines and waited for
the cat was taken up to that
.
light streaming through the

little red flags, popping up,
town near Boston (because they were going
.
stained glass windows high above

to signal success. I heard
away) it got sick; they nursed it back.
.
the chorus and orchestra. I glanced

the sounds that travel through
On the second trip, the cat died.

.

along the sides of the chapel. The

the ice as it freezes; I was

.

.

windows there were not illuminated.

astonished. Later, I was on the

.

.

The tradition of focusing one's

ice as the sun, setting, colored

.

.

attention was being observed. The

both it and the sky. I was

.

.

electric candles were some white and

amazed. I remember I shrank

.

.

some a sort of highway brownish yellow.

in my own estimation. Before

.

.

.

I nearly froze, I collected all

.

.

.

my traps, no fish. I made a

.

What we do, we do without purpose.

.

mental note not to go ice-fishing

.

We are simply invited

.

again without a bottle of cognac.

.

to do it, by someone else

.

On the other hand, there are certain .

.

or by ourselves. And so we do this or that.

.

things I am taught (and I do want
The day before yesterday towards the

.

.

to learn them); for instance: if
middle of the afternoon I noticed

.

.

I will remember not just to touch

I was running out of matches.

•

•

wood but to rub my hand on
I went through pockets, under

•

•

it before I touch metal, then I
papers on tables and finally

•

•

won't get a shock. I had pre-
found a single match. Having

•

•

viously thought that if I picked
lit a cigarette, I decided to

•

We are not doing very much

up my feet as I walked
keep one lit constantly whether

•

of any one thing. We are continually

across the carpet or if I even
I was smoking or not. Oppressed

•

dropping one thing and picking

hopped through the room
by this obligation, I went down-

•

up another. We are, you might

before turning a doorknob or
stairs to the kitchen, found

•

say, concentrated inside and idiotic out.

a light switch that I
nothing, but picked up an

•

•

wouldn't get a shock. That
article by the man at the

•

•

doesn't work. The wood-rubbing
other end of the hall that happened

•

•

does work. The crux of the
to catch my eye. I read it,

•

•

matter is: will I remember
cooked dinner, went on working,

•

•

to rub wood first and, even
and managed through all of this

•

so, just in case I sometime
to light another cigarette be-

.

.

find myself in a situation
fore the burning one burned out.

.

.

where there isn't any wood
I determined to go to the movies

.

.

to rub, shouldn't I just
in order to get some matches.

.

.

decide, here and now, no
However, in the car, I found

.

.

matter where I go, to carry
some partly used folders of them

.

.

a piece of wood with me?
and just went to the movies uselessly.

.

.

Although we speak about going,
The next afternoon, the secretary

.

.

I notice that we spend a lot
came in and asked for a

.

.

of time waiting; that is, I wait.
match. I still had a few

.

.

And when I tell others about it,
left from those I'd found in the

.

He was afraid all along that he

they say they wait too.
car. I realized the situation

.

might lose his mind. He had no

.

was growing ticklish. I left and

.

fear of the cancer which killed him.

.

with the single purpose of getting
He gave rise to two schools, and repudiated

.

matches. I came back with an
them both. *That is partly true. We are*

.

Talking about death, we began
artichoke, a sweet potato, an onion
not just going: we are being swept away.

.

laughing. There had even been an
I didn't need (for I already
How was it she managed to teach me

.

attempted suicide. Which are
had one), three limes, two per-
that the play of her emotions needn't involve

.

you supposed to read: the
simmons, six cans of ale, a box
me? Christmas is here and then

.

article or the advertisements?
of cranberries and an orange, eggs,
shortly we'll be filling out the income tax.

.

I felt so miserable I went to
milk, and cream, and fortunately

.

.

sleep even though I'd just

I remembered the matches. That

.

.

gotten up. I decided to
evening the possibility of lighting

.

.

cancel everything. Instead
a cigarette on an electric stove

.

.

I went out in the woods and
was mentioned, an action

.

.

revived. Going into the unknown
with which I am fully familiar.
You remember the seeds? Well, today,

.

we have no use for value
It is fairly clear that we have
it was rubber bands (not flying

.

judgments. We are only greedy:
changed our direction, but it
through the air, but littering the
There are those who go part way

we want more and more while
is not so clear when we

sidewalk). *It would be so much*
but can't go any farther. And

there's still time. We're getting
did it. Was it in 1913 when
simpler if we were expressing
there is a great interest in going

around to the usefulness of science
Duchamp wrote his piece of music?
ourselves. In that case all you'd
and staying at the same time:

(I don't mean probability) (I mean
And since he didn't tell us, how
need for an understanding of
naturally not in the physical

seeing things just as they are in
did we know? Is what we're
what we're doing would be a
world, but in the world of art.

their state of chaos). And so, if
doing in the air or on the land?
large collection of city directories.
These people want somehow to

you were writing a song, would
When did competition cease?

·

keep alive the traditions and

you write music, or would you
Looking back, it all seems to

·

yet push them forward. It gets

write for a singer? "I can't even
have been done the way we are

·

rather superhuman as a

try," she said, "I can't whistle."
doing it. Even the old bridges.

·

project. The others don't care

·

·

·

so much about tradition, but hang on anyway.

·

·

·

·

·

·

·

·

·

·

·

·

·

·

·

We sometimes leave before we said

we would, and then by things beyond

our control arrive ahead of time. We

then imagine that it will be the same

coming back, and it is. They were in

Why didn't I bring my boots? I

an automobile together on the way to

have several pairs but I left

Oxford. It is remarkable what we are

them all where they are. I could

doing: even though we give the appearance of

•

say that I knew where I was

•

idiots, we are clearing things up considerably.

•

going but didn't know what it

•

Both the turnips and the sweet potatoes

•

would be like when I got there.

•

appeared to have been left to rot.

•

I would have brought some boots

One of the noticeable things about our
So I took some of each without

•

had I thought there was a chance

going is that we're all going
asking. It turned out I should have

•

of going mushrooming. I *did*

in different directions. That's
asked whether or not I might have the

•

bring the basket in which I often

because there's plenty of room.
turnips. No question of will you or

•

throw the boots, but this time

We're not confined to a path
won't you: we are inevitably going.

•

the boots are where they are; and

and so we don't have to follow

•

•

yet I could have put them to

in someone's footsteps even though

•

•

use. Often the reverse situation

that's what we're taught to do. We

•

•

arises: we get into a position

can go anywhere, and if we

•

•

with our art where we have

can't, we concentrate on finding

•

•

a need for something which

a way to get exactly there

•

•

we have never had and of

(if we know where there is).

.

.

the existence of which we have

There's so much to do, it's a

.

.

no knowledge. We then go to

waste of time to run around

.

.

a store that might carry

the house writing twelve-tone

.

.

such things and discover to

music. And that's the only musical

.

.

our delight that the tool was

way to go now if one's going

.

We go foolishly where angels fear
just invented and is in stock.

to go in the same direction

.

to tread (which is not to say that
That was more or less what

others go. That was Schoenberg's business.

.

we do not tremble) and in our
happened to the field of music

.

.

foolishness, we make connections
eleven or twelve years ago.

.

.

where there had been separateness.
And that concomitant going

.

.

We take things that were together
makes us sometimes say that

.

.

and pull them apart. We remove
things are in the air. Or

.

.

the glue but build invisible bridges.
the Lord is working or some

.

.

For the field is not not a field
such statement. The less we

Had a musician to choose between
·

of music, and the acceptance is
hold onto our going, the more

death, deafness, and blindness,
·

not just of the sounds that
this mysterious stream of gifts

which would he choose?
·

had been considered useless, ugly,
surrounds us or comes our

Death's inevitable, does not
·

and wrong, but it is a field
way. Say then that we are

sting, and time shows it's good
·

of human awareness, and the
generally active but not specifically

for music. Blindness would cer-
·

acceptance ultimately is
doing just this but able to employ

tainly sharpen his sense of
Say I've accepted two invitations and they're
of oneself as present mysterious-
for no purpose whatever comes our way.

hearing. Deafness ... well ...

both for the same time. In certain
ly, impermanently, on
·

Beethoven. The lake up above
cases, I could speed up, as it were, and
this limitless occasion.
·

where we live used to be a town.
accept both, spending less time with
·
·

When the people who lived there
each. In another case, it would be
·
·

were told to leave because the
physically impossible to go to both, in which
·
·

waters were being let in, they,
case a choice would have to be made.
Shall I give up mushrooms and
·

most of them, did leave. A few
One obligation is then dropped and every-
study the trees? By all means. They
We are inclined to think that

insisted on staying and had
thing goes smoothly. How, however,

go together almost alarmingly
things are done better when they're

to be rescued from the roofs
do we regain the sense of duty? I told
clearly. What dogged determination
done the first time. That, for

of their homes by policemen
her several times I'd bring her mush-
made my mind shuttle back and
instance, as we go on doing

in rowboats. On the north
rooms; why is it I never have?
forth on one track? We only
the same thing, it gets worse

side of this lake there were here
.
make choices when it's absolutely
rather than better. So many

and there grapevines, not wild,
.
necessary. If we have something
things in history exemplify

but wildly growing, excellent for
.
to do, we don't question whether
this deterioration in going.

jelly. One year I made, if I
.
it is worth while; we just do it.

However, when our eyes get

do say so, good grape jelly
.
The reason we waste our time so
used to the dark, we see that

from those grapes. Next year
.
willingly is that our ideas about
it's not so bad after all.

I gathered a greater quantity
.
usefulness were so limited.
We enjoy hearing about night-

although I was told by an
.
When someone with his nose to the
mares but we feel we are

inspector that it was against
.
grindstone tells us we needn't bother
going along in sunlight doing

regulations. Anyway, while cooking,
.
to do such and such, we get the
the things we do. He said,

I got something else on my
We will not go unless we have no alter-
impression that's something might
when I explained that formerly

mind and the jelly burned—
native. They were the wrong ages and related.
interest us. We study how not to
I had to keep my house and

not with the sugar in it
The doctor who gave the adjustment butchered
stick to our work. Of course, if
desk in order and that my

but before, when I was
the deer. It was an invention? The
we have too much to do,
first work each day consisted

expressing the juice. Now, of
telegram arrived but never departed.
studying being interrupted, we try first
in copying over neatly the

course, all the vines are gone.
The picture on the front page has no caption.
to do everything, and if we
work of the previous day—

They're putting in a parking
.

can't, then, as a last resort,
he said, "That's the way I do

lot and a beach for swimming
He told me about the seeds that whirl
we choose, not so much what
it now." But I made a

so that two thousand people can
and showed me one; I think he
we'll do as, regretfully, what
sweeping gesture around

swim at once. We do not
said they were from the tulip tree—
we won't. But this choice is
the room suggesting the

determine where we go by
and in the wind, he said, they go great
not made on any basis such
embrace of the chaos that one

where we'd like to go. We are
distances. I looked out the window
as "What would please us the most?"
could see there. The house-

too aware of everywhere.
just now. They suggest an innovation in toys.
There again, what we find most
keeper does nothing about

That is, woods, for instance,
.

pleasing is that our tastes are
it because he is instructed

any woods will do for my
.

not limited the way they were.
not to touch any papers.

wandering in them, and

They're getting catholic, we might
There are advantages and

nothing could be more

.

say. Naturally, we don't want
disadvantages. It takes time

frustrating than our necessary

.

to kill ourselves. At the same
to find something you're

long trips that take us quickly

.

time, we realize we're on a sinking
thinking of, but in the course

over large territories, each

.

ship. We come up with a version
of looking for it all sorts of

square foot of which would

.

of the Golden Rule, but we're not
things come up that one was

be suitable for exploration.

.

certain how we'd like to be done
not looking for. You might

Need I say?—Not only woods, but

.

by. We suspect, rather we know,
call living in chaos an

sounds, people, hook-ups, protests.

.

there are pleasures beyond our
exteriorization of the mind.

.

.

cautious past experience. If they
It is as though the things in

.

.

say, for instance, "That music hurt
the room, in the world, in the

.

.

my ears," we immediately think it
woods, were the means of thinking.

.

.

probably didn't, that what were hurt

.

In a grand sense, I do what you

.

were mental attitudes and feelings, and these

.

do and you do what I do.

.

make us rampant. Traffic continues.

.

Thus it is economical for each

.

.

.

one of us to be original. We get

.

.

.

more done by not doing what

.

.

.

someone else is doing. This

.

.

.

way we can speed up history—

.

.

Originally we had in mind what

the one we're making. No need

.

.

you might call an imaginary

for competition, even with

.

.

beauty, a process of basic

oneself. After all, we're all

.

.

emptiness with just a few

the same species and we live on the

.

.

things arising in it. What we

same planet. And I am not who I was.

.

.

had there in mind was not

.

We are trying to go fast enough

.

so much ours (but we thought

.

to catch up with ourselves. This

.

it was) as it was something

We were artisans; now we're
helps to keep us ignorant of

.

like those Japanese gardens

the observers of miracle. All you
knowing where we are going.

.

with a few stones in them.

have to do is go straight on,
Things come in and we send
·
And then when we actually

leaving the path at any moment,
answers. By slow and fast mail,
·
set to work, a kind of

and to the right or to the left,
telegram, and telephone. Now and
·
avalanche came about which

coming back or never, coming
then we appear in person to one
·
corresponded not at all

in, of course, out of the rain.
another. An announcement arrived.
·
with that beauty which had

·
There she was with her back to me painting
·
seemed to appear to us as an

·
with a stick as long as that of a broom.
·
objective. Where do we go

·

·
·
then? Do we turn around?

·
·
·
Go back to the beginning and

·
·
·
change everything? Or do

·
·
·
we continue and give up

·
·
·
what had seemed to be

·
·
·
where we were going? Well,

·
Those signs that are misplaced—
·
what we do is go straight

·
the ones on the street over to the

•

on; that way lies, no doubt,

•

left—the one-way street (there

•

a revelation. I had no idea

•

are two signs, each saying "One way,"

•

this was going to happen. I

•

and they point towards one

•

did have an idea something

•

another—that is, they are at cross

•

else would happen. Ideas

•

purposes): were they misplaced by

•

are one thing and what

•

children? and is that what was

•

happens another. At this

•

meant by the Scripture, that we would

•

point again space between

•

be led by children? I asked

•

things is useful. But we

•

the man at the toll booth

•

are not going into retirement.

•

what would be my best bet:

•

If we are islands, we are

•

he said just go straight ahead.

•

glass ones with no blinds

•

I noted that the road shortly

•

but plenty of old shoes

•

became very confusing. He said,

•

lying around. Also these

•

"Why should it?" A car behind

•

islands are not cubes but

made me proceed against my

·

are spheres: we go out

·

better judgment. We purposefully

·

from them in any direction,

The weather's changing. We are
do what is unnecessary. And

·

not just north, east, south,

busy doing what we do. We take
we have the brass to say that

·

and west. Field therefore is

time, now and then, not to see what
that is exactly what had to be

·

not explicit as a term of

someone's doing but what he did.
done. We have come (or are we
I must say I was surprised
description. And thus a piece

We see that to look at an object,
still going?) (someone wrote that
to read that he had no interest
of paper also falsifies the

a work of art, say, we have to
we've touched bottom—an imper-
in food. If I hadn't been told,
situation. One way or another,

see it as something happening,
manent bottom, he hastened to add, but
I would have surmised that he
we are obliged to be able to go in *all* directions.

not as it did to him who made it,
then added that we truly have
was a gourmet. Not at all. It

·

but as it does while we see it.
touched bottom as far as our
appears that he preferred food to

·

We don't have to go anywhere:
knowledge and tools are concerned).
be the same (providing he found

·

it comes to us. It's a bright
As I was saying: we have come
some he enjoyed), the same each day.

·

sunny day, but that man's
(or are we still going?) to a

·

·

windshield-wipers are working.

WHERE ARE WE GOING? AND WHAT ARE WE DOING?/223

point where it is necessary to
We who speak English were so

.

It looks as though I will one day
speak at cross purposes with what
certain of our language and that

.

be able to look at a tree and speak its
we are saying. It is because what-
we could use it to communicate
We are still going and we are

name, and if that happens, going
ever we were saying so failed to
that we have nearly destroyed
certain that we will never get there.

along with it will be a change
hit the mark. Now at last we know that
its potential for poetry. The
It is just as I thought: the

of attitude towards winter, just
saying one thing requires saying
thing in it that's going to save
children are out playing and

as fungi have given me a
the opposite in order to keep the
the situation is the high percentage
the rest of us are running the

change of attitude towards rain. Getting
whole statement from being like

of consonants and the natural way
danger of not being able to

rid of leaves makes trees visible.
a Hollywood set. Perhaps it would
in which they produce discontinuity.
do what we have to do. And

.

be better to be silent, but a) someone

.

so, to put it bluntly, what

.

else would be speaking; and b) it

.

will we do if we cannot

.

wouldn't keep us from going and we

.

go on with what we are doing?

.

would continue doing what we

.

I congratulate myself that I

.

are doing. I remember once his
What do we like? We do not like
had the good sense to put the car in a garage.

.

saying: "But this opens up
to be pushed around emotionally or to

·

an entirely untouched field
have impressive constructions of re-

·

·

of poetry." And to this day
lationships push us. We can

·

·

neither one of us has budged
manage to do something with

·

·

to move into that untouched
such situations (if we have to

· ɛ

·

open field. I put it away.
be present) such as pinning our

·

·

Today in the newspaper they
attention to some natural event

·

·

bring up the subject, but con-
which is either in the work

·

·

tinue: "Persons who threaten to
or ambient to it but irrelevant

·

·

take their lives and are picked
to its intention. I was asked about

·

·

up by the police here will
the music for the Candlelight Concert

·

·

not be jailed any more, but
and I remarked that it would

·   .

·

will be taken to the hospital instead."
be a pleasure to hear the

·

·

·

motets and the Christmas carols

·

·

·

but that excerpts from the

·

.

oratorio were too much. The

.

.

reply was, "But don't you enjoy

.

.

being moved?" (I enjoy being

.

.

interrupted but not pushed.)

.

.

.

Other people came and some left

.

Dropping everything and going is not

.

and in the conversation my

.

as simple as it sounds. You find

.

answer was given to a person

.

you forgot to go through your

.

who had not asked the question.

. .

pockets; and then again that if

.

I quoted: "The purpose of music

.

you didn't actually take something

.

is to sober and quiet the mind,

.

along, that something stuck to

.

thus making it susceptible to divine

.

you that you failed to notice.

.

influences." Shortly three of us left

.

One might say, "Well, let it, since

.

and were out in the sharp

.

everything goes and there is no
We are doing only what is necessary.
clear winter night. We walked

.

question of value, etc." But
Once when I thought I was going east, I

along and then into the apartment

.

here is a rub: that is only
went west. Do I assume the microscope will be
(not the air-conditioned one) and

.

the case when somehow you've
ruined? Poison ivy this time but not the other.
I asked whether they had music

.

managed to drop everything. **Do**
The appointment is for 9:00 A.M. Friday.
in their Quaker meetings and of

.

we do it and then go? Are our
.
course they don't. And yet his

.

means suitable for this objective?

.

ears are marvelously open when

.

Examine them carefully with accuracy.
.
we walk in the woods. He hears

.

Repeat the examination daily. **This**
.
the different sounds the wind

.

brings up the subject of anonymity.

.

makes, up at the top of the
I was absolutely amazed to hear

But it can be dropped. Here I am.
.
ridge and down by the stream and
him describing to me the beauties

My work is something else.
.
in different trees. He hears them all
of the long line in music, and

.

.

together and distinguishes them. He`
lamenting its absence in the

.

.

told me about the suit he was wear-
pulverized, fragmented modern

We are losing our sense of values
.
ing, a hand-woven tweed, and the
music. And I was amazed

and we are getting increased awareness.
.
difficulties attached to finding a
too that when the nature

We are giving up pride and shame and

.

tie that had the rust color
of the pulverization was pointed

getting interested in whatever comes

.

of one of the threads in the
out, that he continued to

our way or to which we get. Who knows?

.

material. His daughter sent
say something was missing,

If, after thought, I come to the con-

.

him a tie recently, and since
namely the long line.

clusion that *Cantherellus umbonatus* grows

.

she has a fine sense of color, it
(She too had said, "Give me a

most plentifully where there is not

.

matches perfectly, but the suit
line and I'll be able to hang

only the hair-capped moss but also

.

is wearing out. The cleaner in
anything on it.") But the

young junipers, dampness, and some

.

fact said there is nothing more
other one, she who came

sun, how do you explain that to-

.

to be done to save it. Before I left,
from India, was grateful

day in a more or less open field

.

they brought out a dress from Guatemala.
for silence. She could see

we were stepping on them? To be

.

.

easily the possibility of the

sure there was moss, but it was a sit-

.

.

omission of a constant

uation like ones in which I'd only met

.

.

connective. Nothing needs

with failure. While we're on the sub-

.

.

to be connected to anything

ject, how is it I lost interest in the

.

.

else since they are not

Greeks? Now they interest me

.

separated irrevocably to begin

very much. It seems they weren't

.

.

with. Past appearances are

so devoted to the gods after all. Tragedy?

.

to some blinding and to others

.

.

.

clarifying. Right now perhaps

.

.

.

again the children are teaching

.

We are going into the field of frequency

.

us. They have no conception of

.

and that doesn't mean that we are

.

a long line. They have only

.

leaving the notes of the major and minor

.

a short attention span. And

.

scales and the modes, for they are

.

the mass media—they take it

.

in the field we're going into. The

.

for granted that we, like

.

same holds true for the field of

.

children, need to have every-

.

amplitude, the field of timbre, the

.

thing constantly changing. I

.

field of duration, the field of space.

.

can find no example now

.

Though we are not leaving any-

.

in our consciousness of

.

thing, our notations are changing

.

the necessity in us for a long

.

and sometimes even disappearing.

.

line outside of us. (She called

.

Usefulness is uppermost in our

.

it the uncommitted void.) If

.

minds. We begin to be certain

we were really prepared we would

.

that we never were where we

.

need not only boots but roller

.

thought we were, that not only

.

skates too. Then we could visit

.

were mistakes made on occasion,

.

the museums with the long halls

.

noticeable wrong notes, but that the

.

lined with art. Do you suppose

.

whole kit and caboodle was a mis-

.

that eventually they will clear

.

take. The Cuban boy is partly German.

.

everything up? Enough so that

.

.

.

the children will have to stop

.

.

.

playing? There is a fear too

.

Our sense of whether or not we did

.

there that an idea which is

.

what we said we would do is slipping.

.

not in line will somehow

·

What will we do now? I noticed, magnificent

·

cause one to lose the thread.

·

as he is, that he can't tell where he's going.

·

What results is work without

·

·

·

interruption, apologies for

·

·

·

absence of quality, and shortness

'

·

·

of quantity and complaints

·

·

·

that they did something to

·

'

·

it which was not part

·

·

·

of the original intention.

·

·

·

·

·

·

·

·

·

·

·

·

·

·

·

·

·

·

·

We will change direction constantly.

·

·

·

People have arrived from out of town.

.

.

.

We are having two or three gatherings at once.

.

.

.

It was before dawn: I looked out

.

.

.

the window and there he was

.

.

walking down the street in the dark.

.

.

.

It turned out he was not in town at

.

.

.

all. I had seen someone else. We celebrate.

.

Between 1930 or say 1929 and 1942

.

We don't have to make special arrangements.

.

I moved around a good deal.

.

.

.

I got the impression that I

.

.

.

never stayed any place more

.

There is a story that is to the

than a year. I was full of

.

.

point. A man was born in

purpose. Ask me what it was

.

.

Austria. When he came into

and I couldn't really tell you.

.

.

his inheritance, he gave all

Jobs. Actually, I still have

.

.

his money away. He engaged

the same goal in mind. What

.

.

in a wide variety of activities

I've always wanted and still want

.

.

one after the other. When

is a Center for Experimental Music.

.

.

the War came along, he went

Perhaps, some day, maybe when I

.

.

into it. He continued his

can just barely whisper in accept-

.

.

activity during the War and

ance, they'll say, "Why! of course

.

.

even his correspondence. Later

you can have it. Here it is,

.

.

he moved back and forth between

a big, beautiful Center for Ex-

.

.

more or less the same countries

perimental Music, replete with

.

.

and, as I say elsewhere, he

Festivals of Contemporary Music

.

.

started at different times

that'll make America look as

.

.

different schools and repudiated

wide awake as Europe. Make

.

.

both of them which is only

any sounds you like: loud-speakers,

.

.

partly true. He moved around

tape machines; that's nothing,

.

.

a good deal and even came

you can have a super synthe-

I know that if I managed to tell you

•

to America and then he went

sizer. **What more do you**
where we are going, it wouldn't

•

back; he had been at one

want? **You can have it." Well,**
interest you, and it shouldn't except

•

time in Ireland and he

every time I moved, I used to
as conversation. (But I am going

•

began to more and more

look through my papers, letters,
alone; in the Martian anal-

•

include it in the places

music, and so forth, and I threw a-
ysis we are all one happy

•

to which he went and he

way whatever I thought I could
family.) I mentioned that nothing

•

included Norway. He found

just to lighten the travel. **That**
seemed irrelevant and he said, "Yes,

•

a rare mushroom and since

way **I threw away all my**
we see more and more connections."

•

it was in a dry season **he**

earliest work. **There used to**
But we are doing something else:

•

built a protection **for it**

be, for instance, some settings
we are putting separations between

•

and provided it with water.

to choruses from *The Persians* by
each thing and its other. And why is it, when

•

Fulfilling other commitments

Aeschylos and an *Allemande*. **But**
we have no silence, they say, "Why didn't you?"

•

and yet studying the growth

before that there were some

•

•

of the fungus, he involved

short, very short, pieces composed

•

•

himself in many trips of 250 miles

by means of mathematical formulae.

.

.

each. Is that what we are doing?

What do you think, moving off

.

.

.

as we might, all of us, to the

.

.

.

moon, might we not all of us look through

.

.

.

our papers? Father's foot: twice he

.

.

.

went out to pick flowers for Mother

.

We will never have a better

and wounded himself seriously, once

.

.

idea of what we're doing than

up a tree, cutting nearly through his

.

.

we do right now. It is not

wrist; lately in a back yard a

.

.

in the nature of doing to

thorn pierced the flesh of his ankle.

.

It is interesting when we hear
improve but rather to come

It's been a year and a half going on two years.

.

that someone has traveled to a
into being, to continue, to

.

.

foreign country, one he was never
go out of being and to

.

.

in before. It is also interesting
be still, not doing. That

.

.

when we hear that someone has
still not-doing is a

homes in various places all
preparation. It is not

What are we doing about technique?
.
over the world. And if we hear
just static: it is a quiet

We can use it or leave it alone.
.
that someone does not travel
readiness for whatever and

We can remember the old ones and
.
at all, or very little, that too is inter-
the multiplicities are already

invent new ones. If you are o-
.
esting. We heard that they might have
there in the making. We watch

bliged to whistle and can't, there
.
gone to Finland but didn't; that
for signs and accept omens.

remains the possibility of buying
.
was not interesting. We, too,
Everything is an omen, so

a whistle which you can surely

.
have not gone to Finland, and
we continue doing and changing.

blow. We are not bound hand
.
what will be interesting is news
Do we have, if not ideas

and foot even if we were never
.
that someone's actually gone there.
about what we're doing,

taught to sing or to play an in-
.
In our own experience, we some-
feelings about our actions,

strument. We can be silent and
.
times have the impression that
what we've made? We're

so forth. In fact, technically speaking,
.
we are the first ones to ever
losing them because we're

we are in possession of a vast
.
be in a particular place, but
no longer making objects

repertoire of ways of producing
.

we do not trust this impression.
but processes and it is easy

sound. What is it that makes
.

We feel it rising up like an
to see that we are not separate

anyone say, "I can't"? Busy doing
.

atmosphere around us and we
from processes but are in them,

something else? Shall we then
.

find it a kind of hallucination
so that our feelings are not

all gather at the River? Stick
.

which does not let us see clearly
about but *in* them. Criticism

together? We have multiplied
.

where we are. If we want to go
vanishes. Awareness and use

ourselves geometrically and our
.

where no one else has ever gone
and curiosity enter into

inclination is to be alone when-
.

(and still not go out into space),

making our consciousness. We

ever possible, except when loneliness
.

we will have two good bets:
are glad to see that we are

sets in. Sixty people all singing
.

areas environmental to highly
noticing what happens. Asked

in chorus like angels only make
.

attractive points which are
what happened, we have to

us pray that once in Heaven,
.

exceedingly difficult to get to,
say we don't know, or we

God lets us anarchistic be! Why
.

and areas which are unattractive,
could say we see more

did we go in our arts to order and
.

period. It is these latter that are
clearly but we can't tell you what we see.

many people doing the same thing
.

so useful: a) because they're all
.

together, when, given an opportunity
.
around us (Americans); b) because we can
.

for a vacation, we look for a spot
.
actually go to them instead of just
.

where we know (statistically) no
.
talking about going (as we might
.

one we know will be? We go
.
have to do in the other case);
.

into a crowd with a sharp
.
c) because the experience erodes our
.

awareness of the idiosyncrasies
.
preconceptions about what attracts
.

of each person in it, even if
.
us. Nevertheless we would still like
.

they're marching, and we along
.
to have a Center for Experimental Music.

with them. We see, to put it
We can tell very easily whether
.
.

coldly, differences between two things
something we're doing is con-
.
.

that are the same. This enables
temporarily necessary. The way
.
.

us to go anywhere alone or with
we do it is this: if something
.
.

others and any ordinarily too
else happens that ordinarily would
Will we ever again really bother
.

large number of others. We could
be thought to interrupt it
to describe in words or notation
.

take a vacation in a hotel on

doesn't alter it, then it's work-
the details of something that

.

Times Square. But what we do
ing the way it now must. This state-
has not then yet happened? Many

.

see is that we have to give up
ment is in line and can be illustrated
will do this and the changes in sol-

.

our ideas about where we are
by former statements I have
fège that will soon take place in

.

going since if we don't, we
made about painting and music
the schools are alarming just to

.

won't get anywhere. If you'd
but here extend to doing: that
imagine. There will be an

.

asked me a few years ago
is (about painting): if the
increase in the amount of time

.

or even just last year whether
work is not destroyed by

we spend waiting—waiting for

.

I'd like to live in an air-
shadows; and (about music):
machines to do what we planned

.

conditioned suite where I
if the work is not destroyed
for them to do, and then discovering

.

wouldn't be able to open the
by ambient sounds. And so
a mistake was made or the

.

windows, I would have given you a flat No.
the doing not destroyed by
circuits were out, and finally

.

.

simultaneous simisituated
getting an acceptable approximation.

.

.

action. It must then have no
This is not unrelated to thinking

.

.

objective, no goal. Time must be of
the recording, say, of the sound

.

little—I was going to say
of a gong is the sound

.

.

no—consequence. (I pray one
of the gong when it isn't recorded.

.

.

day I may.) But other
It is at this crossroads that

.

.

prayers would be: Dear Lord,
we must change direction, if,

.

.

let me not run out of ink
that is, we are going where we

.

.

(I have committed myself to
are going. (I know perfectly

.

.

quantity); and Dear Lord, do
well I'm wandering but I try to

.

If we really did change, we wouldn't
let me catch up, otherwise
see what there is to see and

.

have to bother about practicing. Of
I will have to become not
my eyes are not as good as

.

course, we'd gradually slip out of doing
contemporary (in my terms)
they were but they're improving.)

.

all the things we practiced. And then when
but ancient (in my terms)
We make then what we do

.

we started going, it would be in a
working like a monk in
virtually unnoticeable, so that

.

state of not knowing. We would be
a tower with a princess
you could even have missed

.

as interested as anybody else. Have
of his own imagination.
the point of its beginning and

.

painters always been looking?
I refuse art if that is what
not be certain about the events

.

Musicians, *mirabile dictu,* **are just**
it is but unless I am cautious
(whether they were "in" or "out" of it) to

.

beginning to listen. (It was some-
that is precisely what it will
say nothing of its ending. Nothing

.

thing else to say it's a good thing the
become (mine, I mean: He came
special. Nothing predetermined. Just

.

children, aged five and seven, are being
in and warned me; and then
something useful to set the
I have just ascertained that

taught solfège.) **Are we on foot**
another and thanked me for
thing going. We could say to
the clock is twenty-five minutes fast.

or in the air? **That's an important**
Mallarmé and job; and then
ourselves: "Beware of setting
That means that I still have

question when it's a question of

I sneezed). I am not obliged
out in search of something
time, probably not enough to

going. **By what bleak chain**
to tell you all of this: I am
interesting"; and, "Beware of doing
finish what I'm doing but

of events did we exchange the
obliged to speak to you and
special things to make two
time. It is extremely unpredictable

chain store for the market place?
that is what we (you and I) are
things more different than they
what will happen next and

Conversation, the food itself, these and
doing. And now I've just heard
are"; "Beware in fact of the
that, of course, is largely

how much else down the drain?
about Marchetti. They've made
tendency to stop and start." "But
due to the weather. We made

.

a mistake. I do hope it isn't
we must have something to do!"
our arrangements very early

.

a mistake. Hidalgo's gone to

.

in advance and they even

.

Paris and Marchetti's gone to

.

include dinner (I have no

.

Milan and Spain is left without

.

idea what we'll eat or

.

anyone. What we need now is not

.

indeed whether I'll get there

.

disarmament and people marching in

.

and whether the plans still

.

the streets but someone, someone

.

hold and whether if they do

.

active active in Spain interested

.

hold I'll be able to get every-

.

in modern art. Why do they all

.

thing done that I have in

.

leave it? What is wrong with Spain?

.

mind to do. This is our

.

.

.

immediate and permanent

.

.

.

condition and we just fail

.

.

.

continually to notice it even

.

.

.

when we think we agree.

.

.

.

If, for instance, as may well

.

What's doing? (Never a dull moment.)

.

have been the case, if someone

It's snowing. It began in the night.

.

procrastinated, then what?

.

The roofs and eaves of the houses

.

The obstacles I foresee to the

.

are white and the natural

.

fulfillment of my obligation

.

tendency of the ends of the

.

which is what we are doing

.

branches of the hemlocks to

.

are only a few. Why don't

.

droop has been encouraged. The

.

I see the others? Don't I

.

traffic continues more or less as

.

have eyes and a head and

.

doggedly as it did yesterday. Are

.

ears? They are not as good

What we need are machines that will
people the way "their land and air

.

as they were and also the

enable us to do all the things we could
is"? If so, should they not have

.

metabolism and perhaps they're

do before we had them plus all the
four or five purposes (instead of one)

.

getting worse. We are now

new things we don't yet know we
and let those interpenetrate with

.

told we'll be able to get so

can do. Perhaps you would say we
one another in some interesting
So often we think that something
far but no further and a

are going mad. We are certainly
natural way? For instance: this
needs to be devious, so that we
day ago we were told it would

aimless or you might say that is

snow is not a proper winter
go to no end of trouble to do
be impossible to go in that

our aim. We are needlessly finicky
snow. It seems more like the
something that could be done
direction because there was no

when it comes to our notice that
last one does just before spring
straightforwardly. (In this particular
money. There was money for

somebody else did it before we
arrives. But the caretaker who
case I am obliged to do four
the eyes but no money for

did it. And generally speaking, it
swept the sidewalk is already
times as much work as I would
the ears. They're going to do

does come to our notice. A little
thinking of the ice to come.
in a conventional fulfillment of the
it anyway and just let the

bit of the scientific attitude, however,
"Those stones are mighty slippery!
same duty.) (Furthermore, I've committed
ears go along with the eyes

and you soon see that what was
There'll be more than one person

myself to thoughts about relevancy
in a kind of slapdash way.

just done was not at all what
falls down this winter!" Bird
and irrelevancy in addition to
Where is their sense of urgency?

was done before except as regards
maddened by the length of its
stories and subjects and where
.

the general situation. There was, by
own winter. But now (as I
are we going and what are we doing.)
.

way of example, a discontinuity of
say elsewhere) the trees are changing
I thought, for instance, when I
.

particles, then there was emptiness
me—my attitude towards winter
first saw the book that it was
.

(which now seems like a melody).
is changing because of the way
probably out of print even
.

Just now there was raw material. Repetition?
one can see the trees in the winter.
though they told me it wasn't.

What I assumed took place
I looked for it in bookstores

Is there a story in the fact that we
in spring has already
and never wrote to the publisher.

call someone to discover that there
taken place: the buds are
Nor did I ask anyone to write

is no answer? And would you say
there on the trees already. With
for me. However, when I met

such a story would be relevant
our eyes and our ears, we do
someone who lived in the town

or irrelevant to our subject: Where
more by doing nothing and just
where the book is published

are we going? Now we have the
giving attention to the natural
I asked him if he'd mind

example of a young composer
busyness. Was what I did
going to the publisher's office

going into the army at a point
interrupted by what happened?
and finding out whether the

in his life when going seemed
If so, it was not contemporary
book was available. I did say,

really unfortunate. And yet it
doing. And equally, it works
"Don't take the trouble until you

has worked out extraordinarily
equally the other way: Does
hear from me." Before writing

well: a great deal of music
what I do interrupt the
to this person, I finally wrote

has been written, lectures given,
changes in weather? This is
directly to the publisher and

and article written and perform-
a corollary to Satie's statement
a week or so later the book

.

ances, live and broadcast, given.
about the necessity for a music
finally arrived. Now the question

.

And a raise, which involved
which would not interrupt the
arises (which I find more and

.

carrying a gun which however
sounds of knives and forks and
more ridiculous, because the

.

is never used and rarely, for
the conversation of friends at table.
answer could be this or that and

.

that reason, requires cleaning.
Put the two together and you
it could be refused or accepted

.

He had done what he could to keep
have an American Picnic.
by something no more solid than

.

from getting in it. But once in,

You know what this absence of
a whim): the question arises:

.

going along as usual with
boredom does? It turns each
What can be said to be

.

changes, very interesting changes.
waking hour musical just as
irrelevant and what can be

.

We are going in such a way that
for years now (on the street), in
said to be relevant and what

.

even if we do what we would
the woods, wherever (I remember
keeps a story from becoming a

.

if we liked (as though entranced),
pavement waiting for a bus), each
subject and indeed vice versa?

.

our activity meets with alter-
place is an active exhibition.

.

.

ation. It is entirely possible that I

.

.

.

cross the room to burst a balloon

.

.

.

which when I was not looking

.

.

.

was removed. In such a case,

.

.

.

would it not have been more

.

.

.

realistic of me to have gone

.

.

.

across the room with nothing in

.

We cannot know now

.

mind about balloons and burst-

.

whether we are continuing or

.

ing them? (They will tell us

.

whether shortly there's going

.

in that case that it is not

.

to be an interruption, after

.

music but some kind of choreo-

.

which we will pick up where

.

graphy.) However, it is music

.

we left off. We have a way

.

the way it's apt to be going.

.

of knowing but we are conscientious-

.

We're not going to go on playing

.

ly not using it. We are

.

games, even if the rules are

.

cultivating disorder in ourselves.

.

downright fascinating. We re-

.

Perhaps this seems ridiculous

.

quire a situation more like

.

but it seems sensible when we

.

it really is—no rules at all.

.

see that the order we cultivated

.

Only when we make them

.

was also of our own making. So
"This has nothing to do with it,"

do it in our labs do crystals

.

in a sense we are simply doing
we say, but it is descriptive

win our games. Do they then? I wonder.

.

what we left undone, but we
of what we are doing and where

.

.

are not extending our knowledge.
we are going that we doubt

.

.

We are learning to say, "I don't
whether we could verify our

.

.

know." Another way to say is:
statement. We know perfectly

.

.

"We don't need a release because
well now that this has

.

.

we are in release." We noticed
something very much to do

.

.

in foreign countries a vast
with everything else. That

.

.

difference between occasions, between
that seems gray, undifferentiated,

.

.

strictness and freedom, and we
inarticulate to us only

.

•

are smoothing out that difference
repeats what nineteenth-century

•

•

mostly by making things which
criticism had to say for

•

•

seem to be boring. ("They are not
the musics of India and

•

•

boring but very interesting.")
China. Everything is articulated.

•

•

I think the knowledge as it
We don't have to do it. In fact,

•

•

gets extended (and you see that
the sharpness increases as we

•

•

I mean information) will get
lay hands off. There are

•

•

into books that will be read
temptations for us to stop

•

•

not by us but by machines, because
what we're doing and make

•

•

there will by that time be too many.
a connection that will

•

•

As it is now, there is only one
be overwhelming. Well, perhaps

•

•

secretary. When the phone
it is. I haven't seen yet.

•

•

rings, she has to run down
I've seen some. But I'm

•

•

the hall to discover whether
losing my ability to make

•

•

so and so is in or out, and

connections because the ones

.

.

then come back alone or
I do make so belittle the

.

.

accompanied as the case may
natural complexity. Now

.

.

be. That is a kind of inefficiency.
and then I'll file things

.

.

The other kind is connected with
away (there is a file and

.

Another thing we're doing is
the fact that the windows
I can use the alphabet, even

.

leaving the things that are in us
cannot be opened. Perhaps telephones
though the secretary only

.

in us. We are leaving our emotions
in graduated sizes would solve the problem.
went as far as S and since

.

where they are in each one of us. One of

.

she's not English-speaking

.

us is not trying to put his emo-

.

by birth—that is, her own

.

tion into someone else. That way

.

alphabet was different from

.

you "rouse rabbles"; it seems on

.

ours—she's got some of

.

the surface humane, but it

.

the letters in the file upside

.

animalizes, and we're not doing

.

down. I can use them, though,

.

it. The cool other thing we

.

right side up or upside down.

•

are also not doing: that is,

•

When I get everything put

•

making constructions of relation-

•

away, then the housekeeper

•

ships that are observed by us.

•

can come in and dust.

•

That faculty of observing relation-

•

By that time I trust the

•

ships we are also leaving in

•

bulbs will have started

•

us, not putting the observation

•

sprouting. Now they are in

•

of one into the other who, it goes

•

the dark where we are. Satie's

•

without saying, see things from his

•

remark to the tree will do but

•

own point of view which is

•

I am not certain any one

•

different from another's. We

•

of us remembers it. Something

•

can of course converse (and do)

•

about never having done any

•

and we can say: "Stand where

•

harm or any good either

•

I stand and look over there and

•

to anyone. It was while

•

see what I see." This is called

•

he was on one of his return

•

lordly entertainment, but we do

nocturnal walks home.

Last year I gave a concert and answered
not thereby pull ourselves up
•

•

questions afterwards. This year some-
by our bootstraps nor do we see.
•

•

one said, "I was present at your lecture
Thus in his teaching, he makes
•

•

and hope to have the chance sometime to
presents silently, and it is only
•

•

hear your music." How can you tell
because I am slow-witted that,
•

•

whether someone's going or staying?
in impatience, he gives hints,
•

•

If he says, speaking of three things,
suggestions. We are all
•

"Put this in the foreground and the others
so busy, we have no time for
•

•

in the background," you know he's
one another. By keeping things
•

•

staying. If, however, he says,
in that are in and letting those
•

•

"I can't find any place to divide
things that are out stay out, a
•

•

it; in fact, I don't know how big
paradox takes place: it becomes
•

•

it is and as a matter of fact I'm
a simple matter to make an
•

•

just using the word 'it' as a
identification with someone or
•

•

convenience because I don't know
something. But this is virtually

.

.

anything about it," you know he's go-
impossible in terms of ideas and

.

.

ing. In the field and where he
feelings. Purposeless play there is un-

.

.

goes, there go we. There are times
Bodhisattvic and only leads to a conflagra-

.

.

when I get out of the house
tion, a more or less catastrophic
That he enjoyed going to the

.

with the jacket on that belongs
social situation, public or
movies is interesting. (She doesn't.)

.

to the pants that are still hanging in the closet.
private, that has brought down
And that he liked to sit in the

.

.
on our heads the arm of the
front row, which gave him the

.

.
law (it was such employment
feeling of a shower bath. Our

.

.
of feelings and ideas letting
family doctor brought himself back

.

.
them go out that brings about
from blindness by sitting in the

.

.
naturally the consequence of
front row at movies (together

.

.
police and don't do this and the
with staring at the sun).

.

.
entire web of rules). But what
Some people are coming out

.

.

we are doing is in our ways of art
of church and others are on their

·

·

to breathe again in our lives anarchistically.
way in. Apparently it's continuous.

·

·

·

·

·

·

·

·

·

·

·

·

·

·

·

·

·

·

·

·

·

·

·

·

·

·

·

·

·

·

·

·

·

·

·

·

·

·

·

·

·

·

·

·

·

·

·

·

·

·

·

·

·

·

·

·

·

·

·

·

·

·

·

·

·

·

·

·

·

·

·

·

When they wanted to photograph

·

·

·

her, they asked her what she could

·

·

·

do. She said she could put on

·

·

·

her hat or take it off. What we

·

·

·

can do is this or that at the

·

·

drop of a hat. Actually what

·

·

we do is drop one hat and pick

·

·

up another. It is as though

·

·

we were painting on silk

·

·

and could not erase. And

·

·

yet erasing quite completely

.

.

.

is one of the easiest things now

.

.

.

for us to do. Are we then

It is not a question of decisions and

.

.

erasing as though it were on

the willingness or fear to make them.

.

.

silk? And do we just abandon

It is that we are impermanently

.

.

rather than finish a work?

part and parcel of all. We are

.

.

It sounds as though that were

involved in a life that passes

.

.

what we are doing but where

understanding and our highest

.

.

would we go if we abandoned

business is our daily life. To draw

.

.

something? We only have to

lines straight or curved anywhere

.

.

change our means of measuring

does not alter the situation, only

.

.

to see how close we are to what

affirms it—if indeed the lines are

.

.

we were doing. It is not an

drawn, I mean materially. If

.

.

object; it is a process and it

not, they were drawn in a mind

.

.

will go on probably for some

to which there is no entry. Let

.

time. It is difficult to know

mysteries remain. Even in desperation

.

.

whether we will ever forget

we fail to convey our thoughts,

.

.

all the things that objects made

our feelings. It is because a

.

.

us memorize. However, let us

line-drawing mind is one bent

.

.

be optimistic and giddy with

on closure whereas the only

.

.

the possibility—the possibility

means of getting out (above or

.

.

of having everything clearly

below) to another is by not

.

.

what it is, going on consuming

drawing lines, by keeping the

.

.

and generously giving and

doors open, by some fluent

.

.

finding time to find our access

disclosure, and then there is no

.

.

to revelation. Now of course

desperation. Another way of

.

everything is canceled, not canceled

saying it is: "Do not be

.

.

but postponed, not on silk

satisfied with approximations

.

.

and not erased. There is

(or just: Do not be satisfied) but insist

.

.

still the question of time and

(as you need not) on what comes

.

.

the old and the new and

to you." This morning, up neither

.

.

whether we'll all get there

early nor late, aware that what-

.

.

where we're going but we'll

ever it is is still with me—a
Therefore, perhaps, we make things

.

never be sure who was coming

feeling that the flesh around my
that are irritatingly worse than

.

in the first place. There'll

eyes is swollen—perhaps a
we would want them to be in our

.

probably be some new faces. We

cold—or the glasses which are
lives, if therapy, a kind of pre-

.

want to get together (if not

new and which the oculist said
ventative therapy. And now the

.

here, in the South) but we're

wouldn't be useful after three
question of structure, the division of a

.

going in different directions. Do

years; at any rate I did get
whole into parts. We no longer

.

you suppose anything will get worked out?

up and was told the telephone
make that and I have given our

.

.

had been ringing and then that
reasons elsewhere (here too). What

.

.

a friend was ready and waiting
it is is a situation in which

.

.

to go mushrooming. The night
grandeur can rub shoulders with

.

.

before I'd scheduled my time for

frivolity. (Now I am speak-

•

•

not just today but the week
ing to the man at the

•

•

and realized clearly that if I'd
other end of the hall.) At any

•

•

just stick to it I'd get it done—
rate, now structure is not put

•

•

this lecture I mean—however,
into a work, but comes up in

•

•

I called and said, "An egg and
the person who perceives it in

•

•

then I'm with you." Presently
himself. There is therefore no problem of

•

•

in the woods and she said
understanding but the possibility of awareness.

•

•

in a few weeks they'd be in

•

•

•

the Caribbean with all the

•

•

•

children. In my mind's eye

•

•

•

I was hunting for tropical fungi.

•

•

•

Now I'm back working. There

•

•

•

was also a biological puzzle and a dis-

•

•

•

cussion of the proper use of knives and forks.

•

•

*Late in September of 1958, in a hotel in Stockholm, I set about writing this
lecture for delivery a week later at the Brussels Fair. I recalled a remark made
years earlier by David Tudor that I should give a talk that was nothing
but stories. The idea was appealing, but I had never acted on it,
and I decided to do so now.*

*When the talk was given in Brussels, it consisted of only thirty stories,
without musical accompaniment. A recital by David Tudor and myself of music
for two pianos followed the lecture. The full title was* Indeterminacy:
New Aspect of Form in Instrumental and Electronic Music.
*Karlheinz Stockhausen was in the audience. Later, when I was in Milan
making the* Fontana Mix *at the Studio di Fonologia, I received a letter from
him asking for a text that could be printed in* Die Reihe No. 5.
I sent the Brussels talk, and it was published.

INDETERMINACY

*The following spring, back in America, I delivered the talk again,
at Teachers College, Columbia. For this occasion I wrote sixty more stories,
and there was a musical accompaniment by David Tudor—material from the*
Concert for Piano and Orchestra, *employing several radios as noise
elements. Soon thereafter these ninety stories were brought out as a Folkways
recording, but for this the noise elements in the* Concert *were tracks
from the* Fontana Mix.

*In oral delivery of this lecture, I tell one story a minute. If it's a short one,
I have to spread it out; when I come to a long one, I have to speak as
rapidly as I can. The continuity of the stories as recorded was not planned.
I simply made a list of all the stories I could think of and checked them off as
I wrote them. Some that I remembered I was not able to write to my
satisfaction, and so they were not used. My intention in putting the stories
together in an unplanned way was to suggest that all things—stories, incidental
sounds from the environment, and, by extension, beings—are related, and
that this complexity is more evident when it is not oversimplified by an
idea of relationship in one person's mind.*

*Since that recording, I have continued to write down stories as I have
found them, so that the number is now far more than ninety. Most concern
things that happened that stuck in my mind. Others I read in books and
remembered—those, for instance, from Sri Ramakrishna and the literature
surrounding Zen. Still others have been told me by friends—Merce Cunningham,
Virgil Thomson, Betty Isaacs, and many more. Xenia, who figures in several
of them, is Xenia Andreyevna Kashevaroff, to whom I was married for
some ten years.*

Some stories have been omitted since their substance forms part of other writings in this volume. Many of those that remain are to be found below. Others are scattered through the book, playing the function that odd bits of information play at the ends of columns in a small-town newspaper. I suggest that they be read in the manner and in the situations that one reads newspapers—even the metropolitan ones—when he does so purposelessly: that is, jumping here and there and responding at the same time to environmental events and sounds.

When I first went to Paris, I did so instead of returning to Pomona College for my junior year. As I looked around, it was Gothic architecture that impressed me most. And of that architecture I preferred the flamboyant style of the fifteenth century. In this style my interest was attracted by balustrades. These I studied for six weeks in the Bibliothèque Mazarin, getting to the library when the doors were opened and not leaving until they were closed. Professor Pijoan, whom I had known at Pomona, arrived in Paris and asked me what I was doing. (We were standing in one of the railway stations there.) I told him. He gave me literally a swift kick in the pants and then said, "Go tomorrow to Goldfinger. I'll arrange for you to work with him. He's a modern architect." After a month of working with Goldfinger, measuring the dimensions of rooms which he was to modernize, answering the telephone, and drawing Greek columns, I overheard Goldfinger saying, "To be an architect, one must devote one's life solely to architecture." I then left him, for, as I explained, there were other things that interested me, music and painting for instance.

Five years later, when Schoenberg asked me whether I would devote my life to music, I said, "Of course." After I had been studying with him for two years, Schoenberg said, "In order to write music, you must have a feeling for harmony." I explained to him that I had no feeling for harmony. He then said that I would always encounter an obstacle, that it would be as though I came to a wall through which I could not pass. I said, "In that case I will devote my life to beating my head against that wall."

When I first moved to the country, David Tudor, M. C. Richards, the Weinribs, and I all lived in the same small farmhouse. In order to get some privacy I started taking walks in the woods. It was August. I began collecting the mushrooms which were growing more or less everywhere. Then I bought some books and tried to find out which mushroom was which. Realizing I needed to get to know someone who knew something about mushrooms, I called the 4-H Club in New City. I spoke to a secretary. She said they'd call me back. They never did.

The following spring, after reading about the edibility of skunk cabbage in Medsger's book on wild plants, I gathered a mess of what I took to be skunk cabbage, gave some to my mother and father (who were visiting) to take home, cooked the rest in three waters with a pinch of soda as Medsger advises, and served it to six people, one of whom, I remember, was from the Museum of Modern Art. I ate more than the others did in an attempt to convey my enthusiasm over edible wild plants. After coffee, poker was proposed. I began winning heavily. M. C. Richards left the table. After a while she came back and whispered in my ear, "Do you feel all right?" I said, "No. I don't. My throat is burning and I can hardly breathe." I told the others to divide my winnings, that I was folding. I went outside and retched. Vomiting with diarrhea continued for about two hours. Before I lost my will, I told M. C. Richards to call Mother and Dad and tell them not to eat the skunk cabbage. I asked her how the others were. She said, "They're not as bad off as you are." Later, when friends lifted me off the ground to put a blanket under me, I just said, "Leave me alone." Someone called Dr. Zukor. He prescribed milk and salt. I couldn't take it. He said, "Get him here immediately." They did. He pumped my stomach and gave adrenalin to keep my heart beating. Among other things, he said, "Fifteen minutes more and he would have been dead."

I was removed to the Spring Valley hospital. There during the night I was kept supplied with adrenalin and I was thoroughly cleaned out. In the morning I felt like a million dollars. I rang the bell for the nurse to tell her I was ready to go. No one came. I read a notice on the wall which said that unless one left by noon he would be charged for an extra day. When I saw one of the nurses passing by I yelled something to the effect that she should get me out since I had no money for a second day. Shortly the room was filled with doctors and nurses and in no time at all I was hustled out.

I called up the 4-H Club and told them what had happened. I emphasized my determination to go on with wild mushrooms. They said, "Call Mrs. Clark on South Mountain Drive." She said, "I can't help you. Call Mr. So-and-so." I called him. He said, "I can't help you, but call So-and-so who works in the A&P in Suffern. He knows someone in Ramsey who knows the mushrooms." Eventually, I got the name and telephone number of Guy G. Nearing. When I called him, he said, "Come over any time you like. I'm almost always here, and I'll name your mushrooms for you."

I wrote a letter to Medsger telling him skunk cabbage was poisonous. He never replied. Some time later I read about the need to distinguish between skunk cabbage and the poisonous helle-bore. They grow at the same time in the same places. Hellebore has pleated leaves. Skunk cabbage does not.

During recent years Daisetz Teitaro Suzuki has done a great deal of lecturing at Columbia University. First he was in the Department of Religion, then somewhere else. Finally he settled down on the seventh floor of Philosophy Hall. The room had windows on two sides, a large table in the middle with ash trays. There were chairs around the table and next to the walls. These were always filled with people listening, and there were generally a few people standing near the door. The two or three people who took the class for credit sat in chairs around the table. The time was four to seven. During this period most people now and then took a little nap. Suzuki never spoke loudly. When the weather was good the windows were open, and the airplanes leaving La Guardia flew directly overhead from time to time, drowning out whatever he had to say. He never repeated what had been said during the passage of the airplane. Three lectures I remember in particular. While he was giving them I couldn't for the life of me figure out what he was saying. It was a week or so later, while I was walking in the woods looking for mushrooms, that it all dawned on me.

Patsy Davenport heard my Folkways record. She said, "When the story came about my asking you how you felt about Bach, I could remember everything perfectly clearly, sharply, as though I were living through it again. Tell me, what did you answer? How do you feel about Bach?" I said I didn't remember what I'd said — that I'd been nonplused. Then, as usual, when the next day came, I got to thinking. Giving up Beethoven, the emotional climaxes and all, is fairly simple for an American. But giving up Bach is more difficult. Bach's music suggests order and glorifies for those who hear it their regard for order, which in their lives is expressed by daily jobs nine to five and the appliances with which they surround themselves and which, when plugged in, God willing, work. Some people say that art should be an instance of order so that it will save them momentarily from the chaos that they know is just around the corner. Jazz is equivalent to Bach (steady beat, dependable motor), and the love of Bach is generally coupled with the love of jazz. Jazz is more seductive, less moralistic than Bach. It popularizes the pleasures and pains of the physical life, whereas Bach is close to church and all that. Knowing as we do that so many jazz musicians stay up to all hours and even take dope, we permit ourselves to become, sympathetically at least, junkies and night owls ourselves: by *participation mystique.* Giving up Bach, jazz, and order is difficult. Patsy Davenport is right. It's a very serious question. For if we do it — give them up, that is — what do we have left?

Once when I was a child in Los Angeles I went downtown on the streetcar. It was such a hot day that, when I got out of the streetcar, the tar on the pavement stuck to my feet. (I was barefoot.) Getting to the sidewalk, I found it so hot that I had to run to keep from blistering my feet. I went into a five and dime to get a root beer. When I came to the counter where it was sold from a large barrel and asked for some, a man standing on the counter high above me said, "Wait. I'm putting in the syrup and it'll be a few minutes." As he was putting in the last can, he missed and spilled the sticky syrup all over me. To make me feel better, he offered a free root beer. I said, "No, thank you."

Betty Isaacs told me that when she was in New Zealand she was informed that none of the mushrooms growing wild there was poisonous. So one day when she noticed a hillside covered with fungi, she gathered a lot and made catsup. When she finished the catsup, she tasted it and it was awful. Nevertheless she bottled it and put it up on a high shelf. A year later she was housecleaning and discovered the catsup, which she had forgotten about. She was on the point of throwing it away. But before doing this she tasted it. It had changed color. Originally a dirty gray, it had become black, and, as she told me, it was divine, improving the flavor of whatever it touched.

George Mantor had an iris garden, which he improved each year by throwing out the commoner varieties. One day his attention was called to another very fine iris garden. Jealously he made some inquiries. The garden, it turned out, belonged to the man who collected his garbage.

Staying in India and finding the sun unbearable, Mrs. Coomaraswamy decided to shop for a parasol. She found two in the town nearby. One was in the window of a store dealing in American goods. It was reasonably priced but unattractive. The other was in an Indian store. It was Indian-made, desirable, but outlandishly expensive. Mrs. Coomaraswamy went back home without buying anything. But the weather continued dry and hot, so that a few days later she went again into town determined to make a purchase. Passing by the American shop, she noticed their parasol was still in the window, still reasonably priced. Going into the Indian shop, she asked to see the one she had admired a few days before. While she was looking at it, the price was mentioned. This time it was absurdly low. Surprised, Mrs. Coomaraswamy said, "How can I trust you? One day your prices are up; the next day they're down. Perhaps your goods are equally undependable." "Madame," the storekeeper replied, "the people across the street are new in business. They are intent on profit. Their prices are stable. We, however, have been in business for generations. The best things we have we keep in the family, for we are reluctant to part with them. As for our prices, we change them continually. That's the only way we've found in business to keep ourselves interested."

There's a street in Stony Point in a lowland near the river where a number of species of mushrooms grow abundantly. I visit this street often. A few years ago in May I found the morel there, a choice mushroom which is rare around Rockland County. I was delighted. None of the people living on this street ever talk to me while I'm collecting mushrooms. Sometimes children come over and kick at them before I get to them. Well, the year after I found the morel, I went back in May expecting to find it again, only to discover that a cinder-block house had been put up where the mushroom had been growing. As I looked at the changed land, all the people in the neighborhood came out on their porches. One of them said, "Ha, ha! Your mushrooms are gone."

We are all part and parcel of a way of life that puts trust in the almighty dollar—so much so that we feel ourselves slipping when we hear that on the international market the West German mark inspires more confidence. Food, one assumes, provides nourishment; but Americans eat it fully aware that small amounts of poison have been added to improve its appearance and delay its putrefaction. None of us wants cancer or skin diseases, but there are those who tell us that's how we get them. It's hard to tell, come December, whether we're celebrating the birth of Christ or whether American business has simply pulled the wool over our eyes. When I hear that an artist whose work I admire gets $7000 for a painting whereas another whose work I don't admire gets twice as much, do I then change my mind? Ten years ago the New York painters were for the most part poor as church mice. Did they then or do they now have a place in American society?

Coming back from an all-Ives concert we'd attended in Connecticut, Minna Lederman said that by separating his insurance business from his composition of music (as completely as day is separated from night), Ives paid full respect to the American assumption that the artist has no place in society. (When Mother first heard my percussion quartet years ago in Santa Monica, she said, "I enjoyed it, but where are you going to put it?") But music is, or was at one time, America's sixth-largest industry—above or below steel, I don't remember which. Schoenberg used to say that the movie composers knew their business very well. Once he asked those in the class who intended to become professional musicians to put up their hands. No one did. (Uncle Walter insisted when he married her that Aunt Marge, who was a contralto, should give up her career.) My bet is that the phenomenal prices paid for paintings in New York at the present time have less to do with art than with business. The lady who lived next door in Santa Monica told me the painting she had in her dining room was worth lots of money. She mentioned an astronomical sum. I said, "How do you know?" She said she'd seen a small painting worth a certain amount, measured it, measured hers (which was much larger), multiplied, and that was that.

Mrs. Coomaraswamy told another story about business methods in India. It seems that early one morning she was at a kind of craftsmen's bazaar. There were fewer shops available than there were craftsmen. So a poetry contest was arranged. The one who made up the best poem got the shop. The losers were going away quite contented reciting the winning poem. She asked them why they were so pleased since they were actually unfortunate. They said, "Oh, it's no matter. When his goods are sold he'll have no use for the shop. Then one more of us will get a chance to sell what he has, and so on."

Lois Long (the Lois Long who designs textiles), Christian Wolff, and I climbed Slide Mountain along with Guy Nearing and the Flemings, including Willie. All the way up and down the mountain we found nothing but *Collybia platyphylla*, so that I began to itch to visit a cemetery in Millerton, New York, where, in my mind's eye, *Pluteus cervinus* was growing. By the time we got back to the cars, our knees were shaking with fatigue and the sun had gone down. Nevertheless, I managed to persuade Lois Long and Christian Wolff to drive over to Millerton. It meant an extra hundred miles. We arrived at the cemetery at midnight. I took a flashlight out of the glove compartment, got out, and first hastily and then carefully examined all the stumps and the ground around them. There wasn't a single mushroom growing. Going back to the car, I fully expected Lois Long and Christian Wolff to be exasperated. However, they were entranced. The aurora borealis, which neither of them had ever seen before, was playing in the northern sky.

I dug up some hog peanuts and boiled them with butter, salt, and pepper for Bob Rauschenberg and Jasper Johns. I was anxious to know what Jasper Johns would think of them because I knew he liked boiled peanuts. I was curious to know whether he would find a similarity between boiled peanuts and hog peanuts. Most people in the North have no experience at all of boiled peanuts. People who've had hog peanuts speak afterwards of the taste of chestnuts and beans. Anyway, Jasper Johns said they were very good but that they didn't taste particularly like boiled peanuts. Then he went down to South Carolina for a few weeks in November. When I saw him after he got back, he said he'd had boiled peanuts again and that they tasted very much like hog peanuts.

Artists talk a lot about freedom. So, recalling the expression "free as a bird," Morton Feldman went to a park one day and spent some time watching our feathered friends. When he came back, he said, "You know? They're not free: they're fighting over bits of food."

I was asked to play my *Sonatas and Interludes* in the home of an elderly lady in Burnsville, North Carolina, the only person thereabouts who owned a grand piano. I explained that the piano preparation would take at least three hours and that I would need a few additional hours for practicing before the performance. It was arranged for me to start work directly after lunch. After about an hour, I decided to take a breather. I lit a cigarette and went out on the veranda, where I found my hostess sitting in a rocking chair. We began chatting. She asked me where I came from. I told her that I'd been born in Los Angeles but that as a child I was raised both there and in Michigan; that after two years of college in Claremont, California, I had spent eighteen months in Europe and North Africa; that, after returning to California, I had moved first from Santa Monica to Carmel, then to New York, then back to Los Angeles, then to Seattle, San Francisco, and Chicago, successively; that, at the moment, I was living in New York in an apartment on the East River. Then I said, "And where do you come from?" She said, pointing to a gas station across the street, "From over there." She went on to say that one of her sons had tried to persuade her to make a second move, for now she lived alone except for the servants, and to come and live with him and his family. She said she refused because she wouldn't feel at home in a strange place. When I asked where he lived, she said, "A few blocks down the street."

On one occasion, Schoenberg asked a girl in his class to go to the piano and play the first movement of a Beethoven sonata, which was afterwards to be analyzed. She said, "It is too difficult.

I can't play it." Schoenberg said, "You're a pianist, aren't you?" She said, "Yes." He said, "Then go to the piano." She did. She had no sooner begun playing than he stopped her to say that she was not playing at the proper tempo. She said that if she played at the proper tempo, she would make mistakes. He said, "Play at the proper tempo and do not make mistakes." She began again, and he stopped her immediately to say that she was making mistakes. She then burst into tears and between sobs explained that she had gone to the dentist earlier that day and that she'd had a tooth pulled out. He said, "Do you have to have a tooth pulled out in order to make mistakes?"

There was a lady in Suzuki's class who said once, "I have great difficulty reading the sermons of Meister Eckhart, because of all the Christian imagery." Dr. Suzuki said, "That difficulty will disappear."

Betty Isaacs went shopping at Altman's. She spent all her money except her last dime, which she kept in her hand so that she'd have it ready when she got on the bus to go home and wouldn't have to fumble around in her purse since her arms were full of parcels and she was also carrying a shopping bag. Waiting for the bus, she decided to make sure she still had the coin. When she opened her hand, there was nothing there. She mentally retraced her steps trying to figure out where she'd lost the dime. Her mind made up, she went straight to the glove department, and sure enough there it was on the floor where she'd been standing. As she stooped to pick it up, another shopper said, "I wish I knew where to go to pick money up off the floor." Relieved, Betty Isaacs took the bus home to the Village. Unpacking her parcels, she discovered the dime in the bottom of the shopping bag.

When David Tudor, Merce Cunningham, Carolyn and Earle Brown, and I arrived in Brus-

sels a year or so ago for programs at the World's Fair, we found out that Earle Brown's *Indices* was not going to be played since the orchestra found it too difficult. So, putting two and two together, we proposed that Merce Cunningham and Carolyn Brown dance solos and duets from Merce Cunningham's *Springweather and People* (which is his title for Earle Brown's *Indices*) and that David Tudor play the piano transcription as accompaniment. With great difficulty, arrangements were made to realize this proposal. At the last minute the authorities agreed. However, just before the performance, the Pope died and everything was canceled.

One day down at Black Mountain College, David Tudor was eating his lunch. A student came over to his table and began asking him questions. David Tudor went on eating his lunch. The student kept on asking questions. Finally David Tudor looked at him and said, "If you don't know, why do you ask?"

When David Tudor and I walked into the hotel where we were invited to stay in Brussels, there were large envelopes for each of us at the desk; they were full of programs, tickets, invitations, special passes to the Fair, and general information. One of the invitations I had was to a luncheon at the royal palace adjacent to the Fair Grounds. I was to reply, but I didn't because I was busy with rehearsals, performances, and the writing of thirty of these stories, which I was to deliver as a lecture in the course of the week devoted to experimental music. So one day when I was coming into the hotel, the desk attendant asked me whether I expected to go to the palace for lunch the following day. I said, "Yes." Over the phone, he said, "He's coming." And then he checked my name off a list in front of him. He asked whether I knew the plans of others on the list, which by that time I was reading upside down. I helped him as best I could. The next morning when I came down for breakfast there was a man from Paris associated as physicist with Schaeffer's studio for *musique concrète*. I said, "Well, I'll be seeing you at luncheon today." He said, "What luncheon?" I said, "At the palace." He said, "I haven't been invited." I said, "I'm sure you are invited. I saw your name on the list. You'd better call them up; they're anxious to know who's coming." An hour later the phone rang for me. It was the director of the week's events. He said, "I've just found out that you've invited Dr. So-and-So to the luncheon." I said I'd seen his name on the list. The director said, "You've made a mistake and I am able to correct it, but what I'd like to know is: How many others have you also invited?"

An Indian woman who lived in the islands was required to come to Juneau to testify in a trial. After she had solemnly sworn to tell the truth, the whole truth, and nothing but the truth, she was asked whether she had been subpoenaed. She said, "Yes. Once on the boat coming over, and once in the hotel here in Juneau."

I took a number of mushrooms to Guy Nearing, and asked him to name them for me. He did. On my way home, I began to doubt whether one particular mushroom was what he had called it. When I got home I got out my books and came to the conclusion that Guy Nearing had made a mistake. The next time I saw him I told him all about this and he said, "There are so many Latin names rolling around in my head that sometimes the wrong one comes out."

A depressed young man came to see Hazel Dreis, the bookbinder. He said, "I've decided to commit suicide." She said, "I think it's a good idea. Why don't you do it?"

David Tudor and I went up to New Haven to do a television class for the New Haven State Teachers College. That college specializes in teaching by means of television. What they do is to make a tape, audio and visual, and then broadcast it at a later date early in the morning. In the course of my talking, I said something about the purpose of purposelessness. Afterwards, one of the teachers said to the head of the Music Department, "How are you going to explain that to the class next Tuesday?" Anyway, we finished the TV business, drove back to the school, and I asked the teachers to recommend some second-hand bookstores in New Haven for David Tudor and me to visit. They did. A half-hour later when we walked into one of them, the book dealer said, "Mr. Tudor? Mr. Cage?" I said, "Yes?" He said, "You're to call the State Teachers College." I did. They said the television class we had recorded had not been recorded at all. Apparently someone forgot to turn something on.

On the way back from New Haven we were driving along the Housatonic. It was a beautiful day. We stopped to have dinner but the restaurants at the river's edge turned out not to be restaurants at all but dark, run-down bars with, curiously, no views of the river. So we drove on to Newtown, where we saw many cars parked around a restaurant that appeared to have a Colonial atmosphere. I said, "All those cars are a good sign. Let's eat there." When we got in, we were in a large dining room with very few other people eating. The waitress seemed slightly giddy. David Tudor ordered some ginger ale, and after quite a long time was served some Coca-Cola, which he refused. Later we both ordered parfaits; mine was to be chocolate, his to be strawberry. As the waitress entered the kitchen, she shouted, "Two chocolate parfaits." When David Tudor explained to her later that he had ordered strawberry, she said, "They made some mistake in the kitchen." I said,

"There must be another dining room in this building with a lot of people eating in it." The waitress said, "Yes. It's downstairs and there are only two of us for each floor and we keep running back and forth."

Then we had to go back to New Haven to do the TV class over again. This time on the way back it was a very hot and humid day. We stopped again in Newtown, but at a different place, for some ice. There was a choice: raspberry, grape, lemon, orange, and pineapple. I took grape. It was refreshing. I asked the lady who served it whether she had made it. She said, "Yes." I said, "Is it fresh fruit?" She said, "It's not fresh, but it's fruit."

Mr. Ralph Ferrara drives a Studebaker Lark which is mashed at both ends. Sometimes the car requires to be pushed in order to run. One Sunday when the mushroom class met at 10:00 A.M. at Suffern, Mr. Ferrara didn't arrive. Next week he told me he'd arrived late, gone to Sloatsburg, gathered a few mushrooms, gone home, cooked dinner, and two of his guests were immediately ill but not seriously. At the last mushroom field trip, November 1, 1959, we ended at my house, drank some stone fences, and ate some *Cortinarius alboviolaceous* that Lois Long cooked. She said to Ralph Ferrara, "Mr. Cage says that there's nothing like a little mushroom poisoning to make people be on time." He said, "Oh, yes. I'm always first in the parking lot."

While I was studying the frozen food department of Gristede's one day, Mrs. Elliott Carter came up and said, "Hello, John. I thought you touched only fresh foods." I said, "All you have to do is look at them and then you come over here." She said, "Elliott and I have just gotten back from Europe. We'd sublet to some intellectuals whose names I won't mention. They had been eating those platters with all sorts of food on them." I said, "Not TV dinners?" She said, "Yes, I found them stuffed around everywhere."

When I came to New York to study with Adolph Weiss and Henry Cowell, I took a job in the Brooklyn YWCA washing walls. There was one other wall-washer. He was more experienced than I. He told me how many walls to wash per day. In this way he checked my original enthusiasm, with the result that I spent a great deal of time simply reading the old newspapers which I used to protect the floors. Thus I had always to be, so to speak, on my toes, ready to resume scrubbing the moment I heard the housekeeper approaching. One room finished, I was to go to the next, but before entering any room I was to look in the keyhole to see whether the occupant's key was in it on the inside. If I saw no key, I was to assume the room empty, go in, and set to work. One morning, called to the office, I was told I had been accused of peeking through the keyholes. I no sooner began to defend myself than I was interrupted. The housekeeper said that each year the wall-washer, no matter who he was, was so accused, always by the same lady.

Standing in line, Max Jacob said, gives one the opportunity to practice patience.

Mr. Romanoff is in the mushroom class. He is a pharmacist and takes color slides of the fungi we find. It was he who picked up a mushroom I brought to the first meeting of the class at the New School, smelled it, and said, "Has anyone perfumed this mushroom?" Lois Long said, "I don't think so." With each plant Mr. Romanoff's pleasure is, as one might say, like that of a child. (However, now and then children come on the field trips and they don't show particular delight over what is found. They try to attract attention to themselves.) Mr. Romanoff said the other day,

"Life is the sum total of all the little things that happen." Mr. Nearing smiled.

Tucker Madawick is seventeen years old. He is Lois Long's son by her first husband. It was dinnertime. He came home from his job in the Good Samaritan Hospital in Suffern and said to his mother, "Well, dear, I won't be seeing you for a couple of days." Lois Long said, "What's up?" Tucker said, "Tomorrow night after work, I'm driving to Albany with Danny Sherwood for a cup of coffee, and I'll be back for work the following day." Lois Long said, "For heaven's sake, you can have a cup of coffee here at home." Tucker Madawick replied, "Don't be a square. Read Kerouac."

Merce Cunningham's parents were going to Seattle to see their other son, Jack. Mrs. Cunningham was driving. Mr. Cunningham said, "Don't you think you should go a little slower? You'll get caught." He gave this warning several times. Finally, on the outskirts of Seattle, they were stopped by a policeman. He asked to see Mrs. Cunningham's license. She rummaged around in her bag and said, "I just don't seem to be able to find it." He then asked to see the registration. She looked for it but unsuccessfully. The officer then said, "Well, what are we going to do with you?" Mrs. Cunningham started the engine. Before she drove off, she said, "I just don't have any more time to waste talking with you. Good-by."

I went to hear Krishnamurti speak. He was lecturing on how to hear a lecture. He said, "You must pay full attention to what is being said and you can't do that if you take notes." The lady on my right was taking notes. The man on her right nudged her and said, "Don't you hear what he's saying? You're not supposed to take notes." She then read what she had written and said, "That's right. I have it written down right here in my notes."

Virgil Thomson and Maurice Grosser were driving across the United States. When they came to Kansas, Virgil Thomson said, "Drive as fast as possible, in no case stop. Keep on going until we get out of it." Maurice Grosser got hungry and insisted on stopping for lunch. Seeing something at the end of the counter, he asked what it was, and the waitress replied, "Peanut butter pie." Virgil Thomson said, "You see what I mean?"

One of Mies van der Rohe's pupils, a girl, came to him and said, "I have difficulty studying with you because you don't leave any room for self-expression." He asked her whether she had a pen with her. She did. He said, "Sign your name." She did. He said, "That's what I call self-expression."

Just before I moved to the country, I called up the Museum of Natural History and asked a man there what poisonous snakes were to be found in Rockland County. Unhesitatingly he replied, "The copperhead and the rattlesnake." Going through the woods, I never see either (now and then a blacksnake or some other harmless reptile down near the stream or even up in the hills). The children across the road warned me that in our woods snakes hang from the trees. A man who works for the Interstate Park and who lives just north of us on Gate Hill told me he'd never seen any poisonous snakes on our land.

On a mushroom walk near Mianus Gorge in Connecticut we came across thirty copperheads basking in the sun. Mr. Fleming put one in a paper bag and carried it home attached to his belt. He is, of course, a specialist with snakes, works for the Bronx Zoo, and makes hunting expeditions in South America. However, he told me once of another snake specialist who worked for the Park his whole life without ever having any trouble, and then, after getting his pension, went out tramping in the woods, was bitten by a copperhead, didn't take the bite seriously, and died of it.

Among those thirty copperheads at Mianus Gorge I noticed three different colorations, so that I have lost faith in the pictures in the books as far as snake identification goes. What you have to do, it seems, is notice whether or not there is a pitlike indentation in each of the snake's cheeks, between the eye and the nostril, in order to be certain whether it's poisonous or not. This is, of course, difficult unless one is already dangerously close.

Over in New Jersey on Bare Fort Mountain and once up at Sam's Point we ran into rattlesnakes. They were larger and more noble in action and appearance than the copperheads. There was only one on each occasion, and each went through the business of coiling, rattling, and spitting. Neither struck.

My new room is one step up from my old kitchen. One fall evening before the gap between the two rooms was closed up, I was shaving at the sink and happened to notice what seemed to be a copperhead making its way into the house five feet away from where I was standing. Never having killed a snake and feeling the urgency of that's being done, I called, "Paul! A copperhead's in the house!" Paul Williams came running over from his house and killed the snake with a bread board. After he left, the snake was still writhing. I cut off its head with a carving knife. With a pair of tongs, I picked up both parts and flushed them down the toilet.

When I told Daniel DeWees what had happened, he said, "That's what I thought. When I was working in the dark under the house the other day putting in the insulation, I had the feeling there was a snake there near me." I said, "Was it just a feeling? Did you imagine it? Or was there something made you certain?" He said, "Well, I thought I heard some hissing."

In 1949 Merce Cunningham and I went to Europe on a Dutch boat. As we were approaching Rotterdam, the fog became so thick that landing was delayed. To expedite matters, the customs officials came aboard the boat. Passengers formed into lines and one by one were questioned. Merce Cunningham was in one line, I was in another. I smoke a great deal, whereas he doesn't smoke at all. However, he was taking five cartons of cigarettes into Europe for me and I had that number myself. We were both traveling through Holland to Belgium and then France, and the customs regulations of all those countries varied with regard to cigarettes. For instance, you could at that time take five cartons per person into France but only two per person into Holland. When I got to my customs officer, all of this was clear to both of us. Out of the goodness of his heart, he was reluctant to deprive me of my three extra cartons or to charge duty on them, but he found it difficult to find an excuse for letting me off. Finally he said, "Are you going to go out of Holland backwards?" I said, "Yes." He was overjoyed. Then he said, "You can keep all the cigarettes. Have a good trip." I left the line and noticed that Merce Cunningham had just reached his customs officer and was having some trouble about the extra cartons. So I went over and told the official that Merce Cunningham was going to go out of Holland backwards. He was delighted. "Oh," he said, "in that case there's no problem at all."

One day when I was studying with Schoenberg, he pointed out the eraser on his pencil and said, "This end is more important than the other." After twenty years I learned to write directly in ink. Recently, when David Tudor returned from Europe, he brought me a German pencil of modern make. It can carry any size of lead. Pressure on a shaft at the end of the holder frees the lead so that it can be retracted or extended or removed and another put in its place. A sharpener came with the pencil. This sharpener offers not one but several possibilities. That is, one may choose the kind of point he wishes. There is no eraser.

During my last year in high school, I found out about the Liberal Catholic Church. It was in a beautiful spot in the Hollywood hills. The ceremony was an anthology of the most theatrical bits and pieces found in the principal rituals, Occidental and Oriental. There were clouds of incense, candles galore, processions in and around the church. I was fascinated, and though I had been raised in the Methodist Episcopal Church and had had thoughts of going into the ministry, I decided to join the Liberal Catholics. Mother and Dad objected strenuously. Ultimately, when I told them of my intention to become an acolyte active in the Mass, they said, "Well, make up your mind. It's us or the church." Thinking along the lines of "Leave your father and mother and follow Me," I went to the priest, told him what had happened, and said I'd decided in favor of the Liberal Catholics. He said, "Don't be a fool. Go home. There are many religions. You have only one mother and father."

Schoenberg always complained that his American pupils didn't do enough work. There was one girl in the class in particular who, it is true, did almost no work at all. He asked her one day why she didn't accomplish more. She said, "I don't have any time." He said, "How many hours are there in the day?" She said, "Twenty-four." He said, "Nonsense: there are as many hours in a day as you put into it."

A crowded bus on the point of leaving Manchester for Stockport was found by its conductress to have one too many standees. She therefore asked, "Who was the last person to get on the bus?" No one said a word. Declaring that the bus

would not leave until the extra passenger was put off, she went and fetched the driver, who also asked, "All right, who was the last person to get on the bus?" Again there was a public silence. So the two went to find an inspector. He asked, "Who was the last person to get on the bus?" No one spoke. He then announced that he would fetch a policeman. While the conductress, driver, and inspector were away looking for a policeman, a little man came up to the bus stop and asked, "Is this the bus to Stockport?" Hearing that it was, he got on. A few minutes later the three returned accompanied by a policeman. He asked, "What seems to be the trouble? Who was the last person to get on the bus?" The little man said, "I was." The policeman said, "All right, get off." All the people on the bus burst into laughter. The conductress, thinking they were laughing at her, burst into tears and said she refused to make the trip to Stockport. The inspector then arranged for another conductress to take over. She, seeing the little man standing at the bus stop, said, "What are you doing there?" He said, "I'm waiting to go to Stockport." She said, "Well, this is the bus to Stockport. Are you getting on or not?"

Alex and Gretchen Corazzo gave a great deal of thought to whether or not they would attend the funeral of a close friend. At the last minute they decided they would go. Hurriedly they dressed, rushed out of the house, arrived late; the services had begun. They took seats at the back of the chapel. When the invitation came to view the body, they again deliberated, finally deciding to do so. Coming to the casket, they discovered they were at the wrong funeral.

Xenia told me once that when she was a child in Alaska, she and her friends had a club and there was only one rule: No silliness.

Xenia never wanted a party to end. Once, in Seattle, when the party we were at was folding, she invited those who were still awake, some of whom we'd only met that evening, to come over to our house. Thus it was that about 3:00 A.M. an Irish tenor was singing loudly in our living room. Morris Graves, who had a suite down the hall, entered ours without knocking, wearing an old-fashioned nightshirt and carrying an elaborately made wooden birdcage, the bottom of which had been removed. Making straight for the tenor, Graves placed the birdcage over his head, said nothing, and left the room. The effect was that of snuffing out a candle. Shortly, Xenia and I were alone.

I enrolled in a class in mushroom identification. The teacher was a Ph.D. and the editor of a publication on mycology. One day he picked up a mushroom, gave a good deal of information about it, mainly historical, and finally named the plant as *Pluteus cervinus*, edible. I was certain that that plant was not *Pluteus cervinus*. Due to the attachment of its gills to the stem, it seemed to me to be an *Entoloma*, and therefore possibly seriously poisonous. I thought: What shall I do? Point out the teacher's error? Or, following school etiquette, saying nothing, let other members of the class possibly poison themselves? I decided to speak. I said, "I doubt whether that mushroom is *Pluteus cervinus*. I think it's an *Entoloma*." The teacher said, "Well, we'll key it out." This was done, and it turned out I was right. The plant was *Entoloma grayanum*, a poisonous mushroom. The teacher came over to me and said, "If you know so much about mushrooms, why do you take this class?" I said, "I take this class because there's so much about mushrooms I don't know." Then I said, "By the way, how is it that you didn't recognize that plant?" He said, "Well, I specialize in the jelly fungi; I just give the fleshy fungi a whirl."

Merce Cunningham's father delights in gardening. Each year he has had to move the shrubs

back from the driveway to protect them from being run over when Mrs. Cunningham backs out. One day Mrs. Cunningham in backing out knocked down but did not hurt an elderly gentleman who had been taking a stroll. Getting out of her car and seeing him lying on the sidewalk, Mrs. Cunningham said, "What are you doing there?"

Generally speaking, suicide is considered a sin. So all the disciples were very interested to hear what Ramakrishna would say about the fact that a four-year-old child had just then committed suicide. Ramakrishna said that the child had not sinned, he had simply corrected an error; he had been born by mistake.

One day while I was composing, the telephone rang. A lady's voice said, "Is this John Cage, the percussion composer?" I said, "Yes." She said, "This is the J. Walter Thompson Company." I didn't know what that was, but she explained that their business was advertising. She said, "Hold on. One of our directors wants to speak to you." During a pause my mind went back to my composition. Then suddenly a man's voice said, "Mr. Cage, are you willing to prostitute your art?" I said, "Yes." He said, "Well, bring us some samples Friday at two." I did. After hearing a few recordings, one of the directors said to me, "Wait a minute." Then seven directors formed what looked like a football huddle. From this one of them finally emerged, came over to me, and said, "You're too good for us. We're going to save you for Robinson Crusoe."

In the poetry contest in China by which the Sixth Patriarch of Zen Buddhism was chosen, there were two poems. One said: "The mind is like a mirror. It collects dust. The problem is to remove the dust." The other and winning poem was actually a reply to the first. It said, "Where is the mirror and where is the dust?"

Some centuries later in a Japanese monastery, there was a monk who was always taking baths. A younger monk came up to him and said, "Why, if there is no dust, are you always taking baths?" The older monk replied, "Just a dip. No why."

While we were sitting on top of Slide Mountain looking out towards Cornell and Wittenberg and the Ashokan Reservoir beyond, Guy Nearing said he had known two women who were bitten by copperheads. "They were just the same after as before," he said, "except they were a little more cranky."

On Christmas Day, Mother said, "I've listened to your record several times. After hearing all those stories about your childhood, I keep asking myself, 'Where was it that I failed?'"

One spring morning I knocked on Sonya Sekula's door. She lived across the hall. Presently the door was opened just a crack and she said quickly, "I know you're very busy: I won't take a minute of your time."

When the depression began, I was in Europe. After a while I came back and lived with my family in the Pacific Palisades. I had read somewhere that Richard Buhlig, the pianist, had years before in Berlin given the first performance of Schoenberg's *Opus 11*. I thought to myself: He probably lives right here in Los Angeles. So I looked in the phone book and, sure enough, there was his name. I called him up and said, "I'd like to hear you play the Schoenberg pieces." He said he wasn't contemplating giving a recital. I said, "Well, surely, you play at home. Couldn't I come over one day and hear the *Opus 11?*" He said, "Certainly not." He hung up.

About a year later, the family had to give up the house in the Palisades. Mother and Dad went to an apartment in Los Angeles. I found an auto court in Santa Monica where, in exchange for doing the gardening, I got an apartment to live in and a large room back of the court over the garages, which I used as a lecture hall. I was nineteen years old and enthusiastic about modern music and painting. I went from house to house in Santa Monica explaining this to the housewives. I offered ten lectures for $2.50. I said, "I will learn each week something about the subject that I will then lecture on."

Well, the week came for my lecture on Schoenberg. Except for a minuet, *Opus 25*, his music was too difficult for me to play. No recordings were then available. I thought of Richard Buhlig. I decided not to telephone him but to go directly to his house and visit him. I hitchhiked into Los Angeles, arriving at his house at noon. He wasn't home. I took a pepper bough off a tree and, pulling off the leaves one by one, recited, "He'll come home; he won't; he'll come home . . ." It always turned out He'll come home. He did. At midnight. I explained I'd been waiting to see him for twelve hours. He invited me into the house. When I asked him to illustrate my lecture on Schoenberg, he said, "Certainly not." However, he said he'd like to see some of my compositions, and we made an appointment for the following week.

Somehow I got through the lecture, and the day came to show my work to Buhlig. Again I hitchhiked into L.A., arriving somewhat ahead of time. I rang the doorbell. Buhlig opened it and said, "You're half an hour early. Come back at the proper time." I had library books with me and decided to kill two birds with one stone. So I went to the library to return the books, found some new ones, and then came back to Buhlig's house and again rang the doorbell. He was furious when he opened the door. He said, "Now you're half an hour late." He took me into the house and lectured me for two hours on the importance of time, especially for one who proposed devoting his life to the art of music.

In 1954 an issue of the United States Lines Paris Review *devoted to humor was being prepared. I was invited to write on the subject of music. I contributed the following article.*

MUSIC LOVERS' FIELD COMPANION

I have come to the conclusion that much can be learned about music by devoting oneself to the mushroom. For this purpose I have recently moved to the country. Much of my time is spent poring over "field companions" on fungi. These I obtain at half price in second-hand bookshops, which latter are in some rare cases next door to shops selling dog-eared sheets of music, such an occurrence being greeted by me as irrefutable evidence that I am on the right track.

The winter for mushrooms, as for music, is a most sorry season. Only in caves and houses where matters of temperature and humidity, and in concert halls where matters of trusteeship and box office are under constant surveillance, do the vulgar and accepted forms thrive. American commercialism has brought about a grand deterioration of the *Psalliota campestris,* affecting through exports even the European market. As a demanding gourmet sees but does not purchase the marketed mushroom, so a lively musician reads from time to time the announcements of concerts and stays quietly at home. If, energetically, *Collybia velutipes* should fruit in January, it is a rare event, and happening on it while stalking in a forest is almost beyond one's dearest expectations, just as it is exciting in New York to note that the number of people attending a winter concert requiring the use of one's faculties is on the upswing (1954: 129 out of 12,000,000; 1955: 136 out of 12,000,000).

In the summer, matters are different. Some three thousand different mushrooms are thriving in abundance, and right and left there are Festivals of Contemporary Music. It is to be regretted, however, that the consolidation of the acquisitions of Schoenberg and Stravinsky, currently in vogue, has not produced a single new mushroom. Mycologists are aware that in the present fungous abundance, such as it is, the dangerous *Amanitas* play an extraordinarily large part. Should not program chairmen, and music-lovers in general, come the warm months, display some prudence?

I was delighted last fall (for the effects of summer linger on, viz. Donaueschingen, C. D. M. I., etc.) not only to revisit in Paris my friend the composer Pierre Boulez, rue Beautreillis, but also to attend the Exposition du Champignon, rue de Buffon. A week later in Cologne, from my vantage point in a glass-encased control booth, I noticed an audience dozing off, throwing, as it were, caution to the winds, though present at a loud-speaker-emitted program of *Elektronische Musik*. I could not help recalling the riveted attention accorded another loud-speaker, rue de Buffon, which delivered on the hour a lecture describing mortally poisonous mushrooms and means for their identification.

But enough of the contemporary musical scene; it is well known. More important is to determine what are the problems confronting the contemporary mushroom. To begin with, I propose that it should be determined which sounds further the growth of which mushrooms; whether these latter, indeed, make sounds of their own; whether the gills of certain mushrooms are employed by appropriately small-winged insects for the production of *pizzicati* and the tubes of the *Boleti* by minute burrowing ones as wind instruments; whether the spores, which in size and shape are extraordinarily various, and in number countless, do not on dropping to the earth produce gamelan-like sonorities; and finally, whether all this enterprising activity which I suspect delicately exists, could not, through technological means, be brought, amplified and magnified, into our theatres with the net result of making our entertainments more interesting.

What a boon it would be for the recording industry (now part of America's sixth largest) if it could be shown that the performance, while at table, of an LP of Beethoven's *Quartet Opus Such-and-Such* so alters the chemical nature of *Amanita muscaria* as to render it both digestible and delicious!

Lest I be found frivolous and light-headed and, worse, an "impurist" for having brought and of the marriage of the again with Euterpe, observe that composers are continually mixing up music with something else. Karlheinz Stockhausen is clearly interested in music and juggling, constructing as he does "global structures," which can be of service only when tossed in the air; while my friend Pierre Boulez, as he revealed in a recent article (*Nouvelle Revue Française*, November 1954), is interested in music and parentheses and *italics*! This combination of interests seems to me excessive in number. I prefer my own choice of the mushroom. Furthermore it is avant-garde.

I have spent many pleasant hours in the woods conducting performances of my silent piece, transcriptions, that is, for an audience of myself, since they were much longer than the popular length which I have had published. At one performance, I passed the first movement by attempting the identification of a mushroom which remained successfully unidentified. The second movement was extremely dramatic, beginning with the sounds of a buck and a doe leaping up to within ten feet of my rocky podium. The expressivity of this movement was not only dramatic but unusually sad from my point of view, for the animals were frightened simply because I was a human being. However, they left hesitatingly and fittingly within the structure of the work. The third movement was a return to the theme of the first, but with all those profound, so-well-known alterations of world feeling associated by German tradition with the A-B-A.

In the space that remains, I would like to emphasize that I am not interested in the relationships between sounds and mushrooms any more than I am in those between sounds and other sounds. These would involve an introduction of logic that is not only out of place in the world, but time-consuming. We exist in a situation demanding greater earnestness, as I can testify, since recently I was hospitalized after having cooked and eaten experimentally some *Spathyema foetida*, commonly known as skunk cabbage. My blood pressure went down to fifty, stomach was pumped, etc. It behooves us therefore to see each thing directly as it is, be it the sound of a tin whistle or the elegant *Lepiota procera*.